Relax.
You've opened the right book.

∴∷∴

Once upon a time, people were wrong. They thought the automobile was an electric death trap that would never replace the buggy, the internet was only for academic shut-ins, and people who used study guides were simply *cheaters*. Then cars stopped exploding every time you started the engine, people realized you could use computers for more than just calculating the digits of *pi*, and the "cheaters" with the study guides… well, they started getting it. They got better grades, got into better schools, and just plain ol' got better. Times change. Rules change. *You snooze, you lose, buggy drivers.*

SparkNotes is different. We've always been thinking ahead. We were the first study guides on the internet back in 1999— you've been to SparkNotes.com haven't you? If not… Why!? This book might be posted online for free! You'll also find busy message boards, diagnostic test-prep, and all kinds of tools you'll need to get your act together and your grades up. And if your act's already together, SparkNotes will help you brutalize the competition. Or work for peace. Your call.

We're inexpensive, not cheap. Not only are our books the best bang for the buck, they're the best bang, period. Our reputation is based on staying smart and trustworthy—one step ahead, making tough topics understandable. We explain, we strategize, we translate. We get you where you want to go: smarter, better, faster than anyone else.

If you've got something to say, tell us. Your input makes us better. Found a mistake? Check www.sparknotes.com/errors. Have a comment? Go to www.sparknotes.com/comments. Did you read all the way to the bottom? Awesome. We love you. You're gonna do just fine.

SPARKNOTES™
SAT Math Level 1
Revised and Updated

SPARK PUBLISHING

Welcome to SparkNotes Test Preparation

The SAT Subject Tests, often referred to as the "evil twin sisters" of the SAT, are required by most selective colleges. And as the competition to get into college becomes more and more intense, the pressure is on to do well and outshine your peers.

At SparkNotes, we believe you should always aim for earning the highest score possible. Our *SAT Math Level 1* book helps you achieve your goals by giving you the exact tools you need to succeed:

- **The exact math topics you need to know for the test.** This book won't teach you all math—only the math you need to know for SAT Math Level 1. We won't waste your time trudging through topics the test doesn't cover. Instead, we tailor our lessons to the content of the test, and we make sure that you actually *understand* (not just memorize) the material.

- **Specific test-taking strategies.** Understanding the fundamentals of math is the most important ingredient to a good score on SAT Math Level 1, but it pays to know how to approach the test as well. We'll teach you specific skills and strategies that can help you net the valuable points that distinguish you from the crowd.

- **Three full-length practice tests, and a study method that teaches you how to transform them into powerful study tools.** Practice tests are an essential part of studying for any standardized test. They help you hone your test-taking skills, track your progress, and become comfortable with the test's format and time limits. Also, by studying the practice test results, you can use the tests as tools to pinpoint and eliminate your weaknesses.

- **General information about SAT Subject Tests.** SparkNotes teaches you everything you need to know to do well on a particular SAT Subject Test, but we also provide helpful information on the SAT Subject Tests in general. The first chapter of the book will help you figure out how colleges use SAT Subject Tests, which tests are right for you, when to take the tests, and how to register for them.

While other companies actually write test prep books to market their expensive courses, SparkNotes' goal is to teach you everything you need to succeed in a straightforward, no-nonsense manner. Our books are written with no hidden agenda, which frees us to help you get the best score you can.

Contents

SAT Math Level 1 Review . . . 31

Practice Tests 261

Orientation

Introduction to the SAT Subject Tests

Chapter Contents

THE SAT SUBJECT TESTS ARE CREATED and administered by the College Board and the Educational Testing Service (ETS), the two organizations responsible for producing the dreaded SAT. The SAT Subject Tests are meant to complement the SAT. Whereas the SAT tests your critical thinking skills by asking math and verbal questions, the SAT Subject Tests examine your knowledge of a particular subject, such as U.S. History, Physics, or Biology. The SAT takes three hours; the Subject Tests take only one hour.

In our opinion, the SAT Subject Tests are better tests than the SAT because they cover a definitive, easily studied topic rather than ambiguous critical thinking skills. However, just because the SAT Subject Tests do a better job of testing your knowledge of a subject doesn't mean the tests are necessarily easier or demand less studying. A "better" test isn't necessarily better for you in terms of how easy it will be.

The Good

- Because SAT Subject Tests cover specific topics, you can study for them effectively. If you don't know a topic in mathematics, such as how to find the slope of a line, you can easily look it up and learn it. The SAT Subject Tests are straightforward: if you know your stuff, you'll do well.

- Often, the classes you've taken in school have already prepared you for the SAT Subject Tests. If you've taken two years of algebra and a year of geometry, you'll have studied the topics covered by the SAT Math Level 1. All you need is some refreshing and refocusing, which this book provides.

- In preparing for the Math, History, or Chemistry SAT tests, you really are learning math, history, and chemistry. In other words, you are gaining valuable, interesting knowledge. If you enjoy learning, you might actually find the process of studying for an SAT Subject Test to be worthwhile and gratifying—few can say the same about studying for the SAT.

The Bad

Because SAT Subject Tests quiz you on specific knowledge, it is much harder to "beat" or "outsmart" an SAT Subject Test than it is to outsmart the SAT. For the SAT, you can use all sorts of tricks or strategies to figure out an answer. There are far fewer strategies to help you on the SAT Subject Tests. To do well on the SAT Subject Tests, you can't just rely on your natural smarts and wits. You need to study.

Colleges and the SAT Subject Tests

We're guessing you didn't sign up to take the SAT Subject Test just for the sheer pleasure of it. You probably want to get into college, and know that the only reason for taking this test is that colleges want or require you to do so.

Colleges care about SAT Subject Tests for two reasons. First, the tests demonstrate your interest, knowledge, and skill in specific subjects. Second, because SAT Subject Tests are standardized, they show how your knowledge of Math (or Biology or U.S. History) measures up to that of high school students nationwide. The grades you get in high school can't be compared in the same way: some high schools are more difficult than others, and students of equal ability might receive different grades, even in classes with relatively similar curriculum.

When it comes down to it, colleges like the SAT Subject Tests because the tests make the colleges' job easier. SAT Subject Tests allow colleges to easily compare you to other applicants, and provide you with an excellent opportunity to shine. If you got a 93% on your Algebra final, and a student at another high school across the country got a 91%, colleges don't know how to compare the two grades. They don't know whose class was harder or whose teacher was a tougher grader. But if you get a 720 on the SAT Math Level 1, and that other kid gets a 650, colleges *will* recognize the difference in your scores.

College Placement

Occasionally, colleges use SAT Subject Tests to determine placement. For example, if you do very well on the SAT Math Level 1, you might be exempted from a basic math class. It's worth finding out whether the colleges you're applying to use the SAT Subject Tests for this purpose.

Scoring the SAT Subject Tests

There are three different versions of your SAT Subject Test score. The "raw score" is a simple score of how you did on the test, like the grade you might receive on a normal test in school. The "percentile score" compares your raw score to all the other raw scores in the country, letting you know how you did on the test in relation to your peers. The "scaled score," which ranges from 200–800, compares your score to the scores received by all students who have ever taken that particular SAT Subject Test.

The Raw Score

You will never know your SAT raw score, because it is not included in the score report. But you should understand how the raw score is calculated, because this knowledge can affect your strategy for approaching the test.

A student's raw score is based solely on the number of questions that student got right, wrong, or left blank:

- You earn 1 point for every correct answer.

- You lose $1/4$ of a point for each incorrect answer.

- You receive zero points for each question left blank.

Calculating the raw score is easy. Count the number of questions you answered correctly and the number of questions answered incorrectly. Then multiply the number of wrong answers by $1/4$, and subtract this value from the number of right answers.

$$\text{raw score } = \text{ \# of correct answers} - \frac{1}{4} \times \text{ \# of wrong answers}$$

The Percentile Score

A student's percentile is based on the percentage of the total test-takers who received a lower raw score than he or she did. Let's say, for example, you had a friend named John Quincy Adams, and he received a score that placed him in the 37th percentile. This percentile score tells John that he scored better on the SAT Subject Test than 36 percent of the other students who took the same test; it also means that 63 percent of the students taking that test scored as well as or better than he did.

The Scaled Score

ETS takes your raw score and uses a formula to turn it into the scaled score of 200–800 that you've probably heard so much about.

The curve to convert raw scores to scaled scores differs from test to test. For example, a raw score of 33 on the Math Level 1 might scale to a 600, while the same raw score of 33 on the Math Level 2 will scale to a 700. In fact, the scaled score can even vary between different editions of the *same* test. A raw score of 33 on the February 2004 Math Level 2 might scale to a 710, while a 33 in June of 2004 might scale to a 690. These differences in scaled scores exist to accommodate varying levels of difficulty and student performance from year to year.

Which SAT Subject Tests to Take

There are three types of SAT Subject Tests: those you must take, those you should take, and those you shouldn't take.

- The SAT Subject Tests you *must* take are those that are required by the colleges you are interested in.

- The SAT Subject Tests you *should* take are tests that aren't required, but which you'll do well on, thereby impressing the colleges looking at your application.

- You *shouldn't* take the unrequired SAT Subject Tests that cover a subject you don't feel confident about.

Determining Which SAT Subject Tests are Required

You'll need to do a bit of research to find out if the colleges you're applying to require that you take a particular SAT Subject Test. Call the schools you're interested in, look at their websites, or talk to your guidance counselor. Often, colleges require that you take the following SAT Subject Tests:

- One of the two Math SAT tests (either Math Level 1 or Math Level 2)

- Another SAT Subject Test in some other subject of your choice

Not all colleges follow these guidelines; you should take the time to verify what tests you need to take in order to apply to the colleges that interest you.

Deciding Which Math SAT to Take

Few students take both Math SAT tests. Instead, you should choose which test to take based on several factors.

- **Test content.** The two tests cover similar topics, but the Math Level 2 covers more material than the Math Level 1 does. Level 1 covers three years of college-preparatory math: two years of algebra and one year of geometry. Level 2 assumes that in addition to those three years, you have also taken a year of trigonometry and/or precalculus.

Math Level 1

Algebra

Plane geometry (lines and angles, triangles, polygons, circles)

Solid geometry (cubes, cylinders, cones, spheres, etc.)

Coordinate geometry (in two dimensions)

Trigonometry (properties and graphs of sine, cosine, and tangent functions, identities)

Algebraic functions

Statistics and sets (distributions, probability, permutations and combinations, groups and sets)

Miscellaneous topics (logic, series, limits, complex and imaginary numbers)

Math Level 2 (covers all areas in Math Level 1 with some additional concepts)

Algebra

Plane geometry

Solid geometry

Coordinate geometry (in two and three dimensions, vectors, polar coordinates, parametric equations)

Trigonometry (cosecant, secant, cotangent functions, inverse functions, in non-right triangles)

Statistics and sets

Miscellaneous topics

- **Question difficulty.** Not only does the Math Level 2 cover additional topics, it also covers the basic topics in more difficult ways than the Math Level 1 does.

- **College choice.** As you choose between the two tests, keep in mind the specific colleges you're applying to. Colleges with a strong focus on math, such as MIT and Cal Tech, require the Math Level 2 test. Most other colleges have no such requirement, but some may prefer that you take the Level 2.

- **Battle of the test curves.** The Level 2 test is scored on a much more liberal curve: you can miss six or seven questions and still achieve a score of 800. On the Level 1 test, however, you would probably need to answer all the questions correctly to get a perfect score. If you wanted to score a 600 on either test, you would need around 20 correct answers on the Level 2 test and 33 on the Level 1 test. Some students with strong math backgrounds think that they can get a marvelous score on the less difficult Math Level 1 while their score on the Level 2 will only be average. But if you get tripped up by just one or two questions on the Math Level 1, your score will not be as impressive as you might expect.

If you have the skills to take the Level 2 test, you should go for it. Some students decide to take the Math Level 1 because it's easier, even though they have taken a precalculus course. We don't recommend this. Colleges will be more impressed by a student who does fairly well on SAT Math Level 2 than one who does very well on SAT Math Level 1. Also, the friendly curve of the Math Level 2 means that if you know enough math to take the Level 2, you might very well get a better score than you would on the Level 1.

If after all this you still can't decide which of the two Math SATs to take, try taking a practice test for each.

Deciding If You Should Take an SAT Subject Test That Isn't Required

There are two rules of thumb for deciding which additional test to take beyond the Math tests:

1. **Go with what you know.** If history is your field, a strong score on the American History test will impress admissions officers far more than a bold but mediocre effort on the Physics test.

2. **Try to show breadth.** Scoring well on similar subject tests such as Math, Biology, and Chemistry will not be as impressive as good scores in more diverse subjects, such as Math, U.S. History, and Spanish.

Of course, you also have to know what is considered a good score, and whether or not you can get that score (or higher).

Below we have included a list of the most popular SAT Subject Tests and the average scaled score on each. If you feel confident that you can get a score that is above the average (50 points or more), taking the test will probably strengthen your college application. Please note that if you are planning to attend an elite school, you might have to score significantly higher than the national average. The following table is just a general guideline. It's a good idea to call the schools that interest you or talk to a guidance counselor to get a more precise idea of what score you should be shooting for.

TEST	AVERAGE SCORE
Literature	590–600
U.S. History	580–590
World History	570–580
Math Level 1	580–590
Math Level 2	655–665
Biology E/M	590–600
Chemistry	605–615
Physics	635–645

As you decide which test to take, be realistic with yourself. Don't just assume you're going to do great without at least taking a practice test and seeing where you stand.

When to Take an SAT Subject Test

The best time to take an SAT Subject Test is right after you've finished a year-long class in that subject. If, for example, you take U.S. History in eleventh grade, then you should take the SAT U.S. History near the end of that year, when the material is still fresh in your mind. (This rule does not apply for the Literature, and Foreign Language SAT tests; it's best to take those after you've had as much study in the area as possible.)

ETS usually sets testing dates for SAT Subject Tests in October, November, December, January, May, and June. However, not every subject test is administered in each of these months. To check when the test you want to take is being offered, visit the College Board website at www.collegeboard.com or do some research in your school's guidance office.

Unless the colleges you're applying to use the SAT Subject Tests for placement purposes, there is no point in taking any SAT tests after November of your senior year, since you won't get your scores back from ETS until after the college application deadline has passed.

Registering for SAT Subject Tests

To register for the SAT Subject Test(s) of your choice, you have to fill out some forms and pay a registration fee. We know, we know—it's ridiculous that *you* have to pay for a test that colleges require you to take in order to make *their* jobs easier. But, sadly, there isn't anything we, or you, can do about it. (It's acceptable here for you to grumble about the unfairness of the world.)

After grumbling, however, you still have to register. There are two ways to go about it: online or by mail. To register online, go to www.collegeboard.com. To register by mail, fill out and send in the forms enclosed in the *Registration Bulletin*, which should be available in your high school's guidance office. You can also request a copy of the *Bulletin* by calling the College Board at (609) 771-7600, or writing to:

College Board SAT Program
P.O. Box 6200
Princeton, NJ 08541-6200

You can register to take up to three SAT Subject Tests for any given testing day. Unfortunately, even if you decide to take three tests in one day, you'll still have to pay a separate registration fee for each.

Introduction to SAT Math Level 1

T HE KEY TO SUCCESS ON ANY TEST IS SIMPLE: know your subject. But just knowing the material isn't enough to guarantee a good score on SAT Math Level 1—if you walked into an exam completely blind, with no preparation besides having read a textbook, and no knowledge of how you'd even be tested, you might spend so much energy trying to figure out *how* to take the test that you'd only get halfway through it.

That's where this chapter comes in handy. We've broken down the Math Level 1 by content and format, giving you a behind-the-scenes look at how your exam is written, organized, and scored. You'll know what to expect before you even enter the testing room.

Content of SAT Math Level 1

The Math Level 1 test covers a variety of topics. ETS, the company that writes the test, provides the following breakdown of coverage:

Topic	Percent of Test	Usual Number of Questions
Algebra	30%	15
Plane Geometry	20%	10
Solid Geometry	6%	3
Coordinate Geometry	12%	6
Trigonometry	8%	4
Functions	12%	6
Statistics and Sets	6%	3
Miscellaneous	6%	3

This breakdown is accurate, but it is too broad to help you direct your studying in any meaningful way. That's why we created this more detailed breakdown of the test:

Topic	Percent of Test	Usual Number of Questions
Algebra	30%	15
Arithmetic	1–3%	1
Equation solving	18–22%	10
Binomials, polynomials, quadratics	5–7%	3
Plane Geometry	20%	10
Lines and angles	3–5%	2
Triangles, polygons, circles	14–18%	8
Solid Geometry	6%	3
Solids (cubes, cylinders, cones, etc.)	7–9%	4
Inscribed solids, solids by rotation	1–3%	1
Coordinate Geometry	12%	6
Lines and distance	7–9%	4
Graphing	1–3%	1
Conic sections (parabolas, circles)	3–5%	2
Trigonometry	8%	4

Topic	Percent of Test	Usual Number of Questions
Basic functions (sine, cosine, tangent)	3–5%	2
Trigonometric identities	1–3%	1
Functions	12%	6
Basic, compound, inverse functions	7–9%	4
Graphing functions	1–3%	1
Domain and range of functions	1–3%	2
Statistics and Sets	1–3%	2
Mean, median, mode	6%	3
Probability	1–3%	1
Permutations and combinations	1–2%	0.5
Group questions, sets	1–2%	0.5
Miscellaneous	6%	3
Arithmetic and geometric series	1–2%	0.5
Logic	1–3%	1
Limits	1–2%	0.5
Imaginary numbers	1–2%	0.5

This book is organized according to these categories, allowing you to focus on each topic to whatever degree you feel necessary. Also, each question in the practice tests at the back of this book is grouped by the above categories, so that you can very precisely identify your weaknesses and then use this book to address them.

Format of SAT Math Level 1

SAT Math Level 1 is a one-hour test composed of 50 multiple-choice questions. The instructions for the test are very simple; you should memorize them so you don't waste time reading them on the day of the test.

> For each of the following problems, decide which is the BEST of the choices given. If the exact numerical value is not one of the choices, select the choice that best approximates this value. Then fill in the corresponding oval on the answer sheet.

Have you read the directions? Have you memorized them? Good. Now here's some specific information about the test's format:

- The 50 questions progress in order of difficulty: the easiest questions come first, the moderately difficult questions are in the middle, and the hardest questions are last.

- You can skip around while taking the test. The ability to skip the occasional question is helpful, as we explain in the next chapter.

- All questions are worth the same number of points, no matter their difficulty.

The Calculator

Unlike the SAT, in which a calculator is permitted but not essential to the test, the Math Level 1 test demands the use of a calculator; some questions on the test are specifically designed to test your calculator-using skills.

It is therefore wise to learn all the essentials about calculators before taking SAT Math Level 1. First, make sure you have the right type of calculator. Virtually any calculator are may be used during the test, including programmable and graphing calculators. Laptops, minicomputers, or any machine that prints, makes noise, or needs to be plugged in are prohibited.

Whatever calculator you use for the test should have all the following functions:

- Exponential powers

- Base-10 logarithms

- Sine, cosine, tangent

Make sure you practice each of these functions on your calculator before taking the test. We tell you more about how to use calculators for the test in the next chapter.

Scoring SAT Math Level 1

Scoring on the SAT Math Level 1 is the same as the scoring for all other SAT Subject Tests. For every right answer, you earn one point. For every wrong answer, you lose $\frac{1}{4}$ of a point. For every answer left blank, you earn zero points. These points combined equal your raw score. ETS converts your raw score to a scaled score according to a special curve tailored to the particular test you take. We have included a generalized version of that curve in a table below. Use this table to convert your raw scores on practice tests into an approximate scaled score.

Average Raw Score	Scaled Score	Average Raw Score	Scaled Score
50	800	18–19	480
49	780	17	470
48	770	16	460
47	760	15	450
46	740	14	440
45	730	13	430
44	720	12	430
43	710	11	420
42	700	10	410
41	690	9	400
40	680	8	390
39	670	7	380
38	660	6	370
37	650	5	370
36	640	4	360
35	630	3	350
34	610	2	340
33	600	1	330
32	590	0	330
31	580	−1	320
30	570	−2	310
29	560	−3	300
28	550	−4	300
27	550	−5	290
26	540	−6	280
25	530	−7	270
24	520	−8	260
23	510	−9	260
22	510	−10	250
21	500	−11	240
20	490	−12	230

As you can see, this curve is not very forgiving. Getting just one question wrong will lower your score by 20 points. Reiterating what we said earlier, you can miss a bunch of questions on the Math Level 2 and still get the same score you would receive on the Math Level 1 if you missed just one. For example, a raw score of 41 on the Math Level 2 test receives an equivalent scaled score as a raw score of 49 on the Math Level 1 test.

But all is not hopeless on the SAT Math Level 1. On a 50-question test, you could score:

- 780 if you answered 49 right, 0 wrong, and left 1 blank
- 740 if you answered 46 right, 0 wrong, and left 4 blank
- 700 if you answered 43 right, 4 wrong, and left 3 blank
- 650 if you answered 39 right, 8 wrong, and left 3 blank
- 650 if you answered 38 right, 4 wrong, and left 7 blank
- 600 if you answered 35 right, 8 wrong, and left 7 blank

These sample scores suggest that when taking the test, you shouldn't imagine your score plummeting with every question you can't confidently answer. Don't get unnecessarily wound up if you run into a difficult question; the key to doing well on SAT Math Level 1 is to follow a strategy that ensures you will see and answer all the questions you can, while intelligently guessing on those slightly fuzzier questions. We discuss these strategies in the next chapter.

Strategies for SAT Math Level 1

A MACHINE, NOT A PERSON, WILL SCORE your SAT Math Level 1 test. The tabulating machine sees only the filled-in ovals on your answer sheet, nothing else. So whether you knew the right answer because you're a math genius or because you took a lucky guess, you'll get a point.

Believe it or not, you can use all this to your advantage. ETS only wants right answers, not the thoughts behind them. So we've organized a few of the basic (and not-so-basic) rules and tips for test-taking that will best enable you to get those right answers quickly.

Basic Rules of SAT Test-Taking

There are some rules of strategy that apply to all SAT Subject Tests. These rules are so obvious that we hesitate to even call them "strategies." Some of these rules will seem more like common sense to you than anything else. We don't disagree. But it is amazing how a timed test can warp and mangle common sense. So we offer the following list.

Avoid Carelessness

There are two types of carelessness, both of which will cost you points. The first type results from sheer overconfidence. If you speed through the test without a second glance, you make yourself vulnerable to misinterpreting questions, overlooking answer choices, and making computational mistakes. As you take the test, make a conscious effort to approach it calmly and methodically, no matter how comfortable you are with the material. There's nothing worse than realizing you lost points due to sloppy mistakes.

Then there's lack of confidence—a defeatist attitude is your worst enemy when taking the SAT Subject Tests, because if you automatically assume you won't be able to answer many of the questions, you'll give up at the first sign of difficulty and sabatoge your score. Even if you don't feel confident about the material, stay on track and use our techniques for test-taking, and you might find you know more (and get a better score) then you thought you would.

Be Careful Gridding In Your Answers

The computer that scores SAT Subject Tests is unmerciful. If you answered a question correctly, but somehow made a mistake in marking your answer grid, the computer will mark that question as wrong. If you skipped question 5, but put the answer to question 6 in row 5, and the answer to question 7 in row 6, etc., thereby throwing off your answers for an entire section . . . it gets ugly.

Some test-prep books advise that you fill in your answer sheet five questions at a time rather than one at a time. Some suggest that you do one question and then fill in the corresponding bubble. We think you should fill out the answer sheet whatever way feels most natural to you; just make sure you're careful while doing it. In our opinion, the best way to ensure that you're being careful is to talk silently to yourself. As you figure out an answer in the test booklet and transfer it over to the answer sheet, say to yourself: "Number 23, B. Number 24, E. Number 25, A."

Know What's in the Reference Area

At the beginning of SAT Math Level 1, there is a reference area that provides you with basic geometric formulas and information.

THE FOLLOWING INFORMATION IS FOR YOUR REFERENCE IN ANSWERING SOME OF THE QUESTIONS IN THIS TEST.

Volume of a right circular cone with radius r and height h: $V = \frac{1}{3}\pi r^2 h$

Lateral area of a right circular cone with circumference of the base c and slant height l: $S = \frac{1}{2}cl$

Volume of a sphere with radius r: $V = \frac{4}{3}\pi r^3$

Surface area of a sphere with radius r: $S = 4\pi r^2$

Volume of a pyramid with base area B and height h: $V = \frac{1}{3}Bh$

You should know all these formulas without needing the reference area; don't neglect to memorize and understand the formulas because you have the reference area as a crutch. Instead, see the reference area as a hint to you about what formulas are likely to be needed on the test. If you know those formulas without having to flip back to the reference area, you'll save time, which puts you one step ahead.

Write All Over Your Test Booklet . . .

Draw diagrams or write out equations to help you think. Mark up graphs or charts as necessary. Cross out answers that can't be right. Basically, the test booklet is yours to write all over, and writing can often help clarify things, allowing you to work more quickly with fewer mistakes.

. . . But Remember That the SAT Rewards Answers, Not Work

That said, we must qualify our advice. Doing math scratchwork can definitely help you avoid careless errors, but doing pristine work, or more work than necessary, can be more time-consuming than it's worth. You must find a balance between speed and accuracy. You need to be able to follow and understand your work, but other people don't. Nobody will look at or reward your work, so don't write it out as if you're being judged.

The Importance of the Order of Difficulty

Imagine that you are taking a test that consists of two questions. After your teacher hands out the test, and before you set to work, a helpful little gnome whispers to you, "The first problem is very simple, the second is much harder." Would the gnome's statement affect the way you approach the two problems? Yes. For a "very simple" question, it seems likely that you should be able to answer it quickly and with little or no agonized second-guessing. You will probably have to spend much more time on a "much harder" question, both to come up with an answer and to check your work to make sure you didn't make an error somewhere along the way.

What about all the other students who didn't hear the gnome? They might labor over the first, easy question, exhaustively checking their work and wasting time that they'll need for the tricky second problem. Then, when those other students do get to the second problem, they might not check their work or be wary of traps, since they have no idea that the problem is so difficult.

The moral here is you should spend less time on the simpler questions that appear early in the test, and devote more time to the harder questions appearing later. Because Math Level 1 questions are ordered by difficulty, it's as if you have that helpful little gnome sitting next to you for the entire test.

Strategies

Knowing When to Be Wary

Most students answer the easy Math Level 1 questions correctly. Only some students get moderate questions right. Very few students get difficult questions right. What does this mean to you? It means that when you are going through the test, you can often trust your first instincts on an easy question. With difficult questions, however, you should be more cautious. There is a reason most people get these questions wrong: not only are they more difficult, containing more sophisticated vocabulary or mathematical concepts, they are also often tricky, full of enticing wrong answers that seem as if they must be correct. But because the SAT orders its questions by difficulty, the test tips you off about when to take a few extra seconds to make sure you haven't been fooled by an answer that only *seems* right.

The tricky answers seem right because they are actually the answers you would get if you were to make a mathematical or logical mistake while working on the problem. For example, let's say you're flying through the test and have to multiply 6 × 8 × 3. So you quickly multiply 6 and 8 to get 42 and then multiply 42 by 3 to get 126. You look down at the answers, and there's 126! You mark it down as your answer and you get the question wrong. 6 × 8 equals 48, *not* 42, making the correct answer 144.

From this example, you should learn that just because the answer you arrived at is among the answers does not mean you definitely have it right. The SAT is designed to punish those who make careless errors. Don't be one of them. After you get an answer, quickly check your work again.

Math Questions and Time

There are often several ways to answer a Math Level 1 question. You can use trial and error, you can set up and solve an equation, and, for some questions, you might be able to answer the question quickly, intuitively, and elegantly, if you can just spot how to do it. These different approaches to answering questions vary in the amount of time they take. Trial and error generally takes the longest, while the elegant method of relying on an intuitive understanding of conceptual knowledge takes the least amount of time.

Take, for example, the following problem:

> Which has a greater area, a square with sides measuring 4 cm or a circle with a radius of the same length?

The most obvious way to solve this problem is simply to plug 4 into the formula for the area of a square and area of a circle. Let's do it: Area of a square = s^2, so the area of this square = $4^2 = 16$. Area of a circle = πr^2, and the area of this circle must therefore be $\pi 4^2 = 16\pi$. 16π is obviously bigger than 16, so the circle must be bigger. That worked nicely. But a faster approach would have been to draw a quick to-scale diagram with the square and circle superimposed.

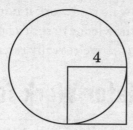

An even quicker way would have been to understand the equations for the area of a square and a circle so well that it was obvious that the circle was bigger, since the equation for the circle will square the 4 and multiply it by π, whereas the equation for the square will only square the 4.

While you may be a math whiz and just *know* the answer, you can learn to look for a quicker route, such as choosing to draw a diagram instead of working out the equation. And, as with the example above, a quicker route is not necessarily a less accurate one. Making such choices comes down to practice, having an awareness that those other routes are out there, and basic mathematical ability.

The value of time-saving strategies is obvious: less time spent on some questions allows you to devote more time to difficult problems. It is this issue of time that separates the students who do terrifically on the math section and those who merely do well. Whether or not the ability to find accurate shortcuts is an actual measure of mathematical prowess is not for us to say (though we can think of arguments on either side), but the ability to find those shortcuts absolutely matters on this test.

Shortcuts Are Really Math Intuition

We've told you all about shortcuts, but now we're going to give you some advice that might seem strange: you shouldn't go into every question searching for a shortcut. If you have to search and search for a shortcut, it might end up taking longer than the typical route. But at the same time, if you're so frantic about calculating out the right answer, you might miss the possibility that a shortcut exists. If you go into each question knowing there might be a shortcut and keep your mind open, you have a chance to find the shortcuts you need.

To some extent, you can teach yourself to recognize when a question might contain a shortcut. From the problem above, you know that there will probably be a shortcut for all those questions that give you the dimensions of two shapes and ask you to compare them. A frantic test-taker might compulsively work out the equations every time. But if you are a little calmer, you can see that drawing a diagram is the best, and quickest, solution.

The fact that we advocate using shortcuts doesn't mean you shouldn't focus on learning how to work out problems. We can guarantee that you're won't find a shortcut for a problem *unless* you know how to work it out the long way. After all, a shortcut requires using your existing knowledge to spot a faster way to answer the question. When we use the term *math shortcut*, we're really referring to your *math intuition*.

Making Your Calculator Work for You

As we've already mentioned, the calculator is a very important part of the Math Level 1 test. You need to have the right kind of calculator, be familiar with its operations, and, above all, know how to use it intelligently.

There are four types of questions on the test: those that are calculator-friendly, calculator-neutral, calculator-unfriendly, and calculator-useless. According to ETS, about 60 percent of the test falls under the calculator-neutral and -friendly categories. That is, calculators are useful or necessary on 30 of the 50 questions on SAT Math Level 1. The other 20 questions are calculator-unfriendly and -useless. The trick is to be able to identify the different types of questions when presented with them on the test. Here's a breakdown of each of the four types, with examples. If you're not certain about the math discussed in the examples, don't worry. We cover all these topics in this book.

Calculator-Friendly Questions

A calculator is extremely helpful and often necessary to solve calculator-friendly questions. Problems demanding exact values for exponents, logarithms, or trigonometric functions will most likely need a calculator. Computations that you can't do easily in your head are prime candidates. Here's an example:

If $f(x) = \sqrt{x} - 2x^2 + 5$, then what is $f(3.4)$?

(A)   −18.73
(B)   −16.55
(C)   −16.28
(D)   −13.32
(E)   −8.42

This is a simple function question in which you are asked to evaluate $f(x)$ at the value 3.4. As you will learn in the Functions chapter, all you have to do to solve this problem is plug in 3.4 for the variable x and carry out the operations in the function. But unless you know the square root and square of 3.4 off the top of your head (which most test-takers wouldn't), this problem is extremely difficult to answer without a calculator.

But with a calculator, all you need to do is take the square root of 3.4, subtract twice the square of 3.4, and then add 5. You get answer choice **C**, −16.28.

Calculator-Neutral Questions

You have two choices when faced with a calculator-neutral question. A calculator is useful for these types of problems, but it's probably just as quick and easy to work the problem out by hand.

If $8x = 4^3 \times 2^3$, what is the value of x?

(A)   2
(B)   3
(C)   5
(D)   7
(E)   8

When you see the variable x as a power, you should think of logarithms. A logarithm is the power to which you must raise a given number to equal another number, so in this case, we need to find the exponent x, such that $8^x = 4^3 \times 2^3$. From the definition of logarithms, we know that if given an equation of the form $a^x = b$, then $\log_a b = x$. So you could type in $\log_8 (4^3 \times 2^3)$ on your trusty calculator and find that $x = 3$.

    Or, you could recognize that 2 and 4 are both factors of 8, and, thinking a step further, that $2^3 = 8$ and $4^3 = 64 = 8^2$. Put together, $4^3 \times 2^3 = 8^2 \times 8 = 8^3$. We come to the same answer that $x = 3$ and that **B** is the right answer.

    These two processes take about the same amount of time, so choosing one over the other is more a matter of personal preference than one of strategy. If you feel quite comfortable with your calculator, then you might not want to risk the possibility of making a mental math mistake and should choose the first method. But if you're more prone to error when working with a calculator, then you should choose the second method.

Calculator-Unfriendly Questions

While it's possible to answer calculator-unfriendly questions using a calculator, it isn't a good idea. These types of problems often have built-in shortcuts—if you know and understand the principle being tested, you can bypass potentially tedious computation with a few simple calculations. Here's a problem that you could solve much more quickly and effectively without the use of a calculator:

$$\frac{\cos^2(3 \times 63°) + \sin^2(3 \times 63°)\}^4}{2} =$$

(A)   .3261
(B)   .5
(C)   .6467
(D)   .7598
(E)   .9238

If you didn't take a moment to think about this problem, you might just rush into it wielding your calculator, calculating the cosine and sine functions, squaring them each and then adding them together, etc. But take a closer look: $\cos^2(3 \times 63°) + \sin^2(3 \times 63°)$ is a trigonometric identity. More specifically, it's a Pythagorean identity: $\sin^2 q + \cos^2 q = 1$ for any angle q. So, the expression $\{\cos^2(3 \times 63°) + \sin^2(3 \times 63°)\}^{4}/2$ simplifies to $1^{4}/2 = \frac{1}{2} = .5$. **B** is correct.

Calculator-Useless Questions

Even if you wanted to, you wouldn't be able to use your calculator on calculator-useless problems. For the most part, problems involving algebraic manipulation or problems lacking actual numerical values would fall under this category. You should be able to easily identify problems that can't be solved with a calculator. Quite often, the answers for these questions will be variables rather than numbers. Take a look at the following example:

$(x + y - 1)(x + y + 1) =$

(A) $(x + y)^2$
(B) $(x + y)^2 - 1$
(C) $x^2 - y^2$
(D) $x^2 + x - y + y^2 + 1$
(E) $x^2 + y^2 + 1$

This question tests you on an algebraic topic—that is, it asks you how to find the product of two polynomials—and requires knowledge of algebraic principles rather than calculator acumen. You're asked to manipulate variables, not produce a specific value. A calculator would be of no use here.

To solve this problem, you need to notice that the two polynomials are in the format of a Difference of Two Squares: $(a + b)(a - b) = a^2 - b^2$. In our case, $a = x + y$ and $b = 1$. As a result, $(x + y - 1)(x + y + 1) = (x + y)^2 - 1$. **B** is correct.

Don't Immediately Use Your Calculator

The fact that the test contains all four of these question types means that you shouldn't get trigger-happy with your calculator. Just because you've got an awesome shiny hammer doesn't mean you should try to use it to pound in thumbtacks. Using your calculator to try to answer every question on the test would be just as unhelpful.

Instead of reaching instinctively for your calculator, first take a brief look at each question and understand exactly what it's asking you to do. That short pause will save you a great deal of time later on. For example, what if you came upon the question:

If $(3, y)$ is a point on the graph of $f(x) = \dfrac{x^2 - 5x + 4}{11x - 44}$, then what is y?

(A)   −3
(B)   −1.45
(C)   0
(D)   .182
(E)   4.87

A trigger-happy calculator user might immediately plug in 3 for x. But the student who takes a moment to think about the problem will probably see that the calculation would be much simpler if the function was simplified first. To start, factor 11 out of the denominator:

$$f(x) = \frac{x^2 - 5x + 4}{11x - 44} = \frac{x^2 - 5x + 4}{11(x - 4)}$$

Then, factor the numerator to its simplest form:

$$f(x) = \frac{x^2 - 5x + 4}{11(x - 4)} = \frac{(x - 4)(x - 1)}{11(x - 4)}$$

The $(x - 4)$ cancels out, and the function becomes $f(x) = (x - 1)/11$. At this point you could shift to the calculator and calculate $f(x) = (3 - 1)/11 = {}^2\!/_{11} = .182$, which is answer **D**. If you were very comfortable with math, however, you would see that you don't even have to work out this final calculation. ${}^2\!/_{11}$ can't work out to any answer other than **D**, since you know that ${}^2\!/_{11}$ isn't a negative number (like answers **A** and **B**), won't be equal to zero (answer **C**), and also won't be greater than 1 (answer **E**).

Approaching Math Level 1 Questions

Though there are four types of questions on the Math Level 1, there is a standard procedure that you should use to approach all of them.

1. Read the question without looking at the answers. Determine what the question is asking and come to some conclusion about how to solve it. Do not look at the answers unless you decide that using the process of elimination is the best way to go.

2. If you think you can solve the problem, go ahead. Once you've derived an answer, only then see if your answer matches one of the choices.

3. Once you've decided on an answer, test it quickly to make sure it's correct, then move on.

Strategies

Working Backward: The Process of Elimination

If you run into difficulty while trying to solve a multiple-choice problem, you might want to try the process of elimination. For every question, the answer is right in front of you, hidden among five answer choices. So if you can't solve the problem directly, you might be able to plug each answer into the question to see which one works.

Not only can this process help you when you can't figure out a question, there are times when it can actually be faster than setting up an equation, especially if you work strategically. Take the following example:

A classroom contains 31 chairs, some of which have arms and some of which do not. If the room contains 5 more armchairs than chairs without arms, how many armchairs does it contain?

(A)   10
(B)   13
(C)   16
(D)   18
(E)   21

Given this question, you could build the equations:

$$\text{total chairs (31)} = \text{armchairs } (x) + \text{normal chairs } (y)$$
$$\text{normal chairs } (y) = \text{armchairs } (x) - 5$$

Then, since $y = x - 5$ you can make the equation:

$$31 = x + (x - 5)$$
$$31 = 2x - 5$$
$$36 = 2x$$
$$x = 18$$

There are 18 armchairs in the classroom.

This approach of building and working out the equations will produce the right answer, but it takes a long time! What if you strategically plugged in the answers instead? Since the numbers ascend in value, let's choose the one in the middle: **C** 16. This is a smart strategic move because if we plug in 16 and discover that it is too small a number to satisfy the equation, we can eliminate **A** and **B** along with **C**. Alternatively, if 16 is too big, we can eliminate **D** and **E** along with **C**.

So our strategy is in place. Now let's work it out. If we have 16 armchairs, then we would have 11 normal chairs and the room would contain 27 total chairs. We needed the total number of chairs to equal 31, so clearly **C** is not the right answer. But because the total number of chairs is too few, we can also eliminate **A** and **B**, the answer choices with smaller numbers of armchairs. If we then plug in **D**, 18, we have 13 normal chairs and 31 total chairs. There's our answer. In this instance, plugging in the answers takes less time, and just seems easier in general.

Now, working backward and plugging in is not always the best method. For some questions it won't be possible to work backward at all. For the test, you will need to build up a sense of when working backward can most help you. Here's a good rule of thumb:

> Work backward when the question describes an equation of some sort and the answer choices are all simple numbers.

If the answer choices contain variables, working backward will often be more difficult than actually working out the problem. If the answer choices are complicated, with hard fractions or radicals, plugging in might prove so complex that it's a waste of time.

Substituting Numbers

Substituting numbers is a lot like working backward, except the numbers you plug into the equation *aren't* in the answer choices. Instead, you have to strategically decide on numbers to substitute into the question to take the place of variables.

For example, take the question:

If p and q are odd integers, then which of the following must be odd?

(A) $p + q$
(B) $p - q$
(C) $p^2 + q^2$
(D) $p^2 \times q^2$
(E) $p + q^2$

It might be hard to conceptualize how the two variables in this problem interact. But what if you chose two odd numbers, let's say 5 and 3, to represent the two variables? You get:

(A) $p + q = 5 + 3 = 8$
(B) $p - q = 5 - 3 = 2$
(C) $p^2 + q^2 = 25 + 9 = 34$
(D) $p^2 \times q^2 = 25 \times 9 = 225$
(E) $p + q^2 = 5 + 9 = 14$

The answer has to be **D**, $p^2 \times q^2$ since it multiplies to 225. (Of course, you could have answered this question without any work at all, as two odd numbers, when multiplied, *always* result in an odd number.)

Substituting numbers can help you transform problems from the abstract to the concrete. However, you have to remember to keep the substitution consistent. If you're using a 5 to represent p, don't suddenly start using 3. Choose numbers that are easy to work with and that fit the definitions provided by the question.

Guessing and the Math Level 1

Should you guess on SAT Math Level 1? We'll answer this question by posing a question of our own:

> G. O. Metry is holding five cards, numbered 1–5. Without telling you, he has selected one of the numbers as the "correct" card. If you pick a single card, what is the probability that you will choose the correct card?

One out of 5, or $\frac{1}{5}$, of course! And that's precisely the situation you're in when you blindly guess the answer on any SAT Math Level 1 question: you have a 1 in 5 chance of getting the question right. If you were to guess on 10 questions, probability says you'll get two questions right and eight questions wrong.

- Two right answers earns you 2 raw points.

- Eight wrong answers gets you –2 raw points ($8 \times -\frac{1}{4}$ points).

Those ten answers, therefore, net you a total of 0 points. And that's exactly what ETS wants. They designed the test to make blind guessing pointless.

Educated Guessing

But suppose you're faced with this question:

> If $x + 2x = 6$, what is the value of x?
>
> (A)   –2
> (B)   2
> (C)   3
> (D)   0
> (E)   1

Let's say you have no idea how to solve this problem. But you look at the answer choices, and realize that 0 multiplied by any number equals 0. If you plug that into the equation, $0 + 2 \times 0$ *cannot* add up to 6. You can eliminate "0" as a possible answer, and now have four choices from which to choose. Now is it worth it to guess? Yes. Probability states that if you are guessing between four choices you will get one question right for every three you get wrong. For that one correct answer, you'll get one point, and for the three incorrect answers, you'll lose a total of $\frac{3}{4}$ of a point: $1 - \frac{3}{4} = \frac{1}{4}$. If you can eliminate even one answer, the odds of guessing turn in your favor: you become more likely to gain points than to lose points.

The rule for guessing on the Math Level 1 test is simple: *if you can eliminate even one answer-choice on a question, you should definitely guess.*

Pacing: The Key to Scoring Well

As we said earlier, the questions on the SAT Math Level 1 test are organized from least to most difficult, with the basic material covered near the beginning and the advanced topics at the end. Make sure you don't spend too much time on the easiest questions, putting yourself in the position of having to leave blank those questions near the end of the test that you could have answered *if only you had more time.*

Answering 50 math questions in 60 minutes is not the easiest of tasks, but if you learn how to pace yourself, you should be able to at least look at every single question on the test. Note that we said "look at" every question, we didn't say "answer."

It is unlikely that you will be able to answer every question on the test. Some questions will stump you completely. Others might demand so much of your time that answering them becomes more trouble than it's worth. While taking five minutes to solve a particularly difficult question might strike you as a moral victory when you're taking the test, you could have used that same time to answer six other questions that would have vastly increased your score. Instead of getting bogged down on individual questions, you will do better if you learn to skip, and leave for later, the very difficult questions either that you can't answer or that will take an extremely long time to solve.

By perfecting your pacing on practice tests, you can make sure that you will see every question on the test, letting you choose which questions you will and will not answer, rather than running out of time before reaching the end of the test.

There are a few simple rules that will make pacing yourself much easier.

- Don't get bogged down on one single question. If you find yourself wasting time on a question, circle it, move on, and come back to it later.

- Answer every question for which you know the answer, and make an educated guess on every question for which you can quickly eliminate at least one answer choice.

- Skip questions in which the question and answers refer to concepts completely foreign to you. If you look at the question and answers and have no idea what topics they cover, you have little chance of making an educated guess. Mark the question in some way to indicate it is very difficult. Return to this type of question only if you have answered everything else. Remember to skip that line on your answer sheet!

Strategies

Setting a Target Score

You can make the job of pacing yourself much easier if you go into the test knowing how many questions you have to answer correctly in order to earn the score you want. So, what score do you want? Obviously, you should strive for the best score possible, but be realistic: consider how much you know about math and how well you usually do on SAT-type tests. You should also consider what exactly defines a good score at the colleges you're applying to: is it a 620? A 680? Talk to their admissions offices, do a little research in college guidebooks, or talk to your guidance counselor. You should also find out the average scores of students already at the schools you want to attend. Take that number and set your target score above it (you want to be *above* average, right?). Then take a look at the chart we showed you earlier.

You'll get:

- 780 if you answered 49 right, 0 wrong, and left 1 blank
- 740 if you answered 46 right, 0 wrong, and left 4 blank
- 700 if you answered 43 right, 4 wrong, and left 3 blank
- 650 if you answered 39 right, 8 wrong, and left 3 blank
- 600 if you answered 35 right, 8 wrong, and left 7 blank

So let's say the average score for SAT Math Level 1 for the school you want to attend is a 600, and you set your target at about 650. According to the chart, you can get 39 questions right, get 8 wrong, leave 3 questions blank, and still achieve your target score.

If you know all these numbers going into the test, you can pace yourself accordingly. You should use practice tests to teach yourself the proper pace, increasing your speed if you find that you aren't getting to answer all the questions you need to, or decreasing your pace if you find that you're rushing and making careless mistakes. If you reach your target score during preparation, give yourself a cookie and take a break for the day. But just because you hit your target score doesn't mean you should stop working altogether. In fact, you should view reaching your target score as a clue that you can do *better* than that score: set a new target 50–100 points above your original, and work to pick up your pace a little bit and skip fewer questions.

By improving your score in manageable increments, you can slowly work up to your top speed, integrating your new knowledge of the test and how to take it without overwhelming yourself. If you can handle working just a little faster without becoming careless and losing points, your score will certainly go up. If you meet your new target score again, repeat the process.

SAT Math Level 1
Review

Math Level 1 Fundamentals

Chapter Contents

O NLY A FEW QUESTIONS (2 to 5 percent) will directly test basic math. But knowledge of basic math is crucial—almost all of the test's 50 questions assume in-depth understanding of it, and you'll need to be able to apply these fundamentals even when answering the most sophisticated questions.

You probably know some of the Math Level 1 Fundamentals like the back of your hand, while others may need a refresher. Either way, it can't hurt to thumb through this chapter. If you know it all, you'll fly right through it. If there's something you don't know, learn it!

Order of Operations

The order of operations is one of the most instrumental and basic principles of arithmetic. It refers to the order in which you must perform the various operations in a given mathematical expression. If operations in an expression could be performed in any random order, a single expression would take on a vast array of values. For example:

Evaluate the expression $3 \times 2^3 + 6 \div 4$.

One student might perform the operations from left to right:

$$3 \times 2^3 + 6 \div 4 = 6^3 + 6 \div 4 = 216 + 6 \div 4 = 222 \div 4 = 55.5$$

Another student might choose to add before executing the multiplication or division:

$$3 \times 2^3 + 6 \div 4 = 3 \times 8 + 6 \div 4 = 3 \times 14 \div 4 = 10.5$$

As you can see, depending on the order in which we perform the required operations, there are a number of possible evaluations of this expression. In order to ensure that all expressions have a single correct value, we have **PEMDAS**—an acronym for determining the correct order of operations in any expression. PEMDAS stands for:

- **P**arentheses: first, perform the operations in the innermost parentheses. A set of parentheses supercedes any other operation.

- **E**xponents: raise any required bases to the prescribed exponent. Exponents include square roots and cube roots, since those two operations are the equivalent of raising a base to the $\frac{1}{2}$ and $\frac{1}{3}$ power, respectively.

- **M**ultiplication and **D**ivision: perform multiplication and division.

- **A**ddition and **S**ubtraction: perform these operations last.

Let's work through a few examples to see how order of operations and PEMDAS work. First, we should find out the proper way to evaluate the expression $3 \times 2^3 + 6 \div 4$. Since nothing is enclosed in parentheses, the first operation we carry out is exponentiation:

$$3 \times 2^3 + 6 \div 4 = 3 \times 8 + 6 \div 4$$

Next, we do all the necessary multiplication and division:

$$3 \times 8 + 6 \div 4 = 24 + 1.5$$

Lastly, we perform the required addition and subtraction. Our final answer is:

$$24 + 1.5 = 25.5$$

Here's another example, which is a bit trickier. Try it on your own, and then compare your results to the explanation that follows:

Evaluate $6\sqrt{2^3 + 4(5-3)}$.

First, resolve the operations under the square root, which is symbolized by $\sqrt{}$ and is also called a **radical**.

But wait, you may be thinking to yourself, I thought we were supposed to do everything within a parentheses before performing exponentiation. Expressions under a radical are special exceptions because they are really an expression within parentheses that has been raised to a fractional power. In terms of math, $6\sqrt{2^3 + 4(5-3)} = 6(2^3 + 4(5-3))^{1/2}$. The radical effectively acts as a large set of parentheses, so the rules of PEMDAS still apply.

To work out this expression, first execute the operations within the innermost set of parentheses:

$$6\sqrt{2^3 + 4(5-3)} = 6\sqrt{2^3 + 4(2)}$$

Next, perform the required exponentiation:

$$6\sqrt{8 + 4(5-3)} = 6\sqrt{8 + 4(2)}$$

Then, multiply:

$$6\sqrt{8 + 4(2)} = 6\sqrt{8 + 8}$$

Finally, add:

$$6\sqrt{8 + 8} = 6\sqrt{16}$$

Now that the operations under the radical have been resolved, we can take the square root.

$$6\sqrt{16} = 6 \times 4 = 24$$

One additional note is important for the division step in the order of operations. When the division symbol $\div$ is replaced by a fraction bar (i.e., the expression includes a fraction), you must evaluate the **numerator** and the **denominator** separately *before* you divide the numerator by the denominator. The fraction bar is the equivalent of placing a set of parentheses around the whole numerator and another for the whole denominator.

Order of Operations and Your Calculator

There are two ways to deal with the order of operations while using a calculator:

Math Level 1 Fundamentals

1. Work out operations one by one on your calculator while keeping track of the entire equation on paper. This is a slow but accurate process.

2. If you have a graphing calculator, you can type the whole expression into your calculator. This method will be faster, but can cause careless errors.

If you want to type full expressions into your graphing calculator, you must be familiar with how your calculator works. You can't enter fractions and exponents into your calculator the way they appear on paper. Instead, you have to be sure to recognize and preserve the order of operations. Practice with the following expression:

$$\frac{(2^2) + 3 \times 4}{\frac{1}{2} \div 2} = ?$$

If you enter this into a graphing calculator, it should look like this:

$$(2^2 + (3 \times 4)) \div ((1 \div 2) \div 2)$$

Numbers

Before you take the Math Level 1, you should know the common types of numbers. Of these types, the most important ones to understand are probably integers and real numbers. They can be spotted in nearly every question on the test and will be explicitly mentioned at times.

- **Whole Numbers.** The set of counting numbers, including zero $\{0, 1, 2, 3, \ldots\}$.

- **Natural Numbers.** The set of all whole numbers except zero $\{1, 2, 3, 4, 5, \ldots\}$.

- **Integers.** The set of all positive and negative whole numbers, including zero. Fractions and decimals are not included $\{\ldots, -3, -2, -1, 0, 1, 2, 3, \ldots\}$.

- **Rational Numbers.** The set of all numbers that can be expressed as a quotient of integers. That is, any number that can be expressed in the form m/n, where m and n are integers. The set of rational numbers includes all integers and all fractions that can be created using integers in the numerator and denominator.

- **Irrational Numbers.** The set of all numbers that cannot be expressed as a quotient of integers. Examples include π, $\sqrt{3}$, $1.01001000100001000001\ldots$.

The sets of irrational numbers and rational numbers are mutually exclusive. Any given number must be either rational or irrational; no number can be both.

- **Real Numbers.** Every number on the number line. The set of real numbers includes all rational and irrational numbers.

- **Imaginary Numbers.** See the "Miscellaneous Math" chapter later in this book.

On the Math Level 1, integers and real numbers will appear far more often than any of the other number types.

Even and Odd Numbers

Even numbers are those numbers that are divisible by two with no remainder.

Only integers can be even or odd, meaning decimals and fractions are not included. Zero, however, is an integer and thus a member of the set.

$$\ldots, -6, -4, -2, 0, 2, 4, 6, \ldots$$

Odd numbers are those numbers not evenly divisible by two.

$$\ldots, -5, -3, -1, 1, 3, 5, \ldots$$

The set of even numbers and the set of odd numbers are mutually exclusive.

A more rigorous definition of even and odd numbers appears below:

Even numbers are numbers that can be written in the form 2n, where n is an integer. Odd numbers are the numbers that can be written in the form 2n + 1, where n is an integer.

This definition is nothing more than a technical repetition of the fact that even numbers are divisible by two, and odd numbers are not. It may come in handy, though, when you need to represent an even or odd number with a variable.

Operations of Odd and Even Numbers

There are a few basic rules regarding the operations of odd and even numbers that you should know well. If you grasp the principles behind the two types of signed numbers, these rules should all come easily.

Addition:

$$even + even = even$$

$$odd + odd = even$$

$$even + odd = odd$$

Subtraction:

$$even - even = even$$

$$odd - odd = even$$

$$even - odd = odd$$

Multiplication and Division:

$$even \times even = even$$

$$odd \times odd = odd$$

$$even \times odd = even$$

Positive and Negative Numbers

Positive and negative numbers are governed by rules similar to those that have to do with even and odd numbers. First, for their quick definitions:

Positive numbers are numbers that are greater than zero. Negative numbers are numbers that are less than zero. The number zero is neither positive nor negative.

Operations of Positive and Negative Numbers

The following rules define how positive and negative numbers operate under various operations.

Addition and Subtraction:

When adding and subtracting negative numbers, it helps to remember the following:
Adding a negative number is the same as subtracting its opposite. For example:

$$3 + (-2) = 3 - 2 = 1$$

Subtracting a negative number is the same as adding its opposite. For example:

$$3 - (-2) = 3 + 2 = 5$$

Multiplication:

$$\text{positive} \times \text{positive} = \text{positive}$$
$$\text{negative} \times \text{negative} = \text{positive}$$
$$\text{positive} \times \text{negative} = \text{negative}$$

Division:

$$\text{positive} \div \text{positive} = \text{positive}$$
$$\text{negative} \div \text{negative} = \text{positive}$$
$$\text{positive} \div \text{negative} = \text{negative}$$

The rules for multiplication and division are exactly the same since any division operation can be written as a form of multiplication: $a \div b = a/b = a \times 1/b$.

Absolute Value

The absolute value of a number is the distance on a number line between that number and zero. Or, you could think of it as the positive "version" of every number. The absolute value of a positive number is that same number, and the absolute value of a negative number is the opposite of that number.

The absolute value of x is symbolized by $|x|$.

If $x = 5$, $|x| = 5$.
If $x = -4.234$, $|x| = 4.234$.
If $x = 0$, $|x| = 0$.

Solving an equation with an absolute value in it can be particularly tricky. As you will see, the answer is often ambiguous. Take a look at the following equation:

$$4|x| + 2 = 10$$

We can simplify the equation in order to isolate $|x|$:

$$4|x| + 2 = 10$$
$$4|x| = 8$$
$$|x| = 2$$

Knowing that $|x| = 2$ means that $x = 2$ and $x = -2$ are both possible solutions to the problem. Keep this in mind; we'll deal more with absolute values in equations later on in the Algebra chapter.

Factors

A **factor** is an integer that divides another integer evenly. If $^a/_b$ is an integer, then b is a factor of a. The numbers 3, 4, and 6, for example, are factors of 12.

Sometimes it is necessary or helpful to factor an integer completely. This means you need to find all the factors of that integer. It's possible that the test will directly require this skill or will make use of it in a more complicated question. In either case, it's something you should know how to do.

Factorization

To find all the factors of a number, write them down in pairs, beginning with 1 and the number you're factoring. We'll factor 24 in this example. One and 24 are both factors of 24. Next, try every integer greater than 1 in increasing order. Here are the factor pairs we find for 24:

- 1 and 24 (1 × 24 = 24)
- 2 and 12 (2 × 12 = 24)
- 3 and 8 (3 × 8 = 24)
- 4 and 6 (4 × 6 = 24)

You know you've found all the factors of a number when the next first factor exceeds its corresponding second factor. For example, after you found that 4 was a factor of 24 and 5 was not, you would see that 6, the next factor of 24, had already been included in a pair of factors. Thus, all the factors have been found.

Prime Numbers

A **prime number** is a number whose only factors are 1 and itself. All prime numbers are positive (because every negative number has −1 as a factor in addition to 1 and itself).

Furthermore, all prime numbers besides 2 are odd. The first few primes, in increasing order, are:

$$2, 3, 5, 7, 11, 13, 17, 19, 23, 29, 31, 37, 41, 43, 47, 53, \ldots$$

To determine whether a number is prime, you shouldn't check whether the number is divisible by every number less than itself. Such an effort would take an incredible amount of time, and you have only an hour for the Math Level 1. Instead, to decide whether a number is prime, all you need to do is estimate the square root of the number, then check all the prime numbers that fall below your estimate. For example, to see if 91 is prime, you should estimate the square root of the number: $\sqrt{91} \approx 10$. Now you should test 91 for divisibility by the prime numbers smaller than 10: 2, 3, 5 and 7.

- Is 91 divisible by 2? No, it does not end with an even number.

- Is 91 divisible by 3? No, 9 + 1 = 10, and 10 is not divisible by 3.

- Is 91 divisible by 5? No, 91 does not end with 0 or 5.

- Is 91 divisible by 7? Yes! 91 ÷ 7 = 13.

Therefore, 91 is not prime.

Prime Factorization

Another form of factorization is called **prime factorization**. The prime factorization of an integer is the listing of the prime numbers whose product is that number.

To find the prime factorization of a number, divide it and all its factors until every remaining integer is prime. This group of prime numbers is the prime factorization of the original integer. As an example, let's find the prime factorization of 36.

$$36 = 2 \times 18 = 2 \times 2 \times 9 = 2 \times 2 \times 3 \times 3$$

It can be helpful to think of prime factorization in the form of a tree:

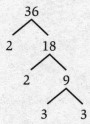

As you may already have noticed, there is more than one way to find the prime factorization of a number. We could have first resolved 36 into 6 × 6, for example, and then determined the prime factorization from there. So don't worry—you can't screw up.

No matter which path you take, you will always get the same result. That is, as long as you do your arithmetic correctly. Just for practice, find the prime factorizations for 45 and 41.

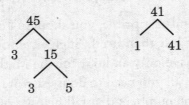

$$3 \times 3 \times 5 = 45 \qquad 1 \times 41 = 41$$

Since the only factors of 41 are 1 and 41, 41 is a prime number. It is therefore its own prime factorization.

Greatest Common Factor

The **greatest common factor** (GCF) of two numbers is the greatest factor that they have in common. Finding the GCF of two numbers is especially useful in certain applications, such as manipulating fractions (we explain why later in this section).

In order to find the GCF of two numbers, we must first produce their prime factorizations. What is the greatest common factor of 18 and 24, for example?

First, their prime factorizations:

$$18 = 2 \times 9 = 2 \times 3 \times 3$$
$$24 = 2 \times 12 = 2 \times 2 \times 6 = 2 \times 2 \times 2 \times 3$$

The greatest common factor is the greatest integer that can be written as a product of common prime factors. That is to say, the GCF is the "overlap," or intersection, of the two prime factorizations. In this case, both prime factorizations contain 2 × 3 = 6. This is their GCF.

Here's another example:

What is the GCF of 96 and 144?

First:

$$96 = 2 \times 48 = 2 \times 2 \times 24 = 2 \times 2 \times 2 \times 12 = 2 \times 2 \times 2 \times 2 \times 6 = 2 \times 2 \times 2 \times 2 \times 2 \times 3 = 2^5 \times 3$$

$$144 = 2 \times 72 = 2 \times 2 \times 36 = 2 \times 2 \times 2 \times 18 = 2 \times 2 \times 2 \times 2 \times 9 = 2 \times 2 \times 2 \times 2 \times 3 \times 3 = 2^4 \times 3^2$$

So, the product of the prime factors that they share is $2^4 \times 3 = 48$, which is their GCF.

For practice, find the GCF of the following pairs of integers:

1. 12 and 15

2. 30 and 45

3. 13 and 72

4. 14 and 49

5. 100 and 80

Compare your answers to the solutions:

1. $12 = 2^2 \times 3$.
   $15 = 3 \times 5$.
   The GCF is 3.

2. $30 = 2 \times 3 \times 5$.
   $45 = 3^2 \times 5$.
   The GCF is $3 \times 5 = 15$.

3. $13 = 1 \times 13$.
   $72 = 2^3 \times 2$.
   There are no common prime factors. The GCF is 1.

4. $14 = 2 \times 7$.
   $49 = 72$.
   The GCF is 7.

5. $100 = 2^2 \times 5^2$.
   $80 = 2^4 \times 5$.
   The GCF is $2^2 \times 5 = 20$.

Relatively Prime Numbers

Two numbers are called **relatively prime** if they have no common prime factors (i.e., if their GCF is 1). This doesn't mean, however, that each number is itself prime. The numbers 8 and 15 are relatively prime because they have no common primes in their prime factorizations ($8 = 2 \times 2 \times 2$ and $15 = 3 \times 5$), but neither number is prime.

Multiples

A **multiple** is an integer that can be evenly divided by another integer. If c/d is an integer, then c is a multiple of d. The numbers 45, 27, and 18, for example, are all multiples of 9. Alternatively, you could define a multiple as an integer with at least one factor. All that really matters is that you understand the concept of multiples, and this is best done with a simple example.

What are some multiples of 4?

- 12, 20, and 96 are all multiples of 4.

How do we know these numbers are multiples of 4?

$$12 = 4 \times 3$$
$$20 = 4 \times 5$$
$$96 = 4 \times 24$$

Also, note that any integer, n, is a multiple of 1 and n, because $1 \times n = n$.

Least Common Multiple

The **least common multiple** (LCM) of two integers is the smallest multiple that the two numbers have in common. The LCM of two numbers is, like the GCF, useful when manipulating fractions:

For example, what is the least common multiple of 4 and 6? We must first find their prime factorizations.

$$4 = 2 \times 2, \text{ and } 6 = 2 \times 3$$

Their LCM is the smallest prime factorization that contains every prime number in each of the two original prime factorizations. For the numbers 4 and 6, this is $2 \times 2 \times 3 = 12$. It is the smallest prime factorization that includes $2 \times 2 \times 3$. Thus, 12 is the LCM of 4 and 6.

Let's try a harder example. What is the LCM of 14 and 38? Again, we start by finding the prime factorizations of both numbers:

$$14 = 2 \times 7$$
$$38 = 2 \times 19$$

Therefore, their LCM is $2 \times 7 \times 19 = 266$.

For some quick practice, find the LCM of the following pairs of integers:

1. 12 and 32

2. 15 and 26

3. 34 and 40

4. 3 and 17

5. 18 and 16

Compare your answers to the solutions:

1. $12 = 2^3 \times 3$.
   $32 = 2^5$.
   The LCM is $2^5 \times 3 = 96$.

2. $15 = 3 \times 5$.
   $26 = 2 \times 13$.
   The LCM is $2 \times 3 \times 5 \times 13 = 390$.

3. $34 = 2 \times 17$.
   $40 = 2^3 \times 5$.
   The LCM is $2^3 \times 5 \times 17 = 680$.

4. $3 = 1 \times 3$.
   $17 = 1 \times 17$.
   The LCM is $3 \times 17 = 51$.

5. $18 = 2 \times 3^2$.
   $16 = 2^4$.
   The LCM is $2^4 \times 3^2 = 144$.

Fractions

Being able to efficiently and correctly manipulate fractions is essential to doing well on the Math Level 1 test. A **fraction** describes a part of a whole. It is composed of two expressions, a numerator and a denominator. The numerator of a fraction is the quantity above the fraction bar, and the denominator is the quantity below the fraction bar. For example, in the fraction ½, 1 is the numerator and 2 is the denominator.

Equivalent Fractions

Two fractions are equivalent if they describe equal parts of the same whole. To determine if two fractions are equivalent, multiply the denominator and numerator of one fraction so that the denominators of the two fractions are equal. For example, ½ = ³/₆ because if you multiply the numerator and denominator of ½ by 3, you get:

$$\frac{1 \times 3}{2 \times 3} = \frac{3}{6}$$

As long as you multiply or divide *both* the numerator and denominator of a fraction by the *same* nonzero number, you will not change the overall value of the fraction. Fractions represent a part of a whole, so if you increase both the part and whole by the same multiple, you will not change their fundamental relationship.

Reducing Fractions

Reducing fractions makes life with fractions a lot simpler. It takes unwieldy fractions such as $450/600$ and makes them into smaller, easier-to-work-with fractions.

To reduce a fraction to its lowest terms, divide the numerator and denominator by their GCF. For example, for $450/600$, the GCF of 450 and 600 is 150. So the fraction reduces down to $3/4$.

A fraction is in reduced form if its numerator and denominator are relatively prime (their GCF is 1). Thus, it makes sense that the equivalent fractions we studied in the previous section all reduce to the same fraction. For example, the equivalent fractions $4/6$ and $8/12$ both reduce to $2/3$.

Comparing Fractions

When dealing with integers, large positive numbers with a lot of digits, like 5,000,000, are greater than numbers with fewer digits, such as 5. But fractions do not work the same way. For example, $200/20,000$ might seem like a big, impressive fraction, but $2/3$ is actually larger, because 2 is a much bigger part of 3 than 200 is of 20,000.

In certain cases, comparing two fractions can be very simple. If the denominators of two fractions are the same, then the fraction with the larger numerator is bigger. If the numerators of the two fractions are the same, the fraction with the smaller denominator is bigger.

However, you'll most likely be dealing with two fractions that have different numerators and denominators, such as $200/20,000$ and $2/3$. When faced with this situation, an easy way to compare these two fractions is to utilize cross-multiplication. All you have to do is multiply the numerator of each fraction by the denominator of the other, then write the product of each multiplication next to the numerator you used to get it. We'll cross-multiply $200/20,000$ and $2/3$:

$$600 = \frac{200}{20,000} \times \frac{2}{3} = 40,000$$

Since 40,000 > 600, $2/3$ is the greater fraction.

Adding and Subtracting Fractions

On SAT Math Level 1, you will need to know how to add and subtract two different types of fractions. Sometimes you will be given two fractions with the same denominator, and other times you will have two fractions with different denominators.

Fractions with the Same Denominators

Fractions can be extremely easy to add and subtract if they have the same denominator. In addition problems, all you have to do is add up the numerators:

$$\frac{1}{20} + \frac{3}{20} + \frac{13}{20} = \frac{17}{20}$$

Subtraction works similarly. If the denominators of the fractions are equal, then you simply subtract one numerator from the other:

$$\frac{13}{20} - \frac{2}{20} = \frac{11}{20}$$

Fractions with Different Denominators

If the fractions do not have equal denominators, the process becomes somewhat more involved. The first step is to make the denominators the same, and then to subtract as described above. The best way to do this is to find the least common denominator (LCD), which is simply the LCM of the two denominators. For example, the LCD of $\frac{1}{2}$ and $\frac{2}{3}$ is 6, since 6 is the LCM of 2 and 3.

The second step, after you've equalized the denominators of the two fractions, is to multiply each numerator by the same value as their respective denominator. Let's take a look at how to do this for our example, $\frac{1}{2} + \frac{2}{3}$. For $\frac{1}{2}$:

$$\text{numerator} = 1 \times 3 = 3$$
$$\text{denominator} = 2 \times 3 = 6$$

So, the new fraction is $\frac{3}{6}$. The same process is repeated for the second fraction, $\frac{2}{3}$:

$$\text{numerator} = 2 \times 2 = 4$$
$$\text{denominator} = 3 \times 2 = 6$$

The new fraction is $\frac{4}{6}$. The final step is to perform the addition or subtraction. In this case, $\frac{3}{6} + \frac{4}{6} = \frac{7}{6}$.

If you think it will be faster, you can always skip finding the LCD and multiply the denominators together to get a common denominator. In some cases, such as our example, the product of the denominators will actually be the LCD ($2 \times 3 = 6 = $ LCD). But, other times, the product of the denominators will be greater than the LCD. For example, if the two denominators are 6 and 8, you could use $6 \times 8 = 48$ as a denominator instead of 24 (the LCD).

The drawback to this second approach is that you will have to work with larger numbers and reduce your answer in the end.

Multiplying Fractions

Multiplying fractions is quite simple. The product of two fractions is the product of their numerators over the product of their denominators. Symbolically, this can be represented as:

$$\frac{a}{b} \times \frac{c}{d} = \frac{ac}{bd}$$

Or, for a numerical example:

$$\frac{3}{7} \times \frac{2}{5} = \frac{3 \times 2}{7 \times 5} = \frac{6}{35}$$

Dividing Fractions

Multiplication and division are inverse operations. It makes sense, then, that to perform division with fractions, all you have to do is flip the second fraction, which is also called taking its reciprocal, and then multiply.

$$\frac{a}{b} \div \frac{c}{d} = \frac{a}{b} \times \frac{d}{c} = \frac{ad}{bc}$$

Here's a numerical example:

$$\frac{1}{2} \div \frac{4}{5} = \frac{1}{2} \times \frac{5}{4} = \frac{5}{8}$$

Mixed Numbers

A **mixed number** is an integer followed by a fraction, like $1\frac{1}{2}$. It is another form of an improper fraction, which is a fraction greater than one. But operations such as addition, subtraction, multiplication, or division can only be performed on the improper fraction form, so you need to know how to convert between mixed numbers and improper fractions.

Let's convert the mixed number 1½ into an improper fraction. First, you multiply the integer portion of the mixed number by the denominator, and add that product to the numerator. So 1 × 2 + 1 = 3, making 3 the numerator of the improper fraction. Now, simply put 3 over the original denominator, 2, and you have your converted fraction.

Here's another example:

$$3\,\frac{2}{13} = \frac{(3 \times 13) + 2}{13} = \frac{39 + 2}{13} = \frac{41}{13}$$

Decimals

Decimals are just another way to express fractions. After all, to produce a decimal, you simply divide the numerator of a fraction by the denominator. For example, ½ = 1 ÷ 2 = .5.

Comparing Decimals

Like fractions, comparing decimals can be a bit deceptive. As a general rule, when comparing two decimals such as .3 with .003, the decimal with more leading zeroes is the smaller one. But if asked to compare .003 with .0009, you might be tempted to overlook the additional zero, and because 9 is the larger integer, choose .0009 as the larger decimal. That would be wrong. Use caution to avoid such mistakes. It might help to line up the decimal points of the two decimals:

- .0009 is clearly smaller than
  .0030

Similarly,

- .000900 is smaller than
  .000925

Converting Decimals to Fractions

Knowing how to convert decimals into fractions and fractions into decimals are useful skills. Sometimes you'll produce a decimal while solving a question, and then you'll have to choose from fractions for test choices. Other times, it may just be easier to work with fractions. Whatever the case, both conversions can be done easily.

To convert a decimal number to a fraction:

1. Remove the decimal point and make the decimal number the numerator.

2. Let the denominator be the number 1 followed by as many zeroes as there are decimal places in the decimal number.

3. Reduce the fraction.

Let's convert .3875 into a fraction. First, we eliminate the decimal point and make 3875 the numerator:

$$.3875 = \frac{3875}{?}$$

Since .3875 has four digits after the decimal point, we put four zeroes in the denominator:

$$.3875 = \frac{3875}{10000}$$

Then, by finding the GCF of 3875 and 10,000, which is 125, we can reduce the fraction:

$$\frac{3875}{10000} = \frac{3875 \div 125}{10000 \div 125} = \frac{31}{80}$$

To convert from fractions back to decimals is a cinch. Simply carry out the necessary division on your calculator, such as for $^3/_5$:

$$\frac{3}{5} = 3 \div 5 = 0.6$$

Percents

A **percent** is another way to describe a part of a whole (which means that percents are also another way to talk about fractions or decimals). Percent literally means "of 100" in Latin, so when you attend school 25 percent of the time, that means you only go to school $^{25}/_{100}$ of the time (or .25).

You would probably fail all your classes if your attendance percentage was that low, so don't get any ideas from our example. Instead, take a look at this question: 3 is what percent of 15?

This question presents you with a whole, 15, and then asks you to determine how much of that whole 3 represents in percentage form. Since a percent is "of 100," to solve the question you have to set the fraction $3/15$ equal to $x/100$:

$$\frac{3}{15} = \frac{x}{100}$$

You then cross-multiply and solve for x:

$$15x = 3 \times 100 = 300$$
$$x = 20$$

Converting Percents into Fractions or Decimals

You should be skilled at converting percents into fractions and decimals, because these problems will definitely come up on the Math Level 1 test.

Percents relate to decimal numbers very simply and directly. A percent is a decimal number with the decimal point moved two decimal places to the left.

For example:

$$50\% \text{ of } 12 = .50 \times 12 = 6$$
$$12\% \text{ of } 120 = .12 \times 120 = 14.4$$

To convert from a decimal number to a percent, move the decimal point two places to the right:

$$.07 \times 1100 = 7\% \text{ of } 1100 = 77$$
$$.97 \times 13 = 97\% \text{ of } 13 = 12.61$$

On an even more simplistic level, we can just say that 50% = .5 or 22.346% = .22346. Percentages greater than 100 exist, too. 235% = 2.35, for example.

To convert from a percent to a fraction, take the percentage number and place it as the numerator over the denominator 100. 58 percent is the same as $58/100$.

To convert from a fraction back to a percent, the easiest method is to convert the fraction into a decimal first and then change the resultant decimal into a percent.

$$\frac{3}{4} = 3 \div 4 = .75 = 75\%$$

Exponents

An exponent defines the number of times a number is to be multiplied by itself. For example, in a^b, where a is the base, and b the exponent, a is multiplied by itself b times. In a numerical example, $2^5 = 2 \times 2 \times 2 \times 2 \times 2$. An exponent can also be referred to as a power: a number with an exponent of 2 is raised to the second power. There are some other terms that you should be familiar with:

- **Base.** The base refers to the 3 in 3^5. It is the number that is being multiplied by itself however many times specified by the exponent.

- **Exponent.** The exponent (or power) is the 5 in 3^5. The exponent tells how many times the base is to be multiplied by itself.

- **Square.** Saying that a number is "squared" means that it has been raised to the second power, i.e., that it has an exponent of 2. In the expression 6^2, 6 has been squared.

- **Cube.** Saying that a number is "cubed" means that it has been raised to the third power, i.e., that it has an exponent of 3. In the expression 4^3, 4 has been cubed.

Math Level 1 Fundamentals

Common Exponents

It may be worth your while to memorize a few common exponents before the test. Knowing these regularly used exponents can save you the time it would take to calculate them during the test. Here is a list of squares from 1 through 10:

$$1^2 = 1$$
$$2^2 = 4$$
$$3^2 = 9$$
$$4^2 = 16$$
$$5^2 = 25$$
$$6^2 = 36$$
$$7^2 = 49$$
$$8^2 = 64$$
$$9^2 = 81$$
$$10^2 = 100$$

Memorizing the first few cubes can be helpful as well:

$$1^3 = 1$$
$$2^3 = 8$$
$$3^3 = 27$$
$$4^3 = 64$$
$$5^3 = 125$$

Math Level 1 Fundamentals

Finally, the first few powers of two are useful for many applications:

$$2^0 = 1$$
$$2^1 = 2$$
$$2^2 = 4$$
$$2^3 = 8$$
$$2^4 = 16$$
$$2^5 = 32$$
$$2^6 = 64$$
$$2^7 = 128$$
$$2^8 = 256$$
$$2^9 = 512$$
$$2^{10} = 1024$$

Adding and Subtracting Numbers with Exponents

In order to add or subtract numbers with exponents, you have to first find the value of each power, and then add the two numbers. For example, to add $3^3 + 4^2$, you must expand the exponents to get $(3 \times 3 \times 3) + (4 \times 4)$, and then, finally, $27 + 16 = 43$.

If you're dealing with algebraic expressions that have the same bases and exponents, such as $3x^4$ and $5x^4$, then they can simply be added and subtracted. For example, $3x^4 + 5x^4 = 8x^4$.

Multiplying and Dividing Numbers with Exponents

To multiply exponential numbers or terms that have the same base, add the exponents together:

$$3^6 \times 3^2 = 3^{(6+2)} = 3^8$$
$$x^4 \times x^3 = x^{(4+3)} = x^7$$

To divide two same-base exponential numbers or terms, just subtract the exponents.

$$\frac{3^6}{3^2} = 3^{(6-2)} = 3^4$$
$$\frac{x^4}{x^3} = x^{(4-3)} = x^1$$

To multiply exponential numbers raised to the same exponent, raise their product to that exponent:

$$4^3 \times 5^3 = (4 \times 5)^3 = 20^3$$
$$a^5 \times b^5 = (a \times b)^5 = ab^5$$

To divide exponential numbers raised to the same exponent, raise their quotient to that exponent:

$$\frac{12^5}{3^5} = \left(\frac{12}{3}\right)^5 = 4^5$$
$$\frac{a^2}{b^2} = \left(\frac{a}{b}\right)^2 = \left(\frac{a}{b}\right)^2$$

If you need to multiply or divide two exponential numbers that do not have the same base or exponent, you'll just have to do your work the old-fashioned way: multiply the exponential numbers out and multiply or divide the result accordingly.

Raising an Exponent to an Exponent

Occasionally you might encounter an exponent raised to another exponent, as seen in the following formats $(3^2)^4$ and $(x^4)^3$. In such cases, multiply the powers:

$$(3^2)^4 = 3^{(2 \times 4)} = 3^8$$
$$(x^4)^3 = x^{(4 \times 3)} = x^{12}$$

Exponents and Fractions

To raise a fraction to an exponent, raise both the numerator and denominator to that exponent:

$$\left(\frac{1}{3}\right)^3 = \frac{1}{27}$$

Exponents and Negative Numbers

As we said in the section on negative numbers, when you multiply a negative number by another negative number, you get a positive number, and when you multiply a negative number by a positive number, you get a negative number. These rules affect how negative numbers function in reference to exponents.

Math Level 1 Fundamentals

- When you raise a negative number to an even-number exponent, you get a positive number. For example $(-2)^4 = 16$. To see why this is so, let's break down the example. $(-2)^4$ means $-2 \times -2 \times -2 \times -2$. When you multiply the first two -2s together, you get $+4$ because you are multiplying two negative numbers. Then, when you multiply the $+4$ by the next -2, you get -8, since you are multiplying a positive number by a negative number. Finally, you multiply the -8 by the last -2 and get $+16$, since you're once again multiplying two negative numbers.

- When you raise a negative number to an odd power, you get a negative number. To see why, all you have to do is look at the example above and stop the process at -8, which equals $(-2)^3$.

These rules can help a great deal as you go about eliminating answer choices and checking potentially correct answers. For example, if you have a negative number raised to an odd power, and you get a positive answer, you know your answer is wrong. Likewise, on that same question, you could eliminate any answer choices that are positive.

Special Exponents

There are a few special properties of certain exponents that you also need to know.

Zero

Any base raised to the power of zero is equal to 1. If you see any exponent of the form x^0, you should know that its value is 1. Note, however, that 0^0 is undefinded.

One

Any base raised to the power of one is equal to itself. For example, $2^1 = 2$, $(-67)^1 = -67$ and $x^1 = x$. This can be helpful when you're attempting an operation on exponential terms with the same base. For example:

$$3x^6 \times x = 3x^6 \times x^1 = 3x^{(6+1)} = 3x^7$$

Fractional Exponents

Exponents can be fractions, too. When a number or term is raised to a fractional power, it is called taking the **root** of that number or term. This expression can be converted into a more convenient form:

$$x^{\left(\frac{a}{b}\right)} = \sqrt[b]{x^a}$$

Or, for example, $2^{13/5}$ is equal to the fifth root of 2 to the thirteenth power:

$$\sqrt[5]{2^{13}} = 6.063$$

The $\sqrt{}$ symbol is also known as the **radical**, and anything under the radical, in this case 2^{13}, is called the **radicand**. For a more familiar example, look at $9^{1/2}$, which is the same as $\sqrt{9}$:

$$\sqrt[2]{9^1} = \sqrt{9} = 3$$

Fractional exponents will play a large role on SAT Math Level 1, so we are just giving you a quick introduction to the topic now. Don't worry if some of this doesn't quite make sense now; we'll go over roots thoroughly in the next section.

Negative Exponents

Seeing a negative number as a power may be a little strange the first time around. But the principle at work is simple. Any number or term raised to a negative power is equal to the reciprocal of that base raised to the opposite power. For example:

$$x^{-5} = \frac{1}{x^5}$$

Or, a slightly more complicated example:

$$\left(\frac{2}{3}\right)^{-3} = \left(\frac{1}{\frac{2}{3}}\right)^3 = \left(\frac{3}{2}\right)^3 = \frac{27}{8}$$

With that, you've got the four rules of special exponents. Here are some examples to firm up your knowledge:

$$5^0 = 1$$

$$x^{\frac{1}{8}} = \sqrt[8]{x^1} = \sqrt[8]{x}$$

$$4^{\frac{2}{3}} \times 4^{\frac{8}{5}} = 4^{\left(\frac{2}{3}+\frac{8}{5}\right)} = 4^{\frac{34}{15}} = \sqrt[15]{4^{34}}$$

$$(3^{-2})^x = 3^{-2x} = \frac{1}{3^{2x}}$$

$$3(xy)^0 = 3$$

$$b^{-1} = \frac{1}{b}$$

$$4^{-2} = \frac{1}{4^2} = \frac{1}{16}$$

$$x^{-\frac{2}{5}} \times z^{-\frac{2}{5}} = (xz)^{-\frac{2}{5}} = \frac{1}{(xz)^{\frac{2}{5}}} = \frac{1}{\sqrt[5]{(xz)^2}}$$

$$1^{\frac{-3v^4}{2w}} = 1 \text{ (one raised to any power is still one)}$$

Roots and Radicals

We just saw that roots express fractional exponents. But it is often easier to work with roots in a different format. When a number or term is raised to a fractional power, the expression can be converted into one involving a root in the following way:

$$x^{\frac{a}{b}} = \sqrt[b]{x^a}$$

with the $\sqrt{}$ sign as the radical sign, and x^a as the radicand.

Roots are like exponents, only backward. For example, to square the number 3 is to multiply 3 by itself: $3^2 = 3 \times 3 = 9$. The root of 9, $\sqrt{9}$, is 3. In other words, the square root of a number is the number that, when squared, is equal to the given number.

Square roots are the most commonly used roots, but there are also cube roots (numbers raised to $\frac{1}{3}$), fourth roots, fifth roots, etc. Each root is represented by a radical sign with the appropriate number next to it (a radical without any superscript denotes a square root). For example, cube roots are shown as $\sqrt[3]{}$, fourth roots as $\sqrt[4]{}$, and so on. These roots of higher degrees operate the same way square roots do. Because $3^3 = 27$, it follows that the cube root of 27 is 3.

Here are a few examples:

$$\sqrt{16} = 4 \text{ because } 4^2 = 16$$
$$\sqrt[4]{81} = 3 \text{ because } 3^4 = 81$$
$$\sqrt{\frac{1}{4}} = \frac{1}{2} \text{ because } \left(\frac{1}{2}\right)^2 = \frac{1}{4}$$
$$\text{If } x^n = y, \text{ then } \sqrt[n]{y} = x$$

The same rules that apply to multiplying and dividing exponential terms with the same exponent apply to roots as well. Look for yourself:

$$\sqrt[n]{x} \times \sqrt[n]{y} = \sqrt[n]{x \times y}$$
$$\sqrt{8} \times \sqrt{2} = \sqrt{8 \times 2} = \sqrt{16} = 4$$

Just be sure that the roots are of the same degree (i.e., you are multiplying or dividing all square roots or all roots of the fifth power).

Scientific Notation

Scientific notation is a convention used to express large numbers. A number written in scientific notation has two parts:

1. A number between 1 and 10.

2. The power of 10 by which you must multiply the first number in order to get the larger number that is being represented.

In the following examples, we'll first write a number and then express it in scientific notation:

$$3{,}000{,}000 = 3.0 \times 10^6$$
$$4{,}123{,}452{,}734 = 4.123452734 \times 10^9$$
$$15 = 1.5 \times 10^1$$
$$13{,}598{,}000 = 1.3598 \times 10^7$$

Scientific notation is particularly useful when a large number contains many zeroes or needs to be approximated because of its unwieldy size. Approximating quantities in scientific notation can prevent unnecessarily messy calculations. Look at the following expression:

$$13{,}234{,}836{,}823{,}436 \times 555{,}317{,}897{,}542{,}222{,}010$$

This is a pretty nasty product to find—even when you're using a calculator. By approximating each number using scientific notation, we can make the problem a lot easier:

$$13{,}234{,}836{,}823{,}436 \times 555{,}317{,}897{,}542{,}222{,}010 \approx$$
$$1.32 \times 10^{13} \times 5.55 \times 10^{17} = (1.32 \times 5.55) \times (10^{13} \times 10^{17}) = 7.33 \times 10^{30}$$

When we compare this approximation to the actual product, we find that we were less than 1% off. Not too shabby.

Also, note the way in which we combined the terms in the last example to make the multiplication a little simpler:

$$1.32 \times 10^{13} \times 5.55 \times 10^{17} = (1.32 \times 5.55) \times (10^{13} \times 10^{17})$$

In general terms:

$$(a \times 10^{x}) \times (b \times 10^{y}) = (a \times b) \times 10^{x+y}$$

Often, this sort of simplification can make your calculations easier.

Scientific Notation and Calculators

On many calculators, scientific notation is written differently from what you've seen here. Instead of 3.1×10^{33}, your calculator might read 3.1 E33. The capital letter "E" has the same role as the " $\times$ 10(power)", only it's a little shorter. In general, scientific notation allows you to work with numbers that might either be very tedious to manipulate or too large to fit on your calculator.

Logarithms

Logarithms are closely related to exponents and roots. A **logarithm** is the power to which you must raise a given number, called the base, to equal another number. For example, $\log_2 8 = 3$ because $2^3 = 8$. In this case, 2 is the base and 3 is the logarithm.

The Math Level 1 likes to use logarithms in algebra problems, mostly in simple equation-solving problems (which we cover in the next chapter). For any of these types of questions, the key thing to remember is that a logarithm problem is really an exponent problem. Keeping this in mind should help reduce the mystery that seems to surround logarithms. In fact, once you get the hang of it, you'll realize that solving logarithmic equations is actually quite simple and easy.

Having defined logarithms in a sentence, let's show one symbolically. The next three equations are equivalent:

$$\log_a x = b, a^b = x, \text{ and } \sqrt[b]{x} = a$$

For example, $\log_4 16 = 2$ because $4^2 = 16$ and $\sqrt{16} = 4$. You should now be able to see why the three topics of exponents, roots, and logarithms are often linked together. Each method provides a way to isolate one of the three variables in these types of equations. In the example above, a is the base, b is the exponent, and x is the product. Finding the root, logarithm, and exponent isolates these values, respectively.

Logarithms and Calculators

Unless the logarithm is a very simple one, you won't be able to mentally calculate it — so the calculator becomes an important tool. But there is one important thing you need to be aware of. On your calculator, the LOG button assumes a base of 10. This means that for the equation $\log_4 16 = 2$, if you punched in LOG 16, you would get $\log_{10} 16$.

Some calculators can calculate a logarithm with any base you want, but less advanced calculators might not. In general, as long as your calculator is scientific, it should be able to calculate logarithms with different bases.

Calculate a few logarithms for practice:

$$\log_{10} 1000 = 3 \text{ because } 10^3 = 1000$$
$$\log_{\frac{1}{2}} \frac{1}{4} = 2 \text{ because } \left(\frac{1}{2}\right)^2 = \frac{1}{4}$$
$$\log_4 \frac{1}{16} = -2 \text{ because } 4^{-2} = \frac{1}{16}$$

Operations on Logarithms

You will rarely see a test question involving basic logarithms such as $\log_{10} 100$, or $\log_2 4$. In particular, on the logarithm questions you'll see in the Algebra chapter, you'll need to be able to manipulate logarithms within equations. So, you should know how to perform the basic operations on logarithms:

- **The Product Rule:** when logarithms of the same base are multiplied, the base remains the same, and the exponents can be added.

$$\log_x jk = \log_x j + \log_x k$$
$$\log_2 4 + \log_2 3 = \log_2 12$$

- **The Quotient Rule:** when logarithms of the same base are divided, the exponents must be subtracted.

$$\log_x \frac{j}{k} = \log_x j - \log_x k$$
$$\log \frac{1}{2} = \log 1 - \log 2$$

- **The Power Rule:** when a logarithm is raised to a power, the exponent can be brought in front and multiplied by the logarithm.

$$\log_x c^n = n \times \log_x c$$
$$\log x^4 = 4 \log x$$

You might have noticed how similar these rules are to those for exponents and roots. This similarity results from the fact that logarithms are just another way to express an exponent.

Review Questions

1. Evaluate the expression $\dfrac{3x^3 + (2x)^2}{\log_x 32}$ for the value $x = 2$.

   (A) $\dfrac{1}{2}$

   (B) 4

   (C) 6

   (D) 8

   (E) $\dfrac{232}{5}$

2. If a is even and negative, b is negative, and c is even, which of the following choices could be equal to $a \times b + c^2 + 1$?

   (A) −71
   (B) −16
   (C) 0
   (D) 4
   (E) 9

3. What is the absolute value of the difference between the LCM and GCF of 24 and 42?

    (A) 18
    (B) 162
    (C) 174
    (D) 498
    (E) 1002

4. Which of the following fractions is not equivalent to the others?

    (A) $\dfrac{6}{14}$

    (B) $\dfrac{-21}{-49}$

    (C) $\dfrac{33}{91}$

    (D) $\dfrac{9}{21}$

    (E) $\dfrac{15}{35}$

5. How many digits are in the number 5^{33}?

    (A) 23
    (B) 24
    (C) 25
    (D) 33
    (E) 38

Explanations

1. **D**

This question tests your understanding of order of operations, exponents, and logarithms. We'll solve it step by step. The numerator simplifies to

$$3(2)^3 + 4 \times 2^2 = 3 \times 8 + 4 \times 4$$
$$= 24 + 16$$
$$= 40$$

The denominator is 5, because $2^5 = 32$. So the answer is $^{40}\!/_5 = 8$.

2. **E**

The product of two negative numbers must be positive, and the product of an even number and any other number is even: therefore, $(a \times b)$ must be even and positive. The square of an even number is even and positive, so c^2 is even and positive. Since two positive even numbers will sum to a positive even number, $(a \times b) + c^2$ must be positive and even. When you add one to this value, the end result is odd and positive. 9 is the only answer choice that is odd and positive.

3. **B**

Find the prime factorizations of 24 and 42 to find their LCM and GCF.

$$24 = 2^3 \times 3$$
$$42 = 2 \times 3 \times 7$$

The LCM of the two numbers is $2^3 \times 3 \times 7 = 168$, and the GCF of the two numbers is $2 \times 3 = 6$. Now you just need to find the absolute value of the difference between the LCM and the GCF: $|168 - 6| = |162| = 162$.

4. **C**

Fractions are equivalent to each other if the numerator and denominator of one fraction can be multiplied by the same scalar, and the result is the other fraction. After reducing the first two fractions, you should have realized that they were both equivalent to $3/7$. As soon as you got to the third one and found that it was already in reduced form and not equal to $3/7$, you could have stopped. If you checked the last two, you found that they, too, are equal to $3/7$.

5. **B**

To answer this problem, use scientific notation. When you type 5^{33} into your calculator, it is approximately 1.16×10^{23}. This means that the decimal point has been moved over 23 decimal places, so there must be $23 + 1 = 24$ digits in the full number.

Algebra

THIS CHAPTER ON ALGEBRA IS A BEHE-
MOTH. It is by far the longest chapter in this book
full of lengthy chapters. There's a reason for our
extensive treatment: algebra is the most tested topic
on the Math Level 1 test. About 30 percent of the
Math Level 1 questions directly test your algebraic
abilities, and some of the questions that focus on
geometry or trigonometry still involve some sort of
algebraic technique or concept.

Before this information all starts to sound overwhelming, there is some good news. First, the algebra
tested on the math subject tests is not all that difficult.
Second, the Math Level 1 test-writers focus on a limited set of algebraic topics. Only the
topics you do need to know are covered in this chapter.

Math Level 1 Algebra Strategies

There are several ways to answer most algebra problems. You could try to solve a
problem by using standard algebra and setting up and solving an equation. Alternatively, you could try to avoid algebra and simply plug the answer choices back into the
question until one of them works out. Or you can pick numbers to substitute into the
various expressions given as answer choices.

None of these methods is necessarily better than the others. Remain flexible in
your approach to each question and choose the method that best suits the problem.
For a problem you know how to solve, using algebra is probably the quickest method.

In contrast, a tough problem that you are unsure how to solve might become easy if you try to plug in some answers. When you study your practice tests and look over the algebra questions you got wrong, you should think about the method you employed. Did you plug in answers when you should have used algebra? Did you use algebra when you should have plugged in answers?

We'll lay out for you the different problem-solving approaches and tell you all you need to know about them. Then you can decide for yourself which method to choose.

Let's use a sample algebra problem to illustrate these separate approaches:

A baseball player travels from his home city, Jasonville, to Giambia City for a baseball game. He drives at 50 miles an hour. After the game, he travels back home and takes a flight that travels at 500 miles an hour. If the distance from Jasonville to Giambia City is 250 miles, and it took him j hours longer to drive than to fly, what is j?

(A)   1
(B)   3.5
(C)   4
(D)   4.5
(E)   12

Using Algebra

This question is a simple rate problem that can be solved with a few basic equations. Since traveling time = distance ÷ speed, it took him:

$$250 \text{ miles} \div 50 \text{ miles an hour} = 5 \text{ hours}$$

to drive to Giambia City. To find the duration of his flight, we use the same rate formula:

$$250 \text{ miles} \div 500 \text{ miles an hour} = 0.5 \text{ hours}$$

It took the player:

$$5 \text{ hours} - .5 \text{ hours} = 4.5 \text{ hours}$$

longer to drive. **D** is the correct answer.

Plugging In Answers

Sometimes you might not be sure how to approach a problem or don't have the time to think out the proper equations. In such instances, plugging in might be the best method for you, especially as you come across the more difficult questions at the end of the test. All you have to do is substitute the answer choices back into the problem, and see whether the given information holds true.

The process of plugging in is simple. First, you should make full use of the fact that the answer choices on Math Level 1 are always presented in ascending value. So start by plugging in answer choice **C**, since if it doesn't turn out to be the answer, you can usually tell whether to try a smaller or larger answer choice. Now, to solve the question: it takes the baseball player $250 \div 50 = 5$ hours to drive to Giambia City. So, if it takes him **C** 4 hours more to drive, than it takes him $5 - 4 = 1$ hour to fly back to Jasonville. But the question tells us that in 1 hour, he could fly 500 miles. Therefore, it must take him longer than 4 hours more to drive than to fly. Next, we try **D** 4.5. It takes him $5 - 4.5 = .5$ hours to fly, which means that he travels $500 \times .5 = 250$ miles on his flight. **D** is the answer.

Picking Numbers

Picking numbers is a variation of plugging in and should only be used when the answer choices contain variables. A modified version of our original sample question shows what kind of problems might lend themselves to picking numbers.

> A baseball player travels from his home city, Jasonville, to Giambia City for a baseball game. He drives at m miles an hour. After the game, he travels back home, and takes a flight instead at p miles an hour. If the distance from Jasonville to Giambia City is v miles, and it took him j longer to drive than to fly, what is j?
>
> (A) $\dfrac{mp}{v}$
>
> (B) $\dfrac{v+p}{v+m}$
>
> (C) $\dfrac{pv-pj}{vj}$
>
> (D) $vm - vp$
>
> (E) $\dfrac{5v}{m-v}$

This question asks you to figure out which set of variables in the answer choices is the right one. But thinking in terms of variables can be confusing to some people. Picking numbers allows you to transform variables into concrete numbers.

To use the picking numbers method, you need to select numbers and plug them into the answer choices. You're essentially testing the relationships between the variables in each given answer and ensuring they remain true. It doesn't matter what specific numbers you plug into a problem. The same answer choice will always surface as long as you plug in consistently and follow all guidelines given by the problem.

For example, in the baseball player problem, let $m = 5$, $v = 100$, and $p = 10$. Clearly, these numbers aren't realistic (who flies at 10 miles an hour?), but your goal is to pick easy-to-manipulate numbers. Using our numbers, it takes the baseball player 100 ÷ 5 = 20 hours to drive and 100 ÷ 10 = 10 hours to fly. So, it takes him 20 − 10 = 10 hours longer to drive. After plugging m, v, and p into all the answer choices, we find that only **D** produces an answer of 10.

Very rarely, more than one answer choice will result in the correct answer for the first set of numbers you picked. When this occurs, simply plug in a different set of numbers. You will almost never have to plug in more than two sets of numbers.

When picking numbers, you must check through all the answer solutions with your chosen numbers. Obviously, this will slow you down, but that's the price you pay for using this method. Picking numbers gives you a mechanical method of solving tricky problems, and it also allows you to check your math for careless calculations, but it is time-consuming.

Finally, when you are picking numbers, avoid 0, 1, or any numbers that appear in the answer choices. Picking these numbers can overly simplify the expressions you are dealing with and cause you to pick the wrong answer.

The Bottom Line

As you can see, there is no "right" method to solving all algebra problems. Some methods work best some times, and others work best at other times. Part of your practice for the Math Level 1 test will be to get comfortable with algebra questions so that you can choose which method you want to use for every question.

Now, we'll review the algebra topics covered in the Math Level 1 Subject Test.

Equation-Solving

There are a number of algebraic terms you should know in order to be able to talk and think about algebra:

- **Variable.** An unknown quantity, written as a letter. The letters x and y are the most commonly used letters for variables, but a variable can be represented by any letter in the English alphabet. Greek letters are also used quite often. Variables will sometimes represent specified quantities, like apples or dollars, for example. Other times, a specific meaning won't be attached to them. You'll need to manipulate variables just to show that you understand certain algebraic principles.

- **Constant.** A quantity that does not change. In other words, a number.

- **Term.** The product of a constant and a variable. Another way to define a term is as any quantity that is separated from other quantities by addition or subtraction. For example, in the equation below, the left side contains four terms $\{x^3, 2x^2, -7x, 4\}$ and the right side contains two terms $\{x, -1\}$. The constants, 4 and –1, are considered terms because they are considered coefficients of variables raised to the zero power. For constant 4, $4 = 4x^0$. So every term, including constants, is the product of a constant and a variable raised to some power.

$$3x^3 + 2x^2 - 7x + 4 = x - 1$$

- **Expression.** Any combination of terms. An expression can be as simple as a single constant term, like 5. Or an expression can be as complicated as the sum or difference of many terms, each of which is a combination of constants and variables, such as $\{(x^2 + 2)^3 - 6x\}/7x^5$. Expressions don't include an equal sign, which is what differentiates expressions from equations. Expressions therefore cannot be solved; they can only be simplified.

- **Equation.** Two expressions linked by an equal sign. A lot of the algebra that you'll have to perform on the SAT Math tests will consist of solving an equation with one variable. Most of this chapter, in fact, deals with different techniques for simplifying expressions and solving different types of equations. First, we'll review how to write an equation.

Writing Equations

For some questions on the Math Level 1 test, you'll need to translate the problem from a language you're used to—English—into a more useful, albeit less familiar language. We're talking about the language of math, of course, and one of your major test-taking responsibilities is being able to write an equation based on the pertinent information you're given by a problem.

In other cases, you'll simply be asked to find an expression for a certain quantity described in a word problem. The best way to learn how to do these things quickly and effectively is to practice. Here's a sample problem:

> In a sack of 50 marbles, there are 20 more red marbles than blue marbles. All of the marbles in the sack are either red or blue. How many blue marbles are in the sack?

To start with, you can write $r + b = 50$, where r is the number of red marbles, and b is the number of blue marbles in the sack. This equation tell us that all of the 50 marbles in the sack are either red or blue.

Now that we have a starting equation, you need to decipher what exactly the question is asking for. This problem gives a clear-cut request: how many blue marbles are in the sack? You must therefore find the value of b.

Unfortunately, you can't do that with just this equation. More information needs to be incorporated. For example, use the knowledge that there are 20 more red marbles than blue marbles. This part of the word problem can be written in the form of an equation as $r = b + 20$. You could also write $b = r - 20$ to signify the same concept.

Let's list the two equations we have so far:

$$r + b = 50$$
$$b = r - 20$$

Using both of these equations, you can solve for b. After a little manipulation, which we'll cover in the coming sections, you'll find that $b = 15$ (and $r = 35$). Don't worry about the solution for now—just focus on how we translated the word problem into equations that lead to the solution.

That problem was easy. Here's a harder one:

> Stan sells oranges for c cents apiece. The minimum number of oranges that Stan will sell to an individual is r, but the first f oranges are free ($f < r$). Find an expression for the price in dollars of 35 oranges, if $35 > r$.

According to the problem, we need to find an expression (notice, not an equation) for the price in dollars of 35 oranges. The key to a problem like this one is working step by step. First, find out how many of the 35 oranges aren't free of charge:

$$\text{number of fare oranges} = 35 - f$$

because f is the number of oranges that are free, and $35 > f$. Next, find the price of those oranges:

$$\text{orange price} = (35 - f) \times c$$

But wait. Did you notice that the question asked for the price of 35 oranges in *dollars*? The writers of the Math Level 1 are a clever bunch, if not a little sneaky. They figure that a good number of test-takers will see only the word *price*, and they will not notice what units are asked for. Be careful not to fall into their carefully laid trap.

We know there are 100 cents per dollar, so we can easily convert the price by dividing by 100:

$$35 \text{ oranges} = \frac{(35 - f)c}{100}$$

Before we move to another problem, note that the variable r didn't appear anywhere in the answer. Egad! It is yet another attempt (and a common one at that) by those devious test-writers to lower your score. You may come across many problems, especially word problems, in which extraneous information is provided only to confuse you. Just because a variable or number appears in a problem doesn't mean that it will be useful in finding the answer.

Here's one last problem:

> Gus needs to paint his house, which has a surface area of x square feet. The brand of paint he buys (at a cost of p dollars a can) comes in cans that cover y square feet each. Gus also needs to buy ten pairs of new jeans (he is uncoordinated and spills often). They cost d dollars a pair. If Gus makes these purchases, what is the difference (in dollars) between the cost of the paint and the cost of the jeans? Assume he doesn't buy any excess paint—that is, the required amount is not a fraction of a can.

This word problem is long and complicated, but you need to carry out just four steps to solve it:

1. Gus must buy x/y cans of paint to cover his house.

2. This will cost him xp/y dollars.

3. The jeans Gus buys cost $10d$ dollars.

4. Thus, the difference, in dollars, between the cost of the paint and the cost of the jeans is $xp/y - 10d$.

For the rest of this chapter, we'll constantly be converting word problems into equations. If you're still uncomfortable doing this, don't worry. You'll get a lot more practice in the sections to come.

Manipulating Equations

Now that you know how to set up the equation, the next thing to do is to solve for the value that the question asks for. First and foremost, the most important thing to remember when manipulating equations is to do exactly the same thing to each side of the equation. If you divide one side of an equation by 3, you must divide the other side by 3. If you take the square root of one side of an equation, take the square root of the other.

By treating the two sides of the equation in the same way, you can rest easy that you won't change the meaning of the equation. You will, of course, change the *form* of the equation—that's the point of manipulating it. But the equation will always remain true as long as you always do the same thing to both sides.

For example, let's look at what happens when you manipulate the equation $3x + 2 = 5$, with $x = 1$.

1. Subtract 2 from both sides:

$$3x + 2 - 2 = 5 - 2$$
$$3x + 0 = 3$$
$$3(1) = 3$$
$$3 = 3$$

2. Multiply both sides by 2:

$$2(3x + 2) = 2(5)$$
$$6x + 4 = 10$$
$$6(1) + 4 = 10$$
$$10 = 10$$

3. Add 4 to both sides:

$$3x + 2 + 4 = 5 + 4$$
$$3x + 6 = 9$$
$$3(1) + 6 = 9$$
$$9 = 9$$

These examples show that you can tamper with the equation in any way you want, as long as you commit the same tampering on both sides. If you follow this rule, you can manipulate the question how you want without affecting the value of its variables.

Solving an Equation with One Variable

To solve an equation with one variable, you must isolate that variable. Isolating a variable means manipulating the equation until the variable is the only thing remaining on one side of the equation. Then, by definition, that variable is equal to everything on the other side, and you have successfully "solved for the variable."

For the quickest results, take the equation apart in the reverse order of operations. That is, first add and subtract any extra terms on the same side as the variable. Then, multiply and divide anything on the same side of the variable. Next, raise both sides of the equation to a power or take their roots according to any exponent attached to the variable. And finally, do anything inside parentheses. This process is PEMDAS in reverse (SADMEP!). The idea is to "undo" everything that is being done to the variable so that it will be isolated in the end. Let's look at an example:

$$\text{Solve for } x \text{ in the equation } \frac{(3x^2 + 5) \times 3}{4} + 1 = 61.$$

In this equation, the variable x is being squared, multiplied by 3, added to 5, etc. We need to do the opposite of all these operations in order to isolate x and thus solve the equation.

First, subtract 1 from both sides of the equation:

$$\frac{(3x^2 + 5) \times 3}{4} + 1 - 1 = 61 - 1$$
$$\frac{(3x^2 + 5) \times 3}{4} = 60$$

Then, multiply both sides of the equation by 4:

$$\frac{(3x^2 + 5) \times 3}{4} \times 4 = 60 \times 4$$
$$(3x^2 + 5) \times 3 = 240$$

Next, divide both sides of the equation by 3:

$$(3x^2 + 5) \times 3 \div 3 = 240 \div 3$$
$$3x^2 + 5 = 80$$

Now, subtract 5 from both sides of the equation:

$$3x^2 + 5 - 5 = 80 - 5$$
$$3x^2 = 75$$

Algebra

Again, divide both sides of the equation by 3:

$$3x^2 \div 3 = 75 \div 3$$
$$x^2 = 25$$

Finally, take the square root of each side of the equation:

$$\sqrt{x^2} = \sqrt{25}$$
$$x = \pm 5$$

We have isolated x to show that $x = \pm 5$.

Sometimes the variable that needs to be isolated is not conveniently located. For example, it might be in a denominator or an exponent. Equations like these are solved the same way as any other equation, except that you may need different techniques to isolate the variable. Let's look at a couple of examples:

Solve for x in the equation $\dfrac{1}{x} + 2 = 4$.

$$\frac{1}{x} + 2 = 4$$
$$\frac{1}{x} = 2$$
$$1 = 2x$$
$$x = \frac{1}{2}$$

The key step is to multiply both sides by x to extract the variable from the denominator. It is not at all uncommon to have to move the variable from side to side in order to isolate it.

Remember, performing an operation on a variable is mathematically no different than performing that operation on a constant or any other quantity.

Here's another, slightly more complicated example:

Solve for x in the equation $2^x = 3^{x+2}$:

$$2^x = 3^{x+2}$$
$$\log 2^x = \log 3^{x+2}$$
$$x \log 2 = (x + 2) \log 3$$
$$x \log 2 = x \log 3 + 2 \log 3$$
$$x \log 2 - x \log 3 = 2 \log 3$$
$$x(\log 2 - \log 3) = 2 \log 3$$
$$x = \frac{2 \log 3}{\log 2 - \log 3}$$
$$x \approx 5.42$$

This question is a good example of how it's not always simple to isolate a variable. (Don't worry about the logarithm in this problem—we'll review these later on in the chapter.) However, as you can see, even the thorniest problems can be solved systematically—as long as you have the right tools. In the next section, we'll discuss factoring and distributing, two techniques that were used in this example.

So, having just given you a very basic introduction to solving equations, we'll reemphasize two things:

1. Do the same thing to both sides.

2. Work backward (with respect to the order of operations).

Now we get into some more interesting tools you will need to solve certain equations.

Distributing and Factoring

Distributing and factoring are two of the most important techniques in algebra. They give you ways of manipulating expressions without changing the expression's value. So it follows that you can factor or distribute one side of the equation without doing the same for the other side of the equation.

The basis for both techniques is the following property, called the distributive property:

$$a \times (b + c + \dots) = a \times b + a \times c + \dots$$

Algebra

Similarly:

$$a \times (-b - c - \dots) = -a \times b - a \times c - \dots$$

a can be any kind of term, from a variable to a constant to a combination of the two.

Distributing

When you distribute a factor into an expression within parentheses, you simply multiply each term inside the parentheses by the factor outside the parentheses. For example, consider the expression $3y(y^2 - 6)$:

$$3y(y^2 - 6) = 3y^3 - 18y$$

If we set the original, undistributed expression equal to another expression, you can see why distributing facilitates the solving of some equations. Solving $3y \, (y^2 - 6) = 3y^3 + 36$ looks quite difficult. But if you distribute the $3y$, you get:

$$3y^3 - 18y = 3y^3 + 36$$

Subtracting $3y^3$ from both sides gives us:

$$-18y = 36$$
$$-y = 2$$

Factoring

Factoring an expression is essentially the opposite of distributing. Consider the expression $4x^3 - 8x^2 + 4x$, for example. You can factor out the GCF of the terms, which is $4x$:

$$4x^3 - 8x + 4x = 4x(x^2 - 2 + 1)$$

The expression simplifies further:

$$4x(x^2 - 2 + 1) = 4x(x - 1)^2$$

See how useful these techniques are? You can group or ungroup quantities in an equation to make your calculations easier. In the last example from the previous section on manipulating equations, we distributed *and* factored to solve an equation. First, we distributed the quantity log 3 into the sum of x and 2 (on the right side of the equation). We later factored the term x out of the expression $x \log 2 - x \log 3$ (on the left side of the equation).

Distributing eliminates parentheses, and factoring creates them. It's your job as a Math Level 1 mathematician to decide which technique will best help you solve a problem.

Let's see a few examples:

$$3(x + y + 4) = 3x + 3y + 12 \quad \text{3 is distributed.}$$
$$2x + 4x + 6x + 8x = 2x(1 + 2 + 3 + 4) \quad \text{$2x$ is factored out.}$$
$$x^2(x - 1) = x^3 - x^2 \quad \text{x^2 is distributed.}$$
$$xy^2(xy^2 + x^2y) = x^2y^4 + x^3y^3 \quad \text{xy^2 is distributed.}$$
$$14xy^2 - 4xy + 22y = 2y(7xy - 2x + 11) \quad \text{$2y$ is factored out.}$$

Combining Like Terms

After factoring and distributing, there are additional steps you can take to simplify expressions or equations. Combining like terms is one of the simpler techniques you can use, and involves adding or subtracting the coefficients of variables that are raised to the same power. For example, by combining like terms, the expression:

$$x^2 - x^3 + 4x^2 + 3x^3$$

can be simplified to:

$$x^3(-1 + 3) + x^2(1 + 4) = 2x^3 + 5x^2$$

by adding the coefficients of the variable x^3 together and the coefficients of x^2 together.

Generally speaking, when you have an expression in which one variable is raised to the same power in different terms, you can factor out the variable and add or subtract the coefficients, combining them into one coefficient and therefore combining the "like" terms into one term. A general formula for combining like pairs looks something like this:

$$ax^k + bx^k + cx^k = x^k(a + b + c)$$

Zero Product

When the product of any number of terms is zero, you know that at least one of the terms is equal to zero. For example, if $xy = 0$, you know that either:

1. $x = 0$, and $y \neq 0$

2. $y = 0$, and $x \neq 0$

3. $x = y = 0$.

This is useful in a situation like the following:

$$(x + 4)(x - 3) = 0$$
$$(x + 4) = 0 \text{ or } (x - 3) = 0$$

In this equation, either $x = -4$ or $x = 3$, since one of the expressions in parentheses must be equal to 0.

Consider this equation:

$$3x^2(x + 2) = 0$$

Again, since $3x^2$ or $(x + 2)$ must equal 0, we know that either $x = 0$ or $x = -2$.

Keep your eye out for a zero product—it's a big time-saver, especially when you have multiple-choice answers to choose from.

Absolute Value

To solve an equation in which the variable is within absolute value brackets, you must divide the equation into two equations.

The most basic example of this is an equation of the form $|x| = c$. In this case, either $x = c$ or $x = -c$.

A slightly more complicated example is this:

$$|x + 3| = 5. \text{ Solve for } x.$$

In this problem, you must solve two equations: First, solve for x in the equation $x + 3 = 5$. In this case, $x = 2$. Then, solve for x in the equation $x + 3 = -5$. In this case, $x = -8$. So the solutions to the equation $|x + 3| = 5$ are $x = \{-8, 2\}$.

Generally speaking, to solve an equation in which the variable is within absolute value brackets, first isolate the expression within the absolute value brackets and then divide the equation into two. Keep one of these two equations the same, while in the other negate one side of the equation. In either case, the absolute value of the expression within brackets will be the same. This is why there are always two solutions to absolute value problems (unless the variable is equal to 0).

Here is one more example:

Solve for x in terms of y in the equation $3\left|\dfrac{x+2}{3}\right| = y^2 - 1$.

First, isolate the expression within the absolute value brackets:

$$\left|\frac{x+2}{3}\right| = \frac{y^2 - 1}{3}$$

Then solve for the variable as if the expression within absolute value brackets were positive:

$$\frac{x+2}{3} = \frac{y^2 - 1}{3}$$
$$x + 2 = y^2 - 1$$
$$x = y^2 - 3$$

Next, solve for the variable as if the expression within absolute value brackets were negative:

$$\frac{x+2}{3} = -\frac{y^2 - 1}{3}$$
$$x + 2 = -y^2 + 1$$
$$x = -y^2 - 1$$

The solution set for x is $\{y^2 - 3, -y^2 - 1\}$.

Inequalities

Before you get too comfortable with expressions and equations, we should introduce inequalities. An inequality is like an equation, but instead of relating equal quantities, it specifies exactly how two quantities are *not* equal. There are four types of inequalities:

1. $x > y$: "x is greater than y."

2. $x < y$: "x is less than y."

3. $x \geq y$: "x is greater than or equal to y."

4. $x \leq y$: "x is less than or equal to y."

Solving inequalities is exactly like solving equations except for one very important difference: when both sides of an inequality are multiplied or divided by a negative number, the direction of the inequality switches.

Here are a few examples:

Solve for x in the inequality $\frac{x}{2} - 3 < 2y$.

$$\frac{x}{2} - 3 < 2y$$
$$\frac{x}{2} < 2y + 3$$
$$x < 2(2y + 3)$$
$$x < 4y + 6$$

Solve for x in the inequality $\frac{4}{x} \geq -2$.

$$\frac{4}{x} \geq -2$$
$$4 \geq -2x$$
$$-2 \leq x$$

Notice that in the last example, the inequality had to be reversed. Another way to express the solution is $x \geq -2$. To help remember that multiplication or division by a negative number reverses the direction of the inequality, remember that if $x > y$, then $-x < -y$, just as $5 > 4$ and $-5 < -4$. Intuitively, this idea makes sense, and it might help you remember this special rule of inequalities.

Absolute Value and Inequalities

When absolute values are included in inequalities, the solutions come in two varieties.

1. If the absolute value is less than a given quantity, then the solution is a single range, with a lower and an upper bound. For example,

Solve for x in the inequality $|2x - 4| \leq 6$.

- First, solve for the upper bound:

$$2x - 4 \leq 6$$
$$2x \leq 10$$
$$x \leq 5$$

- Second, solve for the lower bound:

$$2x - 4 \geq -6$$
$$2x \geq -2$$
$$x \geq -1$$

- Now, combine the two bounds into a range of values for x. $-1 \leq x \leq 5$ is the solution.

2. The other solution for an absolute value inequality involves two disjoint ranges: one whose lower bound is negative infinity and whose upper bound is a real number, and one whose lower bound is a real number and whose upper bound is infinity. This occurs when the absolute value is greater than a given quantity. For example,

Solve for x in the inequality $|3x + 4| > 16$.

- First, solve for the upper range:

$$3x + 4 > 16$$
$$3x > 12$$
$$x > 4$$

- Then, solve for the lower range:

$$3x + 4 < -16$$
$$3x < -20$$
$$x < -\frac{20}{3}$$

- Now combine the two ranges to form the solution, which is two disjoint ranges: $-\infty < x < -{}^{20}\!/_{3}$ or $4 < x < \infty$.

Algebra

When working with absolute values, it is important to first isolate the expression within absolute value brackets. Then, and only then, should you solve separately for the cases in which the quantity is positive and negative.

Ranges

Inequalities are also used to express the range of values that a variable can take. $a < x < b$ means that the value of x is greater than a and less than b. Consider the following word-problem example:

> A very complicated board game has the following recommendation on the box: "This game is only appropriate for people older than 40 but no older than 65." What is the range of the age of people for which the board game is appropriate?

Let a be the age of people for which the board game is appropriate. The lower bound of a is 40, and the upper bound is 65. The range of a does not include its lower bound (it is appropriate for people "older than 40"), but it does include its upper bound ("no older than 65", i.e., 65 is appropriate, but 66 is not). Therefore, the range of the age of people for which the board game is appropriate can be expressed by the inequality:

$$40 < a \leq 65$$

Here is another example:

> A company manufactures car parts. As is the case with any system of mass production, small errors occur on virtually every part. The key for this company to succeed in making viable car parts is to keep the errors within a specific range. The company knows that a particular piece they manufacture will not work if it weighs less than 98% of its target weight or more than 102% of its target weight. If the target weight of this piece is 21.5 grams, in what range of weights must the piece measure for it to function?

The boundary weights of this car part are $.98 \times 21.5 = 21.07$ and $1.02 \times 21.5 = 21.93$ grams. The problem states that the piece cannot weigh *less* than the minimum weight or *more* than the maximum weight in order for it to work. This means that the part will function at boundary weights themselves, and the lower and upper bounds are included. The answer to the problem is $21.07 \leq x \leq 21.93$, where x is the weight of the part in grams.

Finding the range of a particular variable is essentially an exercise in close reading. Every time you come across a question involving ranges, you should carefully peruse the problem to pick out whether a particular variable's range includes its bounds or not. This inclusion is the difference between "less than or equal to" and simply "less than."

Operations on Ranges

Operations like addition, subtraction, and multiplication can be performed on ranges just like they can be performed on variables. For example:

If $4 < x < 7$, what is the range of $2x + 3$?

To solve this problem, simply manipulate the range like an inequality until you have a solution. Begin with the original range:

$$4 < x < 7$$

Then multiply the inequality by 2:

$$8 < 2x < 14$$

Add 3 to the inequality, and you have the answer:

$$11 < 2x + 3 < 17$$

There is one crucial rule you need to know about multiplying ranges: if you multiply a range by a negative number, you *must* flip the greater-than or less-than signs. For instance, if you multiply the range $2 < x < 8$ by -1, the new range will be $-2 > x > -8$. Math Level 1 questions that ask you to perform operations on ranges of one variable will often test your alertness by making you multiply the range by a negative number.

Some range problems on the Math Level 1 will be made slightly more difficult by the inclusion of more than one variable. In general, the same basic procedures for dealing with one-variable ranges applies to adding, subtracting, and multiplying two-variable ranges.

Addition with Ranges of Two or More Variables

If $-2 < x < 8$ and $0 < y < 5$, what is the range of $x + y$?

Simply add the ranges. The lower bound is $-2 + 0 = -2$. The upper bound is $8 + 5 = 13$. Therefore, $-2 < x + y < 13$.

Subtraction with Ranges of Two or More Variables

Suppose $4 < s < 7$ and $-3 < t < -1$. What is the range of $s - t$?

In this case, you have to find the range of $-t$. By multiplying the range of t by -1 and reversing the direction of the inequalities, we find that $1 < -t < 3$. Now we can simply add the ranges again to find the range of $s - t$. $4 + 1 = 5$, and $7 + 3 = 10$. Therefore, $5 < s - t < 10$.

In general, to subtract ranges, find the range of the *opposite* of the variable being subtracted, and then add the ranges as usual.

Multiplication with Ranges of Two or More Variables

If $-1 < j < 4$ and $6 < k < 12$, what is the range of jk?

Algebra

First, multiply the lower bound of one variable by the lower and upper bounds of the other variable:

$$-1 \times 6 = -6$$
$$-1 \times 12 = -12$$

Then, multiply the upper bound of one variable with both bounds of the other variable:

$$4 \times 6 = 24$$
$$4 \times 12 = 48$$

The least of these four products becomes the lower bound, and the greatest is the upper bound. Therefore, $-12 < jk < 48$.

Let's try one more example of performing operations on ranges:

If $3 \leq x < 7$ and $4 \geq y \geq -3$, what is the range of $2(x + y)$?

The first step is to find the range of $x + y$. Notice that the range of y is written backward, with the upper bound to the left of the variable. Rewrite it first:

$$-3 \leq y \leq 4$$

Next add the ranges to find the range of $x + y$:

$$3 + -3 = 0 \text{ and } 7 + 4 = 11$$

We have our bounds for the range of $x + y$, but are they included in the range? In other words, is the range $0 < x + y < 11$, $0 \leq x + y \leq 11$, or some combination of these two?

The rule to answer this question is the following: if either of the bounds that are being added, subtracted, or multiplied is non-inclusive ($<$ or $>$), then the resulting bound is non-inclusive. Only when both bounds being added, subtracted, or multiplied are inclusive ($\leq$ or $\geq$) is the resulting bound also inclusive.

The range of x includes its lower bound, 3, but not its upper bound, 7. The range of y includes both its bounds. Therefore, the range of $x + y$ is $0 \leq x + y < 11$, and the range of $2(x + y)$ is $0 \leq 2(x + y) < 22$.

Algebra

Systems of Equations

Sometimes, a question will have a lone equation containing two variables, and using the methods we've discussed up until now will not be enough to solve for the variables. Additional information is needed, and it must come in the form of another equation.

Say, for example, that a single equation uses the two variables x and y. Try as you might, you won't be able to solve for x or y. But given another equation with the same two variables x and y, then the values of both variables can be found.

These multiple equations containing the same variables are called systems of equations. For the Math Level 1, there are essentially two types of systems of equations that you will need to be able to solve. The first, easier type involves substitution, and the second involves manipulating equations simultaneously.

Substitution

Simply put, substitution is when the value of one variable is found and then substituted into the other equation to solve for the other variable. It can be as easy as this example:

If $x - 4 = y - 3$ and $2y = 6$, what is x?

In this case, we have two equations. The first equation contains x and y. The second contains only y. To solve for x, you must solve for y in the second equation and substitute that value for y in the first equation. If $2y = 6$, then $y = 3$, and then $x = y - 3 + 4 = 3 - 3 + 4 = 4$.

Here is a slightly more complicated example.

Suppose $3x = y + 5$ and $2y - 2 = 12k$. Solve for x in terms of k.

Again, you cannot solve for x in terms of k using just the first equation. Instead, you must solve for y in terms of k in the second equation, and then substitute that value in the first equation to solve for x.

$$2y - 2 = 12k$$
$$2y = 12k + 2$$
$$y = 6k + 1$$

Then substitute $y = 6k + 1$ into the equation $3x = y + 5$.

$$3x = y + 5$$
$$3x = (6k + 1) + 5$$
$$3x = 6k + 6$$
$$x = 2k + 2$$

Simultaneous Equations

Simultaneous equations refer to equations that can be added or subtracted from each other in order to find a solution. Consider the following example:

Suppose $2x + 3y = 5$ and $-1x - 3y = -7$. What is x?

In this particular problem, you can find the value of x by adding the two equations together:

$$\begin{array}{r} 2x + 3y = 5 \\ +(-1x) - 3y = -7 \\ \hline x = -2 \end{array}$$

Here is another example:

$6x + 2y = 11$ and $5x + y = 10$. What is $x + y$?

By subtracting the second equation from the first:

$$\begin{array}{r} 6x + 2y = 11 \\ -(5x + y = 10) \\ \hline x + y = 1 \end{array}$$

Some test-takers might have seen this problem and been tempted to immediately start trying to solve for x and y individually. The better test-taker notices that by subtracting the second equation from the first, the answer is given.

Give this last example a try:

$2x + 3y = -6$ and $-4x + 16y = 13$. What is the value of y?

The question asks you to solve for y, which means that you should find a way to eliminate one of the variables by adding or subtracting the two equations. $4x$ is simply twice $2x$, so by multiplying the first equation by 2, you can then add the equations together to find y.

$$2 \times (2x + 3y = -6) = 4x + 6y = -12$$

Now add the equations and solve for y.

$$\begin{array}{r} 4x + 6y = -12 \\ +(-4x) + 16y = 13 \\ \hline 22y = 1 \\ y = \dfrac{1}{22} \end{array}$$

When you solve for one variable, like we have in this last example, you can solve for the second variable using either of the original equations. If the last question had asked you to calculate the value of xy, for example, you could solve for y, as above, and then solve for x by substitution into either equation. Once you know the independent values of x and y, you can multiply them together.

Simultaneous equations on the Math Level 1 will all be this simple. They will have solutions that can be found easily by adding or subtracting the equations given. Only as a last resort should you solve for one variable in terms of the other and then plug that value into the other equation to solve for the second variable.

Common Word Problems

The writers of the Math Level 1 love word problems. These problems force you to show your range as a mathematician. They demand that you read and comprehend the problem, set up an equation or two, and manipulate the equations to find the solution. Luckily, the Math Level 1 uses only a few types of word problems, and we have the nitty-gritty on all of them.

Rates

A rate is a ratio of related qualities that have different units. For example, speed is a rate that relates the two quantities of distance and time. Here is the general rate formula:

$$\text{quantity } A \text{ (in } x \text{ units)} \times \text{rate } (\text{ in } \frac{y}{x} \text{ units)} = \text{quantity } B \text{ (in } y \text{ units)}$$

No matter the specifics, the key to a rate problem is correctly placing the given information in the three categories. Then, you can substitute the values into the rate formula. We'll look at the three most common types of rate: speed, work, and price.

Speed

In the case of speed, time is quantity a and distance is quantity b. For example, if you traveled for 4 hours at 25 miles per hour, then:

$$4 \text{ hours} \times 25 \ \frac{\text{miles}}{\text{hour}} = 100 \text{ miles}$$

Note that the hour units canceled out, since the hour in the rate is at the bottom of the fraction. But you can be sure that the Math Level 1 test won't simply give you one of the quantities and the rate and ask you to plug it into the rate formula. Because rate questions are in the form of word problems, the information that you'll need to solve the problem will often be given in a less straightforward manner.

Here's an example:

> Jim rollerblades 6 miles per hour. One morning, Jim starts rollerblading and doesn't stop until he has gone 60 miles. How many hours did he rollerblade?

This question provides more information than simply the speed and one of the quantities. We know unnecessary facts such as how Jim is traveling (by rollerblades) and when he started (in the morning). Ignore them and focus on the facts you need to solve the problem.

- **Time a:** x hours rollerblading

- **Rate:** 6 miles per hour

- **Quantity b:** 60 miles

So, we can write:

$$x \text{ hours of rollerblading} = 60 \text{ miles} \div 6 \text{ miles per hour} = 10 \text{ hours}$$

Jim was rollerblading for 10 hours. This problem requires a little analysis, but basically we plugged some numbers into the rate equation and got our answer. Here's a slightly more difficult rate problem:

> At a cycling race, there are 50 cyclists in all, each representing a state. The cyclist from California can cumulatively cycle 528,000 feet per hour. If the race is 480 miles long, how long will it take him to finish the race?

Immediately, you should pick out the given rate of 528,000 feet per hour and notice that 480 miles are traveled. You should also notice that the question presents a units problem: the given rate is in feet cycled per hour, and the distance traveled is in miles.

Sometimes a question will give you inconsistent units, like in this example. Always read over the problem carefully and don't forget to adjust the units—the answer choices are bound to include non-adjusted options, just to throw you off.

For this question, since we know there are 5,280 feet in a mile, we can find the rate for miles per hour:

$$528,000 \text{ feet per hour} \div 5,280 \text{ feet per mile} = 100 \text{ miles per hour}$$

We can now plug the information into the rate formula:

- **Time:** x hours cycling

- **Rate:** 100 miles per hour

- **Distance:** 480 miles

$$480 \text{ miles} \div 100 \text{ miles per hour} = 4.8 \text{ hours}$$

So it takes the cyclist 4.8 hours to finish the race.

Work

In work questions, you will usually find the first quantity measured in time, the second quantity measured in work done, and the rate measured in work done per time. For example, if you knitted for 8 hours and produced two sweaters per hour, then:

$$8 \text{ hours} \times 2 \frac{\text{sweaters}}{\text{hour}} = 16 \text{ sweaters}$$

Here is a sample work problem. It is one of the harder rate questions you might come across on the Math Level 1:

Four men can dig a 40 foot well in 4 days. How long would it take for 8 men to dig a 60 foot well? Assume that these 8 men work at the same pace as the 4 men.

First, let's examine what that problem says: 4 men can dig a 40 foot well in 4 days. We are given a quantity of work of 40 feet and a time of 4 days. We need to create our own rate, using whichever units might be most convenient, to carry over to the 8-men problem. The group of 4 men dig 40 feet in 3 days. Dividing 40 feet by 4 days, you find that the group of 4 digs at a pace of 10 feet per day.

From the question, we know that 8 men dig a 60 foot well. The work done by the 8 men is 60 feet, and they work at a rate of 10 feet per day per 4 men. Can we use this information to answer the question? Yes. The rate of 10 feet per day per 4 men converts to 20 feet per day per 8 men, which is the size of the new crew. Now we use the rate formula:

- **Time:** x days of work

- **Rate:** 20 feet per day per eight men

- **Total Quantity:** 60 feet

$$60 \text{ feet} \div 20 \text{ feet per day per 8 men} = 3 \text{ days of work for 8 men}$$

This last problem required a little bit of creativity—but nothing you can't handle. Just remember the classic rate formula and use it wisely.

Algebra

Price

In rate questions dealing with price, you will usually find the first quantity measured in numbers of items, the second measured in price, and the rate in price per item. Let's say you had 8 basketballs, and you knew that each basketball cost $25 each:

$$8 \text{ basketballs} \times \$25 \frac{\text{price}}{\text{basketball}} = \$200$$

Percent Change

In percent-change questions, you will need to determine how a percent increase or decrease affects the values given in the question. Sometimes you will be given the percent change, and you will have to find either the original value or new value. Other times, you will be given one of the values and be asked to find the percent change. Take a look at this sample problem:

> A professional golfer usually has an average score of 72, but he recently went through a major slump. His new average is 20 percent worse (higher) than it used to be. What is his new average?

This is a percent-change question in which you need to find how the original value is affected by a percent increase. First, to answer this question, you should multiply 72 by .20 to see what the change in score was:

$$72 \times .20 = 14.4$$

Once you know the score change, then you should add it to his original average, since his new average is higher than it used to be:

$$72 + 14.4 = 86.4$$

It is also possible to solve this problem by multiplying the golfer's original score by 1.2. Since you know that the golfer's score went up by twenty percent over his original score, you know that his new score is 120% higher than his old score. If you see this immediately, you can skip a step and multiply $72 \times 1.2 = 86.4$.

Here's another example of a percent-change problem:

> A shirt whose original price was 20 dollars has now been put on sale for 14 dollars. By what percentage did its price drop?

In this case, you have the original price and the sale price and need to determine the percent decrease. All you need to do is divide the amount by which the quantity changed by the original quantity. In this case, the shirt's price was reduced by 20 – 14 = 6 dollars. So, 6 ÷ 20 = .3, a 30% drop in the price of the shirt.

Double Percent Change

A slightly trickier version of the percent-change question asks you to determine the cumulative effect of two percent changes in the same problem. For example:

A bike has an original price of 300 dollars. Its price is reduced by 30%. Then, two weeks later, its price is reduced by an additional 20%. What is the final sale price of the bike?

One might be tempted to say that the bike's price is discounted 30% + 20% = 50% from its original price, but the key to solving double percent-change questions is to realize that each percentage change is dependent on the last. For example, in the problem we just looked at, the second percent decrease is 20 percent of a new, lower price—not the original amount. Let's work through the problem carefully and see. After the first sale, the price of the bike drops 30 percent:

$$300 - (30\% \text{ of } 300) = 300 - .3(300) = 300 - 90 = 210 \text{ dollars}$$

The second reduction in price knocks off an additional 20 percent of the *sale* price, not the original price:

$$210 - (20\% \text{ of } 210) = 210 - .2(210) = 210 - 42 = 168 \text{ dollars}$$

The trickiest of the tricky percentage problems go a little something like this:

A computer has a price of 1400 dollars. Its price is raised 20%, and then lowered 20%. What is the final selling price of the computer?

If this question sounds too simple to be true; it probably is. The final price is not the same as the original. Why? Because after the price was increased by 20 percent, the reduction in price was a reduction of 20 percent of a new, higher price. Therefore, the final price will be lower than the original. Watch and learn:

$$1400 + (20\% \text{ of } 1400) = 1400 + .2(1400) = 1400 + 280 = 1680 \text{ dollars}$$

Now, after the price is reduced by 20%:

$$1680 - (20\% \text{ of } 1680) = 1680 - .2(1680) = 1680 - 336 = 1344 \text{ dollars}$$

Double percent problems can be more complicated than they appear. But solve it step by step, and you'll do fine.

Exponential Growth and Decay

These types of word problems take the concept of percent change even further. In questions involving populations growing in size or the diminishing price of a car over time, you need to perform percent-change operations repeatedly. Solving these problems would be time-consuming without exponents. Here's an example:

If a population of 100 grows by 5% per year, how great will the population be in 50 years?

To answer this question, you might start by calculating the population after one year:

$$100 + .05 \times 100 = 100 + 5 = 105$$

Or use the faster method we discussed in percent increase:

$$1.05 \times 100 = 105$$

After the second year, the population will have grown to:

$$100 \times 1.05 \times 1.05 = 100 \times 1.05^2 = 110.25$$

And so on and so on for 48 more years. You may already see the shortcut you can use to avoid having to do, in this case, 50 separate calculations. The final answer is simply:

$$100 \times 1.05^{50} = 1146.74 \approx 1147$$

In general, quantities like the one described in this problem are said to be growing exponentially. The formula for calculating how much an exponential quantity will grow in a specific number of years is:

$$\text{final amount} = \text{original amount} \times 1 + \text{growth rate}^{(\text{number of changes})}$$

Exponential decay is mathematically equivalent to negative exponential growth. But instead of a quantity growing at a constant percentage, the quantity shrinks at a constant percentage. Exponential decay is a repeated percent decrease. That is why the formulas that model these two situations are so similar. To calculate exponential decay:

$$\text{final amount} = \text{original amount} \times 1 - \text{decay rate}^{(\text{number of changes})}$$

The only difference between the two equations is that the base of the exponent is less than 1, because during each unit of time the original amount is reduced by a fixed percentage. Exponential decay is often used to model population decreases, as well as the decay of physical mass.

Let's work through a few example problems to get a feel for both exponential growth and decay problems.

Simple Exponential Growth Problems

A population of bacteria grows by 35% every hour. If the population begins with 100 specimens, how many are there after 6 hours?

The question, with its growing population of bacteria, makes it quite clear that this is an exponential growth problem. To solve the problem, you just need to plug the appropriate values into the formula for a repeated percent increase. The rate is .035, the original amount is 100, and the time is 6 hours:

$$100 \times 1.35^6 \approx 605 \text{ specimens}$$

Simple Exponential Decay Problem

A fully inflated beach ball loses 6% of its air every day. If the beach ball originally contains 4000 cubic centimeters of air, how many cubic centimeters does it hold after 10 days?

Since the beach ball loses air, we know this is an exponential decay problem. The decay rate is .06, the original amount is 4000 cubic centimeters of air, and the time is 10. Plugging the information into the formula:

$$4000 \times (.94)^{10} \approx 2154 \text{ cubic centimeters}$$

More Complicated Exponential Growth Problem

A bank offers a 4.7% interest rate on all savings accounts, compounded monthly. If 1000 dollars is initially put into a savings account, how much money will the account hold two years later?

This problem is a bit tricky for the simple reason that the interest on the account is compounded monthly. This means that in the 2 years that question refers to, there will be $2 \times 12 = 24$ compoundings of interest. The time variable in the equation is affected by these monthly compoundings: it will be 24 instead of 2. Thus, our answer is:

$$1000 \times 1.047^{24} \approx 3011.07 \text{ dollars}$$

Algebra

Here's another compounding problem:

> Sam puts 2000 dollars into a savings account that pays 5% interest compounded annually. Chris puts 2500 dollars into a different savings account that pays 4% annually. After 15 years, whose account will have more money in it, if no more money is added or subtracted from the principal?

Sam's account will have $2000 × 1.05^{15} ≈ $4157.85 in it after 15 years. Chris's account will have $2500 × 1.04^{15} ≈ $4502.36 in it. So, Chris's account will still have more money in it after 15 years. Notice, however, that Sam's account *is* gaining on Chris's account.

Logarithms

Logarithms have important uses in solving problems with complicated exponential equations. Consider the following example:

> The population of a small town is 1000 on January 1, 2001. It grows at a constant rate of 2% per year. In what year does the population of the town first exceed 1500?

This question is like the exponential growth problems we've just seen but with a twist. Here, we're given the growth rate, the initial quantity, *and* the ending quantity. We need to find the number of percent changes (in this case, the number of years) that links all these values. Since logarithms are the power to which you must raise a given number to equal another number, they are the perfect tool for solving this sort of problem.

$$1000 \times 1.02^x = 1500$$
$$1.02^x = 1.5$$
$$\log 1.02^x = \log 1.5$$
$$x \log 1.02 = \log 1.5$$
$$x = \frac{\log 1.5}{\log 1.02}$$
$$x = 20.47$$

In this case, it will take roughly 20.5 years for the town's population to exceed 1500. So about halfway through the year 2021, the population will first exceed 1500.

The general form for a problem like this one, in which the exponent is unknown, is to isolate the exponential term, take the logarithm of both sides, and then use the power rule of logarithms to bring the variable out of the exponent. You can then isolate the variable on one side of the equation. The base of the logarithms is insignificant. You could choose a base-10 logarithm or a logarithm of any other base, as long as it is consistently used.

Here's a simple example to illustrate this process:

> If $6x = 5^{1000}$, then find the value of x.

This problem would be vastly more difficult if we didn't have logarithms. How would you possibly calculate 5^{1000} anyhow? And how do you solve for x when it's the exponent of a number? But by taking the logarithm of each side of the equation, and utilizing the power rule of logarithms:

$$\log 6^x = \log 5^{1000}$$
$$x \log 6 = 1000 \log 5$$

The confusion clears, and we see that we have a logarithm problem that can be methodically solved.

$$x \log 6 = 1000 \log 5$$
$$x = 1000 \times \frac{\log 5}{\log 6}$$
$$x = 1000 \times \frac{.699}{.778}$$
$$x = 1000 \times .898$$
$$x = 898$$

Polynomials

A **polynomial** is an expression that contains one or more algebraic terms, each consisting of a constant multiplied by a variable raised to a power greater than or equal to zero. For example, $x^2 + 2x + 4$ is a polynomial with three terms (the third term is $4x^0 = 4$. $2x^{-1}$, on the other hand, is not a polynomial because x is raised to a negative power. A **binomial** is a polynomial with exactly two terms: $x + 5$ and $x^2 - 6$ are both binomials.

The rest of this chapter will show you how to perform different operations on and with polynomials.

Multiplying Binomials

There is a very simple acronym that is useful in remembering how to multiply binomials. It is **FOIL**, and it stands for **F**irst, **O**uter, **I**nner, **L**ast. This is the order that you multiply the terms of two binomials to get the right product.

$$(\, x \, + \, 1 \,)\,(\, x \, + \, 3 \,)$$

For example, if asked to multiply the binomials:

$$(x + 1)(x + 3)$$

You first multiply the first terms of each binomial:

$$x \times x = x^2$$

Next, multiply the outer terms of the binomials:

$$x \times 3 = 3x$$

Then, multiply the inner terms:

$$1 \times x = x$$

Finally, multiply the last terms:

$$3 \times -2 = -6$$

Combine like terms and you have your product:

$$2x^2 + -2x + 6x + -6 = 2x^2 + 4x - 6$$

Here are a few more examples:

$$(y + 3)(y - 7) = y^2 - 7y + 3y - 21 = y^2 - 4y - 21$$
$$(-x + 2)(4x + 6) = -4x^2 - 6x + 8x + 12 = -4x^2 + 2x + 12$$
$$(3a + 2b)(6c - d) = 18ac - 3ad + 12bc - 2bd$$

Multiplying Polynomials

Every once in a while, the Math Level 1 test will ask you to multiply polynomials. It may seem like a daunting task. But when the process is broken down, multiplying polynomials requires nothing more than distribution and combining like terms.

Consider the polynomials $(a + b + c)$ and $(d + e + f)$. To find their product, just distribute the terms of the first polynomial into the second polynomial individually and combine like terms to formulate your final answer:

$$(a + b + c)(d + e + f) = a(d + e + f) + b(d + e + f) + c(d + e + f)$$
$$= ad + ae + af + bd + be + bf + cd + ce + cf$$

Here's another example:

$$(x^2 + x + 4)(2x^3 + 5x^2 - 6x - 3)$$
$$= x^2(2x^3 + 5x^2 - 6x - 3) + x(2x^3 + 5x^2 - 6x - 3) + 4(2x^3 + 5x^2 - 6x - 3)$$
$$= 2x^5 + 5x^4 - 6x^3 - 3x^2 + 2x^4 + 5x^3 - 6x^2 - 3x + 8x^3 + 20x^2 - 24x - 12$$
$$= 2x^5 + 7x^4 + 7x^3 + 11x^2 - 27x - 12$$

As you can see, multiplying polynomials is little more than rote multiplication and addition.

Quadratic Equations

A quadratic, or quadratic polynomial, is a polynomial of the form $ax^2 + bx + c$, where $a \neq 0$. The following polynomials are quadratics:

$$x^2 + 3x - 4$$
$$y^2 - 5y + 3$$
$$x^2 - 6x$$
$$x^2 + 1$$
$$t^2$$

A **quadratic equation** sets a quadratic polynomial equal to zero. That is, a quadratic equation is an equation of the form $ax^2 + bx + c = 0$. The values of x for which the equation holds are called the **roots**, or solutions, of the quadratic equation. Most of the questions on quadratic equations involve finding their roots.

There are two basic ways to find roots: by factoring and by using the **quadratic formula**. Factoring is faster, but it can't always be done. The quadratic formula takes longer to work out, but it works for all quadratic equations. We'll study both in detail.

Factoring

To factor a quadratic, you must express it as the product of two binomials. In essence, factoring a quadratic involves a reverse-FOIL process. Take a look at this quadratic:

$$x^2 + 10x + 21$$

In the example above, the leading term has a coefficient of 1 (since $1x^2$ is the same as x^2). Since the two x variables are multiplied together during the FIRST step of foiling to get the first term of the quadratic polynomial, we know that the binomials whose product is this quadratic must be of the form $(x + m)(x + n)$, where m and n are constants. You also know that the sum of m and n is 10, since the $10x$ is derived from multiplying the OUTER and INNER terms of the binomials and then adding the resulting terms together ($10x = mx + nx$, so $m + n$ must equal 10). Finally, you know that the product of m and n equals 21, since 21 is the product of the two last terms of the binomials.

Now you just need to put the pieces together to find the values of m and n. You know that x is the first term of both binomials, and you know that the sum of m and n is 10 and the product of m and n is 21. The pair of numbers that fit the bill for m and n are 3 and 7. Thus, $x^2 + 10x + 21 = (x + 3)(x + 7)$. The quadratic expression has now been factored and simplified.

On the Math Level 1, though, you will often be presented with a quadratic *equation*. The only difference between a quadratic equation and a quadratic expression is that the equation is set equal to 0 ($x^2 + 10x + 21 = 0$). If you have such an equation, then once you have factored the quadratic you can solve it. Because the product of two terms is zero, one of the terms must be equal to zero. Thus, since $x + 3 = 0$ or $x + 7 = 0$, the solutions (also known as the roots) of the quadratic must be $x = -3$ and $x = -7$.

Quadratics with Negative Terms

So far we've dealt only with quadratics in which the terms are all positive. Factoring a quadratic that has negative terms is no more difficult, but it might take slightly longer to get the hang of it, simply because you are less used to thinking about negative numbers.

Consider the quadratic equation $x^2 - 4x - 21 = 0$. There are a number of things you can tell from this equation: the first term of each binomial is x, since the first term of the quadratic is x^2; the product of m and n is -21; and the sum of a and b equals -4. The equation also tells you that either m or n must be negative but that both cannot be negative, because the multiplication of one positive and one negative number can only result in a negative number. Now you need to look for the numbers that fit these requirements for m and n. The numbers that multiply together to give you -21 are: -21 and 1, -7 and 3, 3 and -7, and 21 and -1. The pair that works in the equation is -7 and 3.

Two Special Quadratic Polynomials

There are two special quadratic polynomials that pop up quite frequently on the Math Level 1, and you should memorize them. They are the perfect square and the difference of two squares. If you memorize the formulas below, you may be able to avoid the time taken by factoring.

There are two kinds of perfect square quadratics. They are:

1. $a^2 + 2ab + b^2 = (a + b)(a + b) = (a + b)^2$
   Example: $a^2 + 6ab + 9 = (a + 3)^2$

2. $a^2 - 2ab + b^2 = (a - b)(a - b) = (a - b)^2$
   Example: $a^2 - 6ab + 9 = (a - 3)^2$

Note that when you solve for the roots of a perfect square quadratic equation, the solution for the equation $(a + b)^2 = 0$ will be $-b$, while the solution for $(a + b)^2 = 0$ will be b.

The difference of two squares quadratics follow the form below:

$$(a + b)(a - b) = a^2 - b^2$$
$$\text{Example: } (a + 3)(a - 3) = a^2 - 9$$

Here's an instance where knowing the perfect square or difference of two square equations can help you:

Solve for x: $2x^2 + 20x + 50 = 0$.

To solve this problem by working out the math, you would do the following:

$$2x^2 + 20x + 50 = 0$$
$$2(x^2 + 10x + 25) = 0$$
$$(x + 5)^2 = 0$$
$$(x + 5)(x + 5) = 0$$
$$x = -5$$

If you got to the step where you had $2(x^2 + 10x + 25) = 0$ and realized that you were working with a perfect square of $2(x + 5)^2$, you could immediately have divided out the 2 from both sides of the equation and seen that the solution to the problem is –5.

Practice Quadratics

Since the ability to factor quadratics relies in large part on your ability to "read" the information in the quadratic, the best way to get good is to practice, practice, practice. Just like perfecting a jump shot, repeating the same drill over and over again will make you faster and more accurate. Take a look at the following examples and try to factor them on your own before you peek at the answers.

$$x^2 + x - 2 = 0 \qquad \text{Roots} : \{-2, 1\}$$
$$x^2 + 13x + 42 = 0 \qquad \text{Roots} : \{-7, -6\}$$
$$x^2 - 8x + 15 = 0 \qquad \text{Roots} : \{3, 5\}$$
$$x^2 - 5x - 36 = 0 \qquad \text{Roots} : \{-4, 9\}$$
$$x^2 - 10x + 25 = 0 \qquad \text{Roots} : \{5\}$$
$$x^2 - 25 = 0 \qquad \text{Roots} : \{5, -5\}$$

The Quadratic Formula

Factoring using the reverse-FOIL method is really only practical when the roots are integers. Quadratics, however, can have decimal numbers or fractions as roots. Equations like these can be solved using the quadratic formula. For an equation of the form $ax^2 + bx + c = 0$, the quadratic formula states:

$$x = \frac{-b \pm \sqrt{b^2 - 4ac}}{2a}$$

Consider the quadratic equation $x^2 + 5x + 3 = 0$. There are no integers with a sum of 5 and product of 3. So, this quadratic can't be factored, and we must resort to the quadratic equation. We plug the values, $a = 1$, $b = 5$, and $c = 3$ into the formula:

$$x = \frac{-5 \pm \sqrt{25 - 12}}{2}$$
$$= \frac{-5 \pm \sqrt{13}}{2}$$
$$= \frac{-5 + \sqrt{13}}{2}, \frac{-5 - \sqrt{13}}{2}$$
$$= -4.303, -.697$$

The roots of the quadratic are approximately $\{-4.303, -.697\}$.

Finding the Discriminant:

If you want to find out quickly how many roots an equation has without calculating the entire formula, all you need to find is an equation's discriminant. The **discriminant** of a quadratic is the quantity $b^2 - 4ac$. As you can see, this is the radicand in the quadratic equation. If:

1. $b^2 - 4ac = 0$, the quadratic has one real root and is a perfect square.

2. $b^2 - 4ac > 0$, the quadratic has two real roots.

3. $b^2 - 4ac < 0$, the quadratic has no real roots, and two complex roots.

This information is useful when deciding whether to crank out the quadratic formula on an equation, and it can spare you some unnecessary computation. For example, say you're trying to solve for the speed of a train in a rate problem, and you find that the discriminant is less than zero. This means that there are no real roots (a train can only travel at speeds that are real numbers), and there is no reason to carry out the quadratic formula.

Key Formulas

Distributive Property

$$a(b + c + d + \ldots) = ab + ac + ad + \ldots$$
$$a(-b - c - d - \ldots) = -ab - ac - ad - \ldots$$

Perfect Square of a Binomial

$$(a + b)^2 = a^2 + 2ab + b^2$$
$$(a - b)^2 = a^2 - 2ab + b^2$$

Difference of Two Squares

$$x^2 - y^2 = (x + y)(x - y)$$

Quadratic Formula

In a quadratic equation of the form $ax^2 + bx + c = 0$, where $a \neq 0$:

$$x = \frac{-b \pm \sqrt{b^2 - 4ac}}{2a}$$

Algebra

Review Questions

1. Solve for x in the equation $\dfrac{2 + 3\left(\dfrac{x}{4} - 1\right)}{24} = \dfrac{1}{3}$

   (A) $x = -3$
   (B) $x = 0$
   (C) $x = 6$
   (D) $x = 12$
   (E) $x = 24$

2. Solve for x in the following inequality: $\dfrac{-2x + 8}{6} > 3$

   (A) $x < -13$
   (B) $x \geq -13$
   (C) $x \leq -5$
   (D) $x < -5$
   (E) $x > -5$

3. Solve for x in the following equation: $3 + |2x - 7| = x + 2$

   (A) $x = -6$

   (B) $x = 8$

   (C) $x = \{\frac{8}{3}, 8\}$

   (D) $x = \{6, 8\}$

   (E) $x = \{\frac{8}{3}, 6\}$

4. If $x = 2y - 4$ and $y = 7s + 1$, what is the value of s in terms of x?

   (A) $s = \dfrac{\dfrac{x + 3}{2}}{7}$

   (B) $s = \dfrac{\dfrac{x + 4}{2} - 1}{7}$

   (C) $s = \dfrac{\dfrac{x + 2}{2} - 1}{7}$

   (D) $s = \dfrac{x}{2} + 2 + \dfrac{4}{7}$

   (E) $s = \dfrac{4x}{7}$

Algebra

5. Jim and Ryan run laps around a track which is $^1/_4$ of a mile long. If Jim runs h laps per hour, Ryan runs half as fast as Jim, and Jim starts running half an hour before Ryan, how many miles farther than Ryan has Jim run two hours after Jim starts?

    (A) $\dfrac{1.25h}{4}$

    (B) $\dfrac{2.25h}{4}$

    (C) $\dfrac{5h}{4}$

    (D) $\dfrac{5}{h}$

    (E) $\dfrac{4h}{1.5}$

6. Ken buys a shirt on a 30% sale from its original price of 10 dollars. He then resells it at a 60% increase from the price at which he bought it. How much does Ken sell the shirt for?

    (A) $4.20
    (B) $11.20
    (C) $13.00
    (D) $13.30
    (E) $14.20

7. A train leaves the station traveling due east at a rate of 45 miles per hour. A second train leaves a different station an hour later, traveling due west on the same track, going 60 miles per hour. If the stations are 255 miles apart, how many miles from the halfway point between the stations will the trains collide?

    (A) 0
    (B) 5
    (C) 7.5
    (D) 12.5
    (E) 25

8. A snowman weighing 250 pounds begins to melt in the spring. It loses 4% of its weight every day. How many full days will pass before it weighs less than 100 pounds?

    (A) 17
    (B) 22
    (C) 23
    (D) 27
    (E) 45

9. What is $(a + b + 3c)(2a + 3b + 4c)$?

    (A) $3a + 4b + 7c$
    (B) $2a^2 + 3b^2 + 12c^2$
    (C) $2a^2 + 10ac + 12c^2$
    (D) $2a^2 + 3ab + 10ac + 9bc + 12c^2$
    (E) $2a^2 + 3b^2 + 12c^2 + 5ab + 10ac + 13bc$

10.   Solve for x in the following equations: $3x^2 + 24x - 27 = 0$

(A) $x = 1$
(B) $x = -9$
(C) $x = \{1, -9\}$
(D) $x = \{-1, 9\}$
(E) $x = \{3, 27\}$

Explanations

1.   D

To solve this problem, just isolate the variable:

$$\frac{2 + 3(\frac{x}{4} - 1)}{24} = \frac{1}{3}$$
$$2 + 3(\frac{x}{4} - 1) = 8$$
$$3(\frac{x}{4} - 1) = 6$$
$$\frac{x}{4} - 1 = 2$$
$$\frac{x}{4} = 3$$
$$x = 12$$

2.   D

Solving for a variable in an inequality is similar to solving for a variable in a normal equation, with one big difference: you isolate the variable. But remember that if you multiply or divide an inequality by a negative number, you must reverse the direction of the inequality symbol:

$$\frac{-2x + 8}{6} > 3$$
$$-2x + 8 > 18$$
$$-2x > 10$$
$$x < -5$$

Algebra

3.   **E**

First, isolate the expression within the absolute value brackets:

$$3 + |2x - 7| = x + 2$$
$$|2x - 7| = x - 1$$

Then divide the equation into two equations. In this first case, the expression within absolute value brackets is positive:

$$2x - 7 = x - 1$$
$$2x = x + 6$$
$$x = 6$$

Next, let the expression within absolute value brackets be negative:

$$2x - 7 = -(x - 1)$$
$$2x - 7 = 1 - x$$
$$3x = 8$$
$$x = \frac{8}{3}$$

The two solutions are $x = \{\frac{8}{3}, 6\}$.

4.   **B**

First, solve for s in terms of y:

$$7s + 1 = y$$
$$7s = y - 1$$
$$s = \frac{y - 1}{7}$$

Next, solve for y in terms of x:

$$2y - 4 = x$$
$$2y = x + 4$$
$$y = \frac{x + 4}{2}$$

Finally, substitute this value for y in the equation with s:

$$s = \frac{\frac{x+4}{2} - 1}{7}$$

5. A

This is a rate question, and we are given the input and rate in order to find the output. So, we can plug the known values into the rate formula:

$$\text{input} \times \text{rate} = \text{output}$$

Jim runs h laps per hour for 2 hours, so his total distance traveled is $2h$ laps, which equals $\frac{2h}{4}$ miles. Ryan runs $.5h$ laps per hour for 1.5 hours, so in total he runs $0.75h$ laps. This is equal to $\frac{.75h}{4}$ miles. The difference between the distance traveled by Jim and the distance traveled by Ryan is $\frac{2h}{4} - \frac{.75h}{4} = \frac{1.25h}{4}$ miles.

6. B

This is a double percent-change problem, and so we perform each percent change one by one. First, Ken bought the shirt at a discount of 30%. The price at which he paid was:

$$.7 \times 10 = 7 \text{ dollars}$$

He then sold it for 60% more than he paid:

$$1.6 \times 7 = 11.2 \text{ dollars}$$

He sold the shirt for $11.20.

7. C

The toughest part of this rate problem is translating the word problem into an equation. The point at which the trains will collide is the point at which their combined distance traveled is 255 miles. Using this fact and the rates at which the trains travel, we can find out when the collision occurs, in relation to when the trains left their respec-

Algebra

tive stations. Finally, from this newly calculated information, we can find where the collision occurred. Here is the rate formula we'll be using:

$$\text{Distance} = \text{Rate} \times \text{Time}$$

Let x represent the number of hours before the trains collide. We then have the equation:

$$45x + 60(x - 1) = 255$$

This equation explains the situation before the collision: that the train going 45 miles per hour traveled for x hours and the train traveling 60 miles per hour traveled for $x - 1$ hours. Their combined distance traveled is 255. Now solve the equation for x:

$$45x + 60(x - 1) = 255$$
$$45x + 60x - 60 = 255$$
$$105x = 315$$
$$x = 3$$

3 hours pass before the trains collide. From this, we know that the collision happened $3 \times 45 = 135$ miles from the western station, and $2 \times 60 = 120$ miles from the eastern station. The halfway point between the stations is $\frac{255}{2} = 127.5$ miles from either station, so it happened $135 - 127.5 = 7.5$ miles from the halfway point between the stations.

8. **C**
This problem fits the classic exponential decay model. So we plug the given information into the formula:

$$\text{final amount} = \text{original amount} \times 1 - \text{decay rate}^{(\text{number of changes})}$$

Then we solve:

$$250 \times .96^x = 100$$
$$.96^x = .4$$
$$\log .96^x = \log .4$$
$$x \log .96 = \log .4$$
$$x = \frac{\log .4}{\log .96}$$
$$x = 22.47$$

Thus, it takes approximately 22.5 days to reach the 100 pound mark, or, as the question asked, 23 full days.

9. **E**

To multiply polynomials two at a time, just distribute the terms of one polynomial into the other one individually:

$$(a + b + 3c)(2a + 3b + 4c) = a(2a + 3b + 4c) + b(2a + 3b + 4c) + 3c(2a + 3b + 4c)$$
$$= 2a^2 + 3ab + 4ac + 2ab + 3b^2 + 4bc + 6ac + 9bc + 12c^2$$
$$= 2a^2 + 3b^2 + 12c^2 + 5ab + 10ac + 13bc$$

10. **C**

The equation given is in the form of a quadratic equation $ax^2 + bx + c = 0$, so you can use either the reverse FOIL or the quadratic formula to solve for the roots. Before doing either of those things, first factor out 3 from the equation:

$$3(x^2 + 8x - 9) = 0$$

Factoring takes less time than working out the quadratic formula, so check to see if factoring is possible. It is, and you get:

$$x^2 + 8x - 9 = (x - 1)(x + 9)$$

The solution set for x is {1, −9}.

Algebra

Plane Geometry

Roughly 20 percent of the questions on the Math Level 1 test cover plane geometry. In addition, questions that deal more specifically with solid geometry, coordinate geometry, and trigonometry assume a thorough knowledge of plane geometry. In all, a whopping 45 percent of the Math Level 1 test involves plane geometry either directly or indirectly.

Lines and Angles

A **line** is a collection of points that extends without limit in a straight formation. A line can be named by a single letter, like line l, or it can be named according to two points that it contains, like line AB. The second way of naming a line indicates an important property common to all lines: any two points in space determine a line. For example, given two points, J and K:

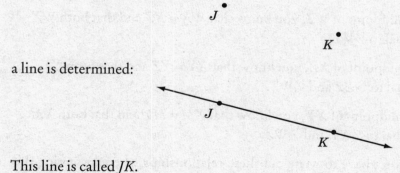

a line is determined:

This line is called JK.

111

Line Segments

A **line segment** is a section of a line. It is named and determined by its endpoints. Unlike a line, whose length is infinite, a line segment has finite length. Line segment *AB* is pictured below.

Distance and Midpoint of a Line Segment

The **midpoint** of a line segment is the point on the segment that is **equidistant** (the same distance) from each endpoint. Because a midpoint splits a line segment into two equal halves, the midpoint is said to *bisect* the line segment.

Because a midpoint cuts a line segment in half, knowing the distance between the midpoint and one endpoint of a line segment allows you to calculate the length of the entire line segment. For example, if the distance from one endpoint to the midpoint of a line segment is 5, the length of the whole line segment is 10.

The Math Level 1 test often asks questions that focus on this property of midpoints. The Math Level 1 writers usually make their questions a little trickier though, by including multiple midpoints. Take a look:

> *X* is the midpoint of *WZ* and *Y* is the midpoint of *XZ*. If *M* is the midpoint of *XY* and *MY* = 3, what is the length of *WX*?

All the midpoints flying around in this question can get quite confusing. Instead of trying to visualize what is being described in your head, draw a sketch of what the question describes.

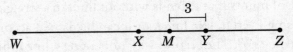

Once you've drawn a sketch, you can see how the three midpoints, and the new line segments that the midpoints create, all relate to each other.

- Since *X* is the midpoint of *WZ*, you know that *WX* = *XZ* and that both *WX* and *XY* are equal to ½*WZ*.

- Since *Y* is the midpoint of *XZ*, you know that *XY* = *YZ* and that both *XY* and *YZ* are equal to ½*XZ* and ¼*WZ*.

- Since *M* is the midpoint of *XY*, you know that *XM* = *MY* and that both *XM* and *MY* are equal to ½*XY* and ⅛*WZ*.

Please note that you don't have to write out these relationships when answering this sort of question. If you draw a good sketch, it's possible to *see* the relationships.

Once you know the relationships, you can solve the problem. For this question, you know that *MY* is equal to ⅛*WZ*. Since, as the question tells you, *MY* = 3, you can calculate that *WZ* = 24. The question asks for the length of *WX*, which is equal to ½*WZ*, so *WX* = 12.

Angles

Technically speaking, an **angle** is the union of two rays (lines that extend infinitely in just one direction) that share an endpoint (called the vertex of the angle). The measure of an angle is how far you must rotate one of the rays such that it coincides with the other.

In this guide and for the Math Level 1, you don't really need to bother with such a technical definition. Suffice it to say, angles are used to measure rotation. One full revolution around a point creates an angle of 360 degrees, or 360°. A half-revolution, also known as a straight angle, is 180° degrees. A quarter revolution, or right angle, is 90°.

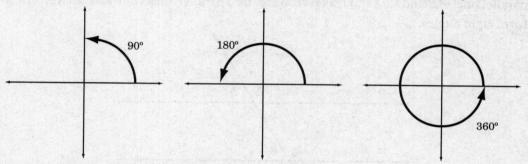

In text, angles can also be indicated by the symbol ∠.

Vertical Angles

When two lines or line segments intersect, two pairs of congruent (equal) angles are created. The angles in each pair of congruent angles created by the intersection of two lines are called vertical angles:

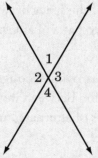

In this figure, ∠1 and ∠4 are vertical angles (and therefore congruent), as are ∠2 and ∠3.

Plane Geometry

Supplementary and Complementary Angles

Supplementary angles are two angles that together add up to 180°. **Complementary angles** are two angles that add up to 90°.

Whenever you have vertical angles, you also have supplementary angles. In the diagram of vertical angles above, $\angle 1$ and $\angle 2$, $\angle 1$ and $\angle 3$, $\angle 2$ and $\angle 4$, and $\angle 3$ and $\angle 4$ are all pairs of supplementary angles.

Parallel Lines Cut by a Transversal

Lines that will never intersect are called **parallel lines**, which are given by the symbol ||. The intersection of one line with two parallel lines creates many interesting angle relationships. This situation is often referred to as "parallel lines cut by a transversal," where the transversal is the nonparallel line. As you can see in the diagram below of parallel lines *AB* and *CD* and transversal *EF*, two parallel lines cut by a transversal will form eight angles.

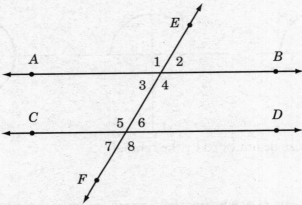

Among the eight angles formed, three special angle relationships exist:

1. **Alternate exterior angles** are pairs of congruent angles on opposite sides of the transversal, outside of the space between the parallel lines. In the figure above, there are two pairs of alternate exterior angles: $\angle 1$ and $\angle 8$, and $\angle 2$ and $\angle 7$.

2. **Alternate interior angles** are pairs of congruent angles on opposite sides of the transversal in the region between the parallel lines. In the figure above, there are two pairs of alternate interior angles: $\angle 3$ and $\angle 6$, and $\angle 4$ and $\angle 5$.

3. **Corresponding angles** are congruent angles on the same side of the transversal. Of two corresponding angles, one will always be between the parallel lines, while the other will be outside the parallel lines. In the

previous figure, there are four pairs of corresponding angles: $\angle 1$ and $\angle 5$, $\angle 2$ and $\angle 6$, $\angle 3$ and $\angle 7$, and $\angle 4$ and $\angle 8$.

In addition to these special relationships between angles, all adjacent angles formed when two parallel lines are cut by a transversal are supplementary. In the previous figure, for example, $\angle 1$ and $\angle 2$ are supplementary.

Math Level 1 questions covering parallel lines cut by a transversal are usually straightforward. For example:

In the figure below, if lines m and n are parallel and $\angle b = 110°$, then $f - g =$

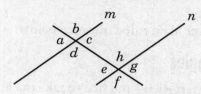

If you know the relationships of the angles formed by two parallel lines cut by a transversal, answering this question is easy. $\angle b$ and $\angle f$ are alternate exterior angles, so $\angle f = 110°$. $\angle g$ is adjacent to $\angle f$, so it must be equal to $180° - 110° = 70°$. From here, it's easy to calculate that $f - g = 110° - 70° = 40°$.

Perpendicular Lines

Two lines that intersect to form a right (90°) angle are called **perpendicular lines**. Line segments AB and CD are perpendicular.

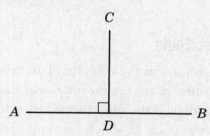

A line or line segment is called a perpendicular bisector when it intersects a line segment at the midpoint, forming vertical angles of 90° in the process. For example, in the figure above, since $AD = DB$, CD is the perpendicular bisector of AB.

Keep in mind that if a single line or line segment is perpendicular to two different lines or line segments, then those two lines or line segments are parallel. This is actually just another example of parallel lines being cut by a transversal (in this case, the transversal is perpendicular to the parallel lines), but it is a common situation when dealing with polygons. We'll examine this type of case later.

Triangles

The importance of triangles to the plane geometry questions on the Math Level 1 test cannot be overstated. Not only will you encounter numerous questions specifically about triangles, you will also need a solid understanding of triangles in order to answer other questions about polygons, coordinate geometry, and trigonometry. Luckily for you, the essential rules governing triangles are few and simple to master.

Basic Properties

Every triangle adheres to four main rules, outlined below:

1. Sum of the Interior Angles

If you were trapped on a desert island and had to take the Math Level 1 test, this is the one rule about triangles you should bring along: the sum of the measures of the interior angles is 180°. With this rule, if you know the measures of two of a triangle's angles, you will be able to find the third. Helpful, don't you think?

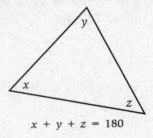

$$x + y + z = 180$$

2. Measure of an Exterior Angle

Another property of triangles is that the measure of an exterior angle of a triangle is equal to the sum of the measures of the remote interior angles.

    An exterior angle of a triangle is the angle formed by extending one of the sides of the triangle past a vertex (the point at which two sides meet). An exterior angle is always supplementary to the interior angle with which it shares a vertex, and equal in measure to the sum of the measures of the remote interior angles. Take a look at the figure below, in which d, the exterior angle, is supplementary to interior angle c:

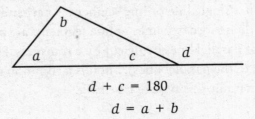

$$d + c = 180$$
$$d = a + b$$

It doesn't matter which side of a triangle you extend to create an exterior angle; the exterior angle will always be supplementary to the interior angle with which it shares a vertex and therefore (because of the 180° rule) equal to the sum of the remote interior angles.

3. Triangle Inequality

The third important property of triangles is the triangle inequality rule, which states: the length of a side of a triangle is less than the sum of the lengths of the other two sides and greater than the difference of the lengths of the other two sides.

Observe the figure below:

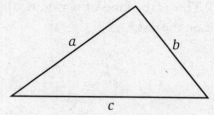

From the triangle inequality, we know that $c - b < a < c + b$. The exact length of side a depends on the measure of the angle created by sides b and c. If this angle is large (close to 180°) then a will be large (close to $b + c$). If this angle is small (close to 0°), then a will be small (close to $b - c$).

For an example, take a look at this triangle:

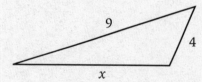

Using the triangle inequality, we can tell that $9 - 4 < x < 9 + 4$, or $5 < x < 13$. The exact value of x depends on the measure of the angle opposite side x.

4. Proportionality of Triangles

This brings us to the last basic property of triangles, which has to do with the relationships between the angles of a triangle and the lengths of the triangle's sides. In every triangle, the longest side is opposite the largest angle and the shortest side is opposite the smallest angle.

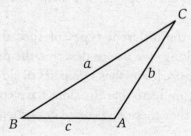

In this figure, side *a* is clearly the longest side and ∠*A* is the largest angle. Conversely, side *c* is the shortest side and ∠*C* is the smallest angle. It follows, therefore, that $c < b < a$ and $C < B < A$. This proportionality of side lengths and angle measures holds true for all triangles.

We did not assign measures and lengths to the angles and sides for the figure above. If we had limited information about those values, however we could make certain assumptions about the other unknown side lengths and angles measures. For example, if we knew the measures of two of the angles in the triangle, we could find the measure of the third angle and therefore decide which side is the longest (it would be the side opposite the largest angle). This is the kind of reasoning that you might have to use when dealing with triangles on the test.

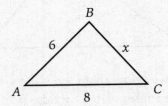

What is one possible value of *x* if angle $C < A < B$?

(A)   1
(B)   6
(C)   7
(D)   10
(E)   15

The largest angle in triangle *ABC* is ∠*B* , which is opposite the side of length 8. The smallest angle in triangle *ABC* is ∠*C* , which is opposite the side of length 6. This means that the third side, of length *x*, measures between 6 and 8 units in length. The value 7 is the only choice that fits the criteria.

Special Triangles

There are several special triangles that have particular properties. Knowing these triangles and what makes each of them special will help you immeasurably on the Math Level 1 test.

But before getting into the different types of special triangles, we must take a moment to explain the markings we use to describe the properties of each particular triangle. For example, the figure below has two pairs of sides of equal length and three congruent angle pairs: these indicate that the sides have equal length. The arcs drawn into ∠*A* and ∠*B* indicate that these angles are congruent. In some diagrams, there might be more than one pair of equal sides or congruent angles. In this case, double hash marks or double arcs can be drawn into a pair of sides or angles to indicate that they are equal to each other, but not necessarily equal to the other pair of sides or angles:

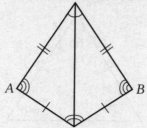

Now, on to the special triangles.

Scalene Triangles

A **scalene triangle** has no equal sides and no equal angles.

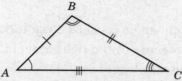

In fact, the special property of scalene triangles is that they don't really have any special qualities. Scalene triangles almost never appear on the Math Level 1.

Isosceles Triangles

A triangle that contains two sides of equal length is called an **isosceles triangle**. In an isosceles triangle, the two angles opposite the sides of equal length are congruent. These angles are usually referred to as base angles. In the isosceles triangle below, side $a = b$ and $\angle A = B$:

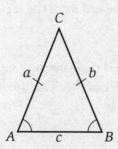

If you know the value of one of the base angles in an isosceles triangle, you can figure out all the angles. For example, if one base angle of an isosceles triangle is 35°, then you know that the other base angle is also 35°. Since the three angles in a triangle must add up to 180°, you can figure out the value of the third angle: 180° – 35° – 35° = 110°.

Equilateral Triangles

A triangle whose sides are all of equal length is called an **equilateral triangle**. All three angles in an equilateral triangle are congruent as well; the measure of each is 60°.

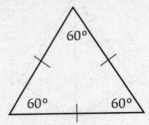

If you know that a triangle has three equal sides, then the proportionality rule states that the triangle must also have three equal angles. Similarly, if you know that a triangle has three equal angles, then you know it has three equal sides.

Right Triangles

A triangle that contains a right angle is called a **right triangle**. The side opposite the right angle is called the hypotenuse of the right triangle, and the other two sides are called legs. The angles opposite the legs of a right triangle are complementary.

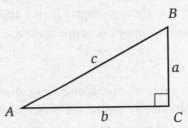

In the figure above, $\angle C$ is the right angle (as indicated by the box drawn in the angle), side c is the hypotenuse, and sides a and b are the legs.

The Pythagorean Theorem

The Pythagorean theorem is crucial to answering most of the right-triangle questions that you'll encounter on the Math Level 1. The theorem will also come in handy later on, as you study coordinate geometry and trigonometry. The theorem states that in a right triangle $a^2 + b^2 = c^2$:

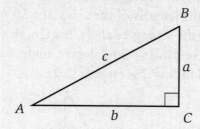

where c is the length of the hypotenuse, and a and b are the lengths of the two legs. The theorem states that the square of the hypotenuse is equal to the sum of the squares of the two legs.

If you know the measures of two sides of a right triangle, you can always use the Pythagorean theorem to find the third.

Pythagorean Triples

Because right triangles obey the Pythagorean theorem, only a few have side lengths which are all integers. For example, a right triangle with legs of length 3 and 5 has a hypotenuse of length $\sqrt{3^2 + 5^2} = \sqrt{9 + 25} = \sqrt{34} = 5.83$.

The few sets of three integers that do obey the Pythagorean theorem and can therefore be the lengths of the sides of a right triangle are called Pythagorean triples. Here are some common ones:

$$\{3, 4, 5\}$$
$$\{5, 12, 13\}$$
$$\{7, 24, 25\}$$
$$\{8, 15, 17\}$$

In addition to these Pythagorean triples, you should also watch out for their multiples. For example, $\{6, 8, 10\}$ is a Pythagorean triple, since it is a multiple of $\{3, 4, 5\}$.

The Math Level 1 is full of right triangles whose side lengths are Pythagorean triples. Study the ones above and their multiples. If you can recognize a Pythagorean triple on a triangle during the test, you can drastically reduce the amount of time you need to spend on the problem since you won't need to do any calculations.

Special Right Triangles

Right triangles are pretty special in their own right. But there are two *extra*special right triangles that appear frequently on the Math Level 1. They are 30-60-90 triangles and 45-45-90 triangles.

Plane Geometry

30-60-90 Triangles

A 30-60-90 triangle is a triangle with angles of 30°, 60°, and 90°. What makes it special is the specific pattern that the lengths of the sides of a 30-60-90 triangle follow. Suppose the short leg, opposite the 30 degree angle, has length x. Then the hypotenuse has length $2x$, and the long leg, opposite the 60 degree angle, has length $x\sqrt{3}$. The sides of every 30-60-90 triangle will follow this ratio of $1 : 2 : \sqrt{3}$.

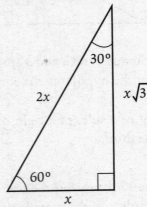

The constant ratio of the lengths of the sides of a 30-60-90 triangle means that if you know the length of one side in the triangle, you will immediately know the lengths of all the sides. If, for example, you know that the side opposite the 30° angle is 2 meters long, then by using the $1 : 2 : \sqrt{3}$ ratio, you will know that the hypotenuse is 4 meters long, and the leg opposite the 60° angle is $2\sqrt{3}$ meters. On the Math Level 1, you will quite often encounter a question that will present you with an unnamed 30-60-90 triangle, allowing you to use your knowledge of this special triangle. You could solve these questions by using the Pythagorean theorem, but that method takes a lot longer than simply knowing the proper 30-60-90 ratio.

45-45-90 Triangles

A 45-45-90 triangle is a triangle with two 45° angles and one right angle. This type of triangle is also sometimes referred to as an isosceles right triangle, since it's both isosceles and right. Like the 30-60-90 triangle, the lengths of the sides of a 45-45-90 triangle also follow a specific pattern that you should know. If the legs are of length x (they are always equal), then the hypotenuse has length $x\sqrt{2}$. Take a look at this diagram:

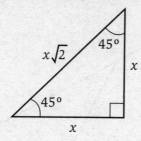

As with 30-60-90 triangles, knowing the 1: 1: $\sqrt{2}$ ratio for 45-45-90 triangles can save you a great deal of time on the Math Level 1.

Similar Triangles

Two triangles are called similar if the ratio of the lengths of their corresponding sides is constant. In order for this to be true, the corresponding angles of each triangle must be congruent. In essence, similar triangles have exactly the same shape but not necessarily the same size. Take a look at a few similar triangles:

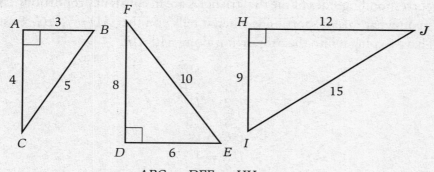

$$ABC \sim DEF \sim HIJ$$

As you may have assumed from the above figure, the symbol for "is similar to" is ~. So if triangle ABC is similar to triangle DEF, you will write $ABC \sim DEF$.

When you say that two triangles are similar, it is important to know which sides of each triangle correspond to each other. After all, the definition of similar triangles is that "the ratio of the lengths of their corresponding sides is constant." So, considering that $ABC \sim DEF$, you know that the ratio of the short sides equal the ratio of the larger sides. $^{AB}/_{DE} = {^{BC}/_{EF}} = {^{CA}/_{FD}}$.

Just as similar triangles have corresponding sides, they also have corresponding angles. If $ABC \sim DEF$, then $\angle A = \angle D$, $\angle B = \angle E$, and $\angle C = \angle F$.

Occasionally, the Math Level 1 may present you with two separate triangles and tell you that the two are similar. More often, the Math Level 1 will present you with a single triangle that contains a line segment parallel to one base. This line segment creates a second, smaller, similar triangle. In the figure below, for example, line segment *DE* is parallel to *CB*, and triangle *ABC* is similar to triangle *AED*.

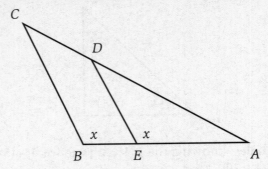

After presenting you with a diagram like the one above, the Math Level 1 will test whether you understand similarity by asking a question like:

If $BC = 6$ and $AD = \frac{2}{3}AC$, what is DE?

This question doesn't tell you outright that *DE* and *CB* are parallel, but it implicitly tells you that the two lines are parallel by indicating that both lines form the same angle, $x°$, when they intersect with *BA*. Once you realize that *ABC ~ AED*, you know that the corresponding sides of the two triangles are in constant proportion. The question tells you what this proportion is when it tells you that $AD = \frac{2}{3} AC$. To solve for *DE*, you have to plug it into the proportion along with *CB*:

$$\frac{2}{3} = \frac{DE}{CB}$$
$$\frac{2}{3} = \frac{DE}{6}$$
$$3 \times DE = 12$$
$$DE = 4$$

Area of a Triangle

It's quite likely that you will have to calculate the area of a triangle for the Math Level 1. The formula for the area of a triangle is:

$$A = \frac{1}{2}bh$$

where b is the length of a base of the triangle, and h is height (also called the altitude).

In the previous sentence we said "a base" instead of "the base" because you can actually use any of the three sides of the triangle as the base; a triangle has no particular side that is the base until you designate one. The height of the triangle depends on the base, which is why the area formula always works, no matter which side you choose to be the base. The heights of a few triangles are pictured with their altitudes drawn in as dotted lines.

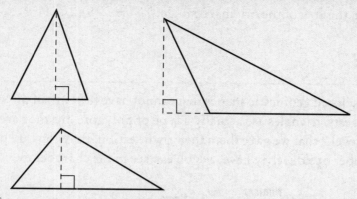

Study the triangle on the right. Its altitude does not lie in the interior of the triangle. This is why the altitude of a triangle is defined as a line segment perpendicular to *the line containing the base* and not simply as perpendicular to the base. Sometimes the endpoint of the altitude does not lie on the base; it can be outside of the triangle, as is the case of the second example above.

On the Math Level 1, you may be tested on the area of a triangle in a few different ways. You might be given the altitude of a triangle along with the length of the base, but it's unlikely you'd get such an easy question. It's more probable that the altitude would have to be found, using other tools and techniques from plane geometry. For example, try to find the area of the triangle below:

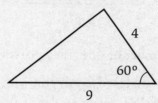

To find the area of this triangle, draw in the altitude from the base (of length 9) to the opposite vertex. Notice that now you have two triangles, and one of them (the smaller one on the right) is a 30-60-90 triangle.

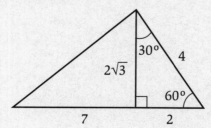

Plane Geometry

The hypotenuse of this 30-60-90 triangle is 4, so the short side is 2 and the medium side, which is also the altitude of the original triangle, is $2\sqrt{3}$. Now you can use the area formula to find the area of the original triangle: $\frac{1}{2}bh = \frac{1}{2}(9)(2\sqrt{3}) = 9\sqrt{3} \approx 15.6$.

Polygons

Polygons are enclosed geometric shapes that cannot have fewer than three sides. As this definition suggests, triangles are actually a type of polygon, but they are so important on the Math Level 2 that we gave them their own section. Polygons are named according to the number of sides they have, as you can see in the chart below.

Number of Sides	Name
3	triangle
4	quadrilateral
5	pentagon
6	hexagon
7	heptagon
8	octagon
9	nonagon
10	decagon
12	dodecagon
n	n-gon

All polygons, no matter the number of sides they possess, share certain characteristics:

- The sum of the interior angles of a polygon with n sides is $(n - 2)\,180°$. So, for example, the sum of the interior angles of an octagon is $(8 - 2)\,180° = 6(180°) = 1080°$.

- The sum of the exterior angles of any polygon is $360°$.

- The perimeter of a polygon is the sum of the lengths of its sides. The perimeter of the hexagon below, for example, is 35.

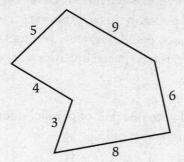

Regular Polygons

Most of the polygons with more than four sides that you'll deal with on the Math Level 2 will be regular polygons—polygons whose sides are all of equal length and whose angles are all congruent (neither of these conditions can exist without the other). Below are diagrams, from left to right, of a regular pentagon, a regular octagon, and a square (also known as a regular quadrilateral):

Area of a Regular Polygon

There is one more characteristic of polygons with which to become familiar. It has to do specifically with regular hexagons. A regular hexagon can be divided into six equilateral triangles, as the figure below shows:

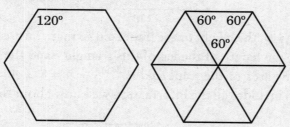

If you know the length of just one side of a regular hexagon, you can use that information to calculate the area of the equilateral triangle that uses the side. To find the area of the hexagon, simply multiply the area of that triangle by 6.

Plane Geometry

Quadrilaterals

The most frequently seen polygon on the Math Level 1 is the **quadrilateral**, which is a general term for a four-sided polygon. In fact, there are five types of quadrilaterals that pop up on the test: trapezoids, parallelograms, rectangles, rhombuses, and squares. Each of these five quadrilaterals has special qualities, as shown in the sections below.

Trapezoids

A **trapezoid** is a quadrilateral with one pair of parallel sides and one pair of nonparallel sides. Below is an example of a trapezoid:

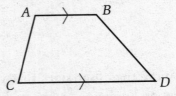

In the trapezoid pictured above, AB is parallel to CD (shown by the arrow marks), whereas AC and BD are not parallel.

The area of a trapezoid is:

$$A = \frac{s_1 + s_2}{2} h$$

where s_1 and s_2 are the lengths of the parallel sides (also called the bases of the trapezoid), and h is the height. In a trapezoid, the height is the perpendicular distance from one base to the other.

Try to find the area of the trapezoid pictured below:

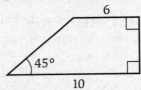

To find the area, draw in the height of the trapezoid so that you create a 45-45-90 triangle. You know that the length of the leg of this triangle—and the height of the trapezoid—is 4. Thus, the area of the trapezoid is $^{6+10}\!/_2$ × 4 = 8 × 4 = 32. Check out the figure below, which includes all the information we know about the trapezoid:

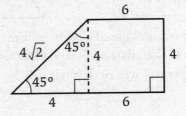

Parallelogram

A **parallelogram** is a quadrilateral whose opposite sides are parallel. The figure below shows an example:

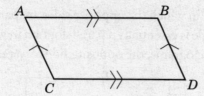

Parallelograms have three very important properties:

1. Opposite sides are equal.

2. Opposite angles are congruent.

3. Adjacent angles are supplementary (they add up to 180°).

To visualize this last property, simply picture the opposite sides of the parallelogram as parallel lines and one of the other sides as a transversal:

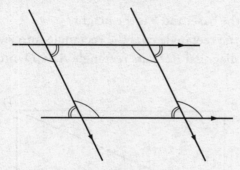

The area of a parallelogram is given by the formula:

$$\text{Area} = bh$$

where b is the length of the base, and h is the height.

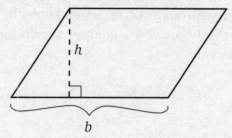

In area problems, you will likely have to find the height using techniques similar to the one used in the previous example problem with trapezoids.

The next three quadrilaterals that we'll review—rectangles, rhombuses, and squares—are all special types of parallelograms.

Rectangles

A **rectangle** is a quadrilateral in which the opposite sides are parallel and the interior angles are all right angles. A rectangle is essentially a parallelogram in which the angles are all right angles. Also similar to parallelograms, the opposite sides of a rectangle are equal.

The formula for the area of a rectangle is:

$$A = bh$$

where b is the length of the base, and h is the height.

A diagonal through the rectangle cuts the rectangle into two equal right triangles. In the figure below, the diagonal BD cuts rectangle $ABCD$ into congruent right triangles ABD and BCD.

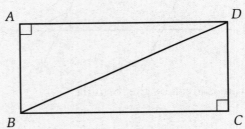

Because the diagonal of the rectangle forms right triangles that include the diagonal and two sides of the rectangle, if you know two of these values, you can always calculate the third with the Pythagorean theorem. If you know the side lengths of the rectangle, you can calculate the diagonal; if you know the diagonal and one side length, you can calculate the other side.

Rhombuses

A **rhombus** is a quadrilateral in which the opposite sides are parallel and the sides are of equal length.

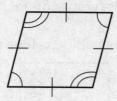

The formula for the area of a rhombus is:

$$A = bh$$

where b is the length of the base, and h is the height.

To find the area of a rhombus, use the same methods as used to find the area of a parallelogram. For example:

If *ABCD* is a rhombus, *AC* = 4, and *ABD* is an equilateral triangle, what is the area of the rhombus?

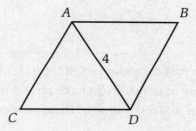

If *ABD* is an equilateral triangle, then the length of a side of the rhombus is 4, and angles *ADB* and *ABD* are 60°. Draw an altitude from *a* to *DC* to create a 30-60-90 triangle, and you can calculate the length of this altitude to be $2\sqrt{3}$. The area of a rhombus is bh, so the area of this rhombus is $4 \times 2\sqrt{3} = 8\sqrt{3}$.

Squares

A **square** is a quadrilateral in which all the sides are equal and all the angles are right angles. A square is a special type of rhombus, rectangle, and parallelogram:

Plane Geometry

The formula for the area of a square is:

$$A = s^2$$

where s is the length of a side of the square. Because all the sides of a square are equal, it is also possible to provide a simple formula for the perimeter: $P = 4s$, where s is, once again, the length of a side.

A diagonal drawn into the square will always form two congruent 45-45-90 triangles:

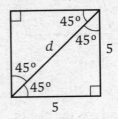

From the properties of a 45-45-90 triangle, we know that $d = s\sqrt{2}$. In other words, if you know the length of one side of the square, you can easily calculate the length of the diagonal. Similarly, if you know the length of the diagonal, you can calculate the length of the sides of the square.

Circles

Circles are another popular plane-geometry test topic. Unlike polygons, all circles are the same shape and vary only in size. Circles have certain basic characteristics, and test questions will focus on your understanding of these properties.

Basic Definitions of Circles

A **circle** is the collection of all points equidistant from a given point, called the center. A circle is named after its center point. The distance from the center to any point on the circle is called the **radius**, (r), which is the most important measurement in a circle. If you know the radius of a circle, you can figure out all its other characteristics. The **diameter** (d) of a circle is twice as long as the radius ($d = 2r$), and stretches between end-points on the circle, making sure to pass through the center. A **chord** also extends from endpoint to endpoint on the circle, but it does not necessarily pass through the center. In the figure below, point C is the center of the circle, r is the radius, and AB is a chord.

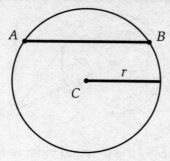

Tangent Lines

A line that intersects the circle at only one point is called a **tangent** line. The radius whose endpoint is the intersection point of the tangent line and the circle is always perpendicular to the tangent line.

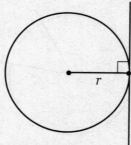

Every point in space outside the circle can extend exactly two tangent lines to the circle. The distance from the origin of the two tangents to the points of tangency are always equal. In the figure below, $XY = XZ$.

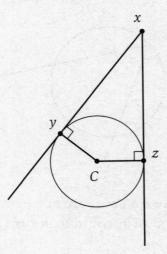

The Math Level 1 often includes tangent lines in the test. For example:

What is the area of triangle *QRS*, if *RS* is tangent to circle *Q*?

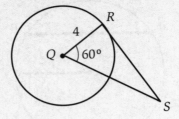

If *RS* is tangent to circle *Q*, then *QR* is perpendicular to *RS*, and therefore *QRS* is a 30-60-90 triangle. Given that *QR* = 4, we know that *RS* = $4\sqrt{3}$, and the area of triangle *QRS* is $\frac{1}{2}(4)(4\sqrt{3}) = 8\sqrt{3}$.

Central Angles and Inscribed Angles

An angle whose vertex is the center of the circle is called a **central angle**.

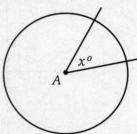

The degree of the circle (the slice of pie) cut by a central angle is equal to the measure of the angle. If a central angle is 25°, then it cuts a 25° arc in the circle.

An **inscribed angle** is an angle formed by two chords in a circle that originate from a single point.

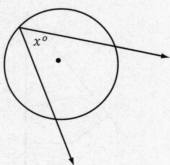

An inscribed angle will always cut out an arc in the circle that is twice the size of the degree of the inscribed angle. If an inscribed angle has a degree of 40°, it will cut an arc of 80° in the circle.

If an inscribed angle and a central angle cut out the same arc in a circle, the central angle will be twice as large as the inscribed angle.

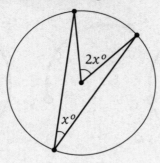

Circumference of a Circle

The **circumference** of a circle is the length of the 360° arc that forms the circle. In other words, if you were to trace around the edge of the circle, it is the distance from a point on the circle back to itself. The circumference is the perimeter of the circle. The formula for circumference is:

$$C = 2\pi r$$

where r is the radius. The formula can also be written $C = \pi d$, where d is the diameter. Using the formula, try to find the circumference of the circle below:

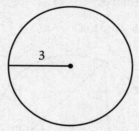

Plugging the radius into the formula, $C = 2\pi r = 2\pi\,(3) = 6\pi$.

Arc Length

An **arc** is part of a circle's circumference. An arc contains two endpoints and all the points on the circle between the endpoints. By picking any two points on a circle, two arcs are created: a major arc, which is by definition the longer arc, and a minor arc, which is the shorter one.

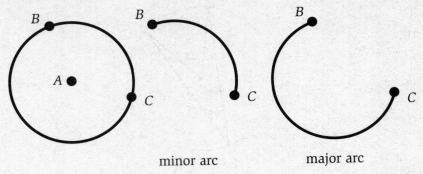

minor arc   major arc

Since the degree of an arc is defined by the central or inscribed angle that intercepts the arc's endpoints, you need only know the measure of either of those angles and the measure of the radius of the circle to calculate the arc length. The arc length formula is:

$$\text{arc length} = \frac{n}{360} \times 2\pi r$$

where n is the measure of the degree of the arc, and r is the radius. The formula could be rewritten as arc length = $^n/_{360} \times C$, where C is the circumference of the circle.

A Math Level 1 question might ask:

Circle D has radius 9. What is the length of arc AB?

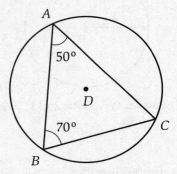

In order to figure out the length of arc AB, you need to know the radius of the circle and the measure of $\angle C$, which is the inscribed angle that intercepts the endpoints of AB. The question tells you the radius of the circle, but it throws you a little curveball by not providing you with the measure of $\angle C$. Instead, the question puts $\angle C$ in a triangle and tells you the measures of the other two angles in the triangle. Using this information you can figure out the measure of ∠c. Since the three angles of a triangle must add up to 180°, you know that:

$$\angle c = 180° - (50° + 70°)$$
$$\angle c = 180° - 120°$$
$$\angle c = 60°$$

Since angle *c* is an inscribed angle, arc *AB* must be 120°. Now you can plug these values into the formula for arc length

$$AB = \frac{120}{360} \times 2\pi 9$$
$$AB = \frac{1}{3} \times 18\pi$$
$$AB = 6\pi$$

Area of a Circle

The area of a circle depends on the radius of the circle. The formula for area is:

$$\text{Area} = \pi r^2$$

where *r* is the radius. If you know the radius, you can always find the area.

Area of a Sector

A **sector** of a circle is the area enclosed by a central angle and the circle itself. It's shaped like a slice of pizza. The shaded region in the figure below is a sector:

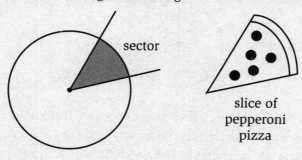

sector

slice of
pepperoni
pizza

The area of a sector is related to the area of a circle the same way that the length of an arc is related to circumference. To find the area of a sector, simply find what fraction of 360° the sector comprises and multiply this fraction by the area of the circle.

$$\text{Area of Sector} = \frac{n}{360} \times \pi r^2$$

where n is the measure of the central angle which forms the boundary of the sector, and r is the radius.

Try to find the area of the sector in the figure below:

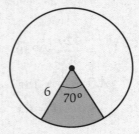

The sector is bounded by a 70° central angle in a circle whose radius is 6. Using the formula, the area of the sector is:

$$A = \frac{70}{360} \times \pi(6)^2 = \frac{7}{36} \times 36\pi = 7\pi$$

Polygons and Circles

You could potentially see a question or two on the Math Level 1 that involve polygons and circles in the same figure. Here's an example:

What is the length of major arc *BE* if the area of rectangle *ABCD* is 18?

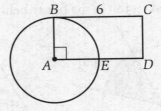

To find the length of major arc *BE*, you must know two things: the measure of the central angle that intersects the circle at its endpoints and the radius of the circle. Because *ABCD* is a rectangle, and rectangles only have right angles, figuring out the measure of the central angle is simple. ∠*BAD* is 90°, so the measure of the central angle is 360° − 90° = 270°.

Finding the radius of the circle is a little tougher. From the diagram, you can see that it is equal to the height of the rectangle. To find the height of the rectangle, you can use the fact that the area of the rectangle is 18, and the length is 6. Since $A = bh$, and you know the values of both a and b,

$$h = A \div b$$
$$= 18 \div 6$$
$$= 3$$

With a radius of 3, we can use the arc length formula to find the length of major arc BE.

$$BC = \frac{270}{360} \times 2\pi(3)$$
$$= \frac{3}{4} \times 6\pi$$
$$= \frac{9\pi}{2}$$

Key Formulas

Pythagorean Theorem

$a^2 + b^2 = c^2$, where a and b are the lengths of the legs of a right triangle, and c is the length of the hypotenuse.

Area of a Triangle

Area $= \frac{1}{2}bh$, where b is the length of the base and h is height.

Sum of the Interior Angles of a Polygon

The sum of the interior angles of a polygon is $(n - 2)180°$, where n is the number of sides in the polygon.

Area of a Trapezoid

Area $= \frac{s_1 + s_2}{2}h$, where s_1 and s_2 are the lengths of the bases of the trapezoid, and h is the height.

Area of a Parallelogram, Rectangle, and Rhombus

Area = bh, where b is the length of the base, and h is the height.

Area of a Square

Area = s^2, where s is the length of a side of the square.

Circumference of a Circle

Circumference = $2\pi r$, where r is the radius of the circle.

Arc Length

Arc Length = $\dfrac{n}{360°} \times 2\pi r$, where n is the measure of the degree of the arc, and r is the radius of the circle.

Area of a Circle

Area = πr^2, where r is the radius of the circle.

Area of a Sector

Area of Sector = $\dfrac{n}{360°} \times \pi r^2$, where n is the measure of the central angle which forms the boundary of the sector, and r is the radius of the circle.

Plane Geometry

Review Questions

1. In the figure below, lines l and m are parallel, and $AB = 5$. What is the perpendicular distance between lines l and m?

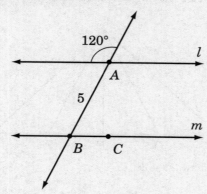

Note: Figure may not be drawn to scale.

(A) $\dfrac{5}{2}$

(B) $\dfrac{5\sqrt{2}}{2}$

(C) $\dfrac{5\sqrt{3}}{2}$

(D) $5\sqrt{2}$

(E) $5\sqrt{3}$

2. In the figure below, line *CF* is the perpendicular bisector of *AB*, and the area of triangle *CDB* is equal to the area of triangle *CEA*. Which of the following statements must be true?

> I.   Line *CF* is the perpendicular bisector of *ED*.
> II. *E* and *D* are the midpoints of *BF* and *AF*, respectively.
> III. Triangles *CEB* and *CDA* have the same area.

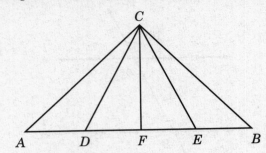

Note: Figure may not be drawn to scale.

(A) I only
(B) II only
(C) III only
(D) I and II only
(E) I and III only

3. A triangle and a square have the same base and equal areas. If the length of the common base is *x* and the height of the triangle is *h*, what is the height of the triangle in terms of *x*?

(A) $\dfrac{x}{4}$

(B) $\dfrac{2x}{3}$

(C) $2x$

(D) $\dfrac{3x}{2}$

(E) $4x$

4.   If *ABCD* is a rhombus and *ABD* is an equilateral triangle, what is the area of the rhombus?

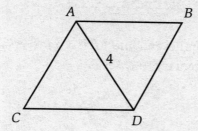

Note: Figure may not be drawn to scale.

(A) $4\sqrt{2}$

(B) $4\sqrt{3}$

(C) $\dfrac{16}{\sqrt{3}}$

(D) $8\sqrt{3}$

(E)   16

5.   Circle *D* has radius 8. What is the length of arc *AB* in terms of *a*, *b*, and *c*?

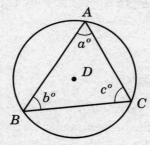

Note: Figure may not be drawn to scale.

(A) $\dfrac{(a+b+c)\pi}{30}$

(B) $\dfrac{(a+b)\pi}{45}$

(C) $\dfrac{c\pi}{45}$

(D) $\dfrac{4c\pi}{45}$

(E) $\dfrac{2\pi}{45c}$

Explanations

1. **C**

Because lines l and m are parallel and line AB is a transversal, the angle whose measure is labeled as 120° is supplementary to $\angle ABC$.

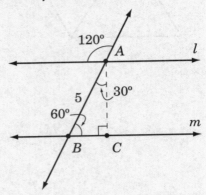

Now we have a 30-60-90 triangle whose longer leg, AC, is also the distance between lines l and m. Using the $1:2:\sqrt{3}$ side ratios for 30-60-90 triangles you can use the hypotenuse length to calculate the lengths of the other two legs. The short leg has a $1:2$ ratio to the hypotenuse, so its length is $5/2$. The long leg has a $\sqrt{3}:1$ ration to the short leg, so its length is $5\sqrt{3}/2$.

2. **E**

Let's analyze each statement separately.

I. This statement implies that $DF = EF$. We know that $BF = AF$ because it is given that line CF is the perpendicular bisector of AB, and by definition, F is the midpoint of AB. It is also given that the area of triangle CDB is equal to the area of triangle CEA. These two triangles share the same height, and since the area of a triangle is found by the formula $\frac{1}{2} b \times h$, it follows that if their areas are equal, their bases are equal too. If $BD = AE$, then by subtracting DE from each segment, we have $BE = AD$ and thus $EF = DF$. So statement I is true.

II. This statement is simply not backed by any evidence. All we know is that $BE = AD$, $EF = DF$, and $BF = AF$. As long as points E and D are equidistant from F, all these conditions hold, so there is no guarantee that they are the midpoints of BF and AF, respectively. E and D could be anywhere along BF and AF, respectively, as long as they are equidistant from F. Thus, this statement is not necessarily true.

III. Triangles *CDB* and *CEA* are equal in area; this is given. By subtracting the area of triangle *CED* from each of these triangles, we see that triangles *CEB* and *CDA* must have the same area. This statement is true.

Only statements I and III must be true.

3.   **C**

The area of a triangle with base *x* and height *h* is given by the formula ½*xh*. The area of a square with sides of length *x* is x^2. Since you know the two shapes have equal areas, you can set the two expressions equal to each other and solve for *h*:

$$\frac{1}{2}xh = x^2$$
$$xh = 2x^2$$
$$h = 2x$$

The correct answer is *h* = 2*x*.

4.   **D**

If *ABD* is an equilateral triangle, then *AD* = *AB* = *BD* = 4, and all the sides of the rhombus have a length of 4 (by definition of a rhombus, all sides are congruent). Also, by definition of a rhombus, opposite angles are congruent, so $\angle ABD = \angle ACD = 60°$. Draw an altitude from *a* to *DC* to create a 30-60-90 triangle, and from the length ratio of $x : \sqrt{3}\,x : 2x$ among the sides, you can calculate the length of this altitude to be $2\sqrt{3}$. The area of a rhombus is *bh*, so the area of this rhombus is $4 \times 2\sqrt{3} = 8\sqrt{3}$.

5.   **D**

The length of the arc depends on the circumference of the circle and the measure of the central angle that intercepts that arc. The formula is:

$$\text{arc length} = \frac{n}{360} \times 2\pi r$$

where *n* is the measure of the central angle that intercepts the arc and *r* is the radius.

Angle c is the inscribed angle or one-half as large as the central angle that intercepts the circle at the same points. So the measure of this angle is $2c°$.

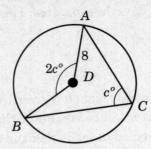

Now simply plug the values into the formula: the length of arc AB is:

$$\frac{2c}{360} \times 2\pi(8) = \frac{32c\pi}{360} = \frac{4c\pi}{45}$$

Solid Geometry

Solid geometry adds literally another dimension to the plane geometry explained in the previous chapter—instead of squares and circles, we now have cubes and spheres. These three-dimensional shapes may be more difficult to visualize, but there are only a few specific solids that you'll need to know about for the Math Level 1. We'll review them one by one.

Prisms

Most of the solids you'll see on the Math Level 1 test are prisms, or variations on prisms. A **prism** is defined as a geometric solid with two congruent bases that lie in parallel planes. You can create a prism by dragging any two-dimensional triangle, circle, or polygon through space without rotating or tilting it. The three-dimensional space defined by the moving triangle or polygon is the body of the prism. The prism's two bases are the planes where the two-dimensional shape begins and ends. The perpendicular distance between the bases is the height of the prism.

Solid Geometry

The figures below are all prisms. The bases of these prisms are shaded, and the altitude (the height) of each prism is marked by a dashed line:

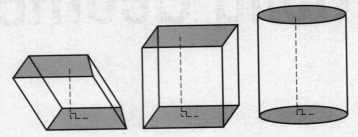

There are two main aspects of geometric solids that are relevant for the Math Level 1: volume and surface area.

Volume of a Prism

The **volume** of a prism is the amount of space taken up by that prism. The general formula for calculating the volume of a prism is very simple:

$$\text{Volume} = Bh$$

where B is the area of the base, and h is the prism's height. Certain geometric solids have slightly different formulas for calculating volume that we will cover on a case-by-case basis.

Surface Area

The **surface area** of a prism is the sum of the areas of all the prism's sides. The formula for the surface area of a prism therefore depends on the type of prism with which you are dealing. As with volume, we cover the specifics of calculating surface area as we cover each type of geometric solid.

Rectangular Solids

A **rectangular solid** is a prism with a rectangular base and lateral edges that are perpendicular to its base. In short, a rectangular solid is shaped like a box.

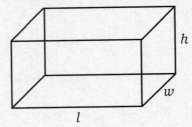

A rectangular solid has three important dimensions: length (*l*), width (*w*), and height (*h*). If you know these measurements, you can find the solid's surface area, volume, and diagonal length.

Volume of a Rectangular Solid

The volume of a rectangular solid is given by the following formula:

$$\text{Volume} = lwh$$

where *l* is the length, *w* is the width, and *h* is the height. Notice how this formula corresponds with the general formula for the volume of a prism: the product *lw* is the area of the base. Now try to find the volume of the prism in the following example:

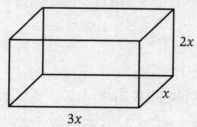

In this solid, $l = 3x$, $w = x$, and $h = 2x$. Simply plug the values into the formula given for volume, and you would find Volume $= (3x)(2x)(x) = 6x^3$.

Surface Area

The surface area of a rectangular solid is given by the following formula:

$$\text{Surface Area} = 2lw + 2lh + 2wh$$

where *l* is the length, *w* is the width, and *h* is the height.

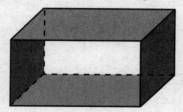

The six faces of a rectangular solid consist of three congruent pairs. The surface area formula is derived by simply adding the areas of the faces—two faces have areas of $l \times w$, two faces have areas of $l \times h$, and two faces have areas of $w \times h$.

To practice, try to find the surface area of the rectangular solid we used as an example for volume. Here's the figure again:

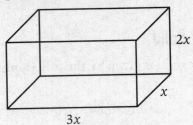

All you have to do is enter the given values into the formula for surface area:

$$\begin{aligned} \text{Surface Area} &= 2lw + 2lh + 2wh \\ &= 2(3x)(x) + 2(3x)(2x) + 2(x)(2x) \\ &= 6x^2 + 12x^2 + 4x^2 \\ &= 22x^2 \end{aligned}$$

Diagonal Length of a Rectangular Solid

The diagonal of a rectangular solid, d, is the line segment whose endpoints are opposite corners of the solid. Every rectangular solid has four diagonals, each with the same length, that connect each pair of opposite vertices. Here's one diagonal drawn in:

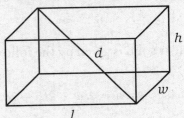

The formula for the length of a diagonal is:

$$d = \sqrt{l^2 + w^2 + h^2}$$

where l is the length, w is the width, and h is the height.

You can look at this formula as the Pythagorean theorem in three dimensions. In fact, you can derive this formula using the Pythagorean theorem. First, find the length of the diagonal along the base. This is $\sqrt{l^2 + w^2}$. Then use the Pythagorean theorem again, incorporating height to find the length of the diagonal from one corner to the other: $d^2 = \left(\sqrt{l^2 + w^2}\right)^2 + h^2$. Thus, $d^2 = l^2 + w^2 + h^2$ and $d = \sqrt{l^2 + w^2 + h^2}$. A Math Level 1 question might ask you:

What is the length of diagonal *AH* in the rectangular solid below if *AC* = 5, *GH* = 6, and *CG* = 3?

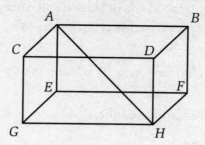

The question gives the length, width, and height of the rectangular solid, so you can just plug those numbers into the formula:

$$AH = \sqrt{5^2 + 6^2 + 3^2} = \sqrt{25 + 36 + 9} = \sqrt{70}$$

The length of the diagonal *AH* (as well as *BG*, *CF*, and *DE*) is $\sqrt{70}$.

Cubes

Just as a square is a special kind of rectangle, a cube is a special kind of rectangular solid. A **cube** is a rectangular solid whose edges are each the same length. In other words, the length, width, and height are equal, and each of its six faces is a square.

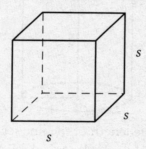

Volume of a Cube

The formula for finding the volume of a cube is essentially the same as the formula for the volume of a rectangular volume. However, since a cube's length, width, and height are all equal, the cube volume formula is:

$$\text{Volume of a Cube} = s^3$$

where *s* is the length of one edge of the cube.

Solid Geometry

Surface Area of a Cube

Since a cube is just a rectangular solid whose sides are all equal, the formula for finding the surface area of a cube is the same as that for a rectangular solid, except with $s = l = w = h$:

$$\text{Surface Area of a Cube} = 6s^2$$

where s is the length of one edge of the cube.

Diagonal Length of a Cube

The same is true for measuring the diagonal length of a cube. The formula for the diagonal of a cube is simply adapted from the formula for the diagonal length of a rectangular solid, with $s = l = w = h$:

$$\sqrt{3s^2} = s\sqrt{3}$$

where s is the length of one edge of the cube.

Cylinders

A **cylinder** is a prism with circular bases.

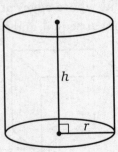

The height of a cylinder, h, is the length of the line segment whose endpoints are the centers of the bases. The radius of a cylinder, r, is the radius of its base. If you know the height and radius of a cylinder, you can easily calculate its volume and surface area.

Volume of a Cylinder

The volume of a cylinder is the product of the area of its base and its height. Because a cylinder has a circular base, the volume of a cylinder is:

$$\text{Volume of a Cylinder} = \pi r^2 h$$

where r is the radius of the circular base and h is the height. Try to find the volume of the cylinder below:

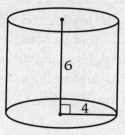

This cylinder has a radius of 4 and a height of 6. Using the volume formula:

$$\text{Volume} = \pi(4)^2(6) = 96\pi$$

Surface Area of a Cylinder

The surface area of a cylinder is the sum of the areas of the two bases and the lateral face of the cylinder. The bases are congruent circles, so their areas can be found easily. The lateral face is the tubing that connects the two bases. When "unrolled," the lateral base is simply a rectangle whose length is the circumference of the base and whose width is the height of the cylinder. Therefore, the surface area of a cylinder is given by this formula:

$$\text{Surface Area} = 2\pi r^2 + 2\pi rh$$

where r is the radius and h is the height. As with finding the volume of a cylinder, finding the surface area involves plugging the height and radius of the base into the formula. To find the surface area of the cylinder in the practice example on volume,

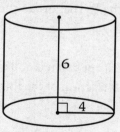

just plug the values into the formula:

$$
\begin{aligned}
\text{Surface Area} &= 2\pi(4)^2 + 2\pi(4)(6) \\
&= 32\pi + 48\pi \\
&= 80\pi
\end{aligned}
$$

Solids That Aren't Prisms

Some of the solids that appear on the Math Level 1 do not have two congruent bases that lie in parallel planes, so they cannot be considered prisms. As with prisms, you need to know how to calculate the volume and surface area of these non-prisms. The formulas for the volume and surface area of the non-prisms are a little more complex than those for the prisms, but not too difficult.

Cones

A **cone** is not a prism, but it is similar to a cylinder. A cone is essentially a cylinder in which one of the bases is collapsed into a single point at the center of the base.

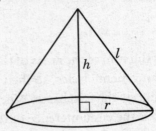

The radius of a cone is the radius of its one circular base. The height of a cone is the distance from the center of the base to the apex (the point on top). The lateral height, or slant height, of a cone is the distance from a point on the edge of the base to the apex. In the figure above, these three measurements are denoted by r, h, and l, respectively.

Notice that the height, radius, and lateral height of a cone form a right triangle. This means that if you know the value for any two of these measurements, you will always be able to find the third by using the Pythagorean theorem.

Volume of a Cone

Since a cone is similar to a cylinder except that it is collapsed to a single point at one end, the formula for the volume of a cone is a fraction of the formula for the volume of a cylinder:

$$\text{Volume of a Cone} = \frac{1}{3}\text{Volume of a Cylinder}$$
$$= \frac{1}{3}\pi r^2 h$$

where r is the radius and h is the height.

For practice, find the volume of the cone pictured below:

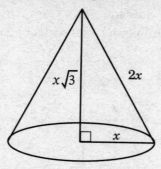

To answer this question, just use the formula for the volume of a cone with the following values plugged in: $r = x$, $l = 2x$, and $h = x\sqrt{3}$. The volume is:

$$\frac{1}{3}\pi(x^2)(x\sqrt{3}) = \frac{\sqrt{3}x^3\pi}{3}$$

Surface Area of a Cone

The surface area of a cone consists of the lateral surface area and the area of the base. Because the base is a circle, it has an area of πr^2. The lateral surface is the cone "unrolled," which, depending on the shape of the cone, can be the shape of a triangle with a curved base, a half-circle, or a "Pacman" shape. The area of the lateral surface is related to the circumference of the circle times the lateral height, l. This is the formula:

Lateral Surface Area of a Cone $= \pi r l$

where r is the radius and l is the lateral height.

The total surface area is the sum of the base area and lateral surface area:

Total Surface Area of a Cone $= \pi r^2 + \pi r l$

When you are finding the surface area of a cone, be careful not to find only the lateral surface area and then stop. Students often forget the step of adding on the area of the circular base. Practice by finding the total surface area of the cone pictured below:

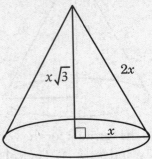

The total surface area is equal to the area of the base plus the area of the lateral surface. The area of the base = πx^2. The lateral surface area = $\pi x \times 2x$. The total surface area therefore equals $\pi x^2 + \pi 2x^2 = 3\pi x^2$.

Pyramids

A **pyramid** is like a cone, except that it has a polygon for a base. Though pyramids are not tested very often on the Math Level 1 test, you should be able to recognize them and calculate their volume.

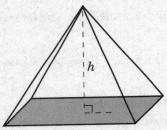

The shaded area in the figure above is the base, and the height is the perpendicular distance from the apex of the pyramid to its base.

Volume of a Pyramid

The formula for calculating the volume of a pyramid is:

$$\text{Volume} = \frac{1}{3}Bh$$

where B is the area of the base and h is the height. Try to find the volume of the pyramid below:

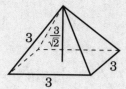

The base is just a square with a side of 3, and the height is $3\sqrt{2}/2$. $B = 3^2 = 9$, and the total volume of the pyramid is:

$$\begin{aligned}
\text{Volume} &= \frac{1}{3} \times (9)\left(\frac{3\sqrt{2}}{2}\right) \\
&= \frac{1}{3} \times \frac{27}{\sqrt{2}} \\
&= \frac{9\sqrt{2}}{2}
\end{aligned}$$

Surface Area of a Pyramid

The surface area of a pyramid is rarely tested on the Math Level 1 test. If you come across one of those rare questions that covers the topic, you can calculate the area of each face individually using techniques from plane geometry, since the base of a pyramid is a square and the sides are triangles. Practice by finding the surface area of the same pyramid in the figure below:

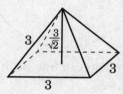

To calculate the surface area, you need to add together the area of the base and the areas of the four sides. The base is simply a square, and we've seen that $B = 3^2 = 9$. Each side is an equilateral triangle, and we can use the properties of a 30-60-90 triangle to find their areas:

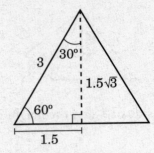

For each triangle, Area $= {}^1/_2 \times 3 \times {}^{3\sqrt{3}}/_2 = {}^{9\sqrt{3}}/_4$. The sum of the areas of the four triangles is $4 \times {}^{9\sqrt{3}}/_4 = 9\sqrt{3}$. The total surface area of the pyramid is $9 + 9\sqrt{3}$.

Spheres

A **sphere** is the collection of points in three-dimensional space that are equidistant from a fixed point, the center of the sphere. Essentially, a sphere is a 3-D circle. The main measurement of a sphere is its radius, r, the distance from the center to any point on the sphere.

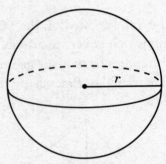

If you know the radius of a sphere you can find both its volume and surface area. The equation for the volume of a sphere is:

$$\text{Volume of a Sphere} = \frac{4}{3}\pi r^3$$

The equation for the surface area of a sphere is:

$$\text{Surface Area of a Sphere} = 4\pi r^2$$

Relating Length, Surface Area, and Volume

The Math Level 1 tests not only whether you've memorized the formulas for the different geometric solids, but also whether you understand those formulas. The test gauges your understanding by asking you to calculate the lengths, surface areas, and volumes of various solids. The Math Level 1 will ask you about the relationship between these three properties. The Math Level 1 includes two kinds of questions covering these relationships.

Comparing Dimensions

The first way the Math Level 1 will test your understanding of the relationship among the basic measurements of geometric solids is by giving you the length, surface area, or volume of different solids and asking you to compare their dimensions. The math needed to answer comparing-dimensions questions isn't that hard. But in order to do the math, you need to have a good grasp of the formulas for each type of solid and be able to relate those formulas to one another algebraically. For example,

> The surface area of a sphere is the same as the volume of a cylinder. What is the ratio of the radius of the sphere to the radius of the cylinder?

This question tells you that the surface area of a sphere and the volume a cylinder are equal. A sphere's surface area is $4\pi(r_s)^2$, where r_s is the radius of the sphere.

A cylinder's volume is $\pi(r_c)^2 \times h$, where r_c is the radius of the cylinder, and h is its height. Therefore,

$$4\pi(r_s)^2 = \pi(r_c)^2 \times h$$

The question asks for the ratio between the radii of the sphere and the cylinder. This ratio is given by r_s/r_c. Now you can solve the equation $4\pi r_s^2 = \pi r_c^2 \times h$ for the ratio r_s/r_c.

$$4\pi(r_s)^2 = \pi(r_c)^2 \times h$$
$$4(r_s)^2 = h(r_c)^2$$
$$\frac{(r_s)^2}{(r_c)^2} = \frac{h}{4}$$
$$\frac{r_s}{r_c} = \sqrt{\frac{h}{4}}$$

Changing Measurements

The second way the Math Level 1 will test your understanding of the relationships among length, surface area, and volume is by changing one of these measurements by a given factor, and then asking how this change will influence the other measurements.

When the lengths of a solid in the question are increased by a single constant factor, a simple rule can help you find the answer:

- If a solid's length is multiplied by a given factor, then the solid's surface area is multiplied by the square of that factor, and its volume is multiplied by the cube of that factor.

Remember that this rule holds true only if *all* of a solid's dimensions increase in length by a given factor. So for a cube or a sphere, the rule holds true when just a side or the radius changes, but for a rectangular solid, cylinder, or other solid, all of the length dimensions must change by the same factor. If the dimensions of the object do not increase by a constant factor—for instance, if the height of a cylinder doubles but the radius of the base triples—you will have to go back to the equation for the dimension you are trying to determine and calculate by hand.

Example 1

If you double the length of the side of a square, by how much do you increase the area of that square?

If you understand the formula for the area of a square, this question is simple. The formula for the area of a square is $A = s^2$, where s is the length of a side. Replace s with $2s$, and you see that the area of a square quadruples when the length of its sides double: $(2s)^2 = 4s^2$.

Example 2

If a sphere's radius is halved, by what factor does its volume decrease?

The radius of the sphere is multiplied by a factor of $\frac{1}{2}$ (or divided by a factor of 2), and so its volume multiplies by the cube of that factor: $(\frac{1}{2})^3 = \frac{1}{8}$. Therefore, the volume of the sphere is multiplied by a factor of $\frac{1}{8}$ (divided by 8), which is the same thing as decreasing by a factor of 8.

Example 3

A rectangular solid has dimensions $x \times y \times z$ (these are its length, width, and height), and a volume of 64. What is the volume of a rectangular solid of dimensions $x/2 \times y/2 \times z$?

If this rectangular solid had dimensions that were all one-half as large as the dimensions of the solid whose volume is 64, then its volume would be $(\frac{1}{2})^3 \times 64 = \frac{1}{8} \times 64 = 8$. But dimension z is not multiplied by $\frac{1}{2}$ like x and y. To answer a question like this one, you should use the volume formula for rectangular solids: Volume $= l \times w \times h$. It is given in the question that $xyz = 64$. So, $x/2 \times y/2 \times z = \frac{1}{4} \times xyz = \frac{1}{4} \times 64 = 16$.

Inscribed Solids

An **inscribed solid** is a solid placed inside another solid, with the edges of the two solids touching. The figures below are, from left to right, a cylinder inscribed in a sphere, a sphere inscribed in a cube, and a rectangular solid inscribed in a sphere.

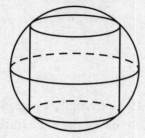 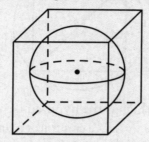 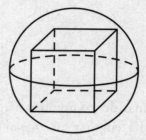

Math Level 1 questions that involve inscribed solids don't require any techniques other than those you've already learned. These questions do require an ability to visualize inscribed solids and an awareness of how certain line segments relate to both of the solids in a given figure.

Most often, an inscribed-solid question will present a figure of an inscribed solid and give you information about one of the solids. For example, you may be given the radius of a cylinder, and then be asked to find the volume of the other solid, say a rectangular solid. Using the figure as your guide, you need to use the radius of the cylinder to find the dimensions of the other solid so that you can answer the question. Here's an example:

In the figure below, a cube is inscribed in a cylinder. If the length of the diagonal of the cube is $4\sqrt{3}$ and the height of the cylinder is 5, what is the volume of the cylinder?

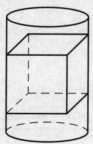

The formula for the volume of a cylinder is $\pi r^2(h)$. The question states that $h = 5$, but there is no value given for r. So in order to solve for the volume of the cylinder, we need to first find the value of r.

The key step in this problem is to recognize that the diagonal of a face of the cube is also the diameter, or twice the radius, of the cylinder. To see this, draw a diagonal, d, in either the top or bottom face of the cube.

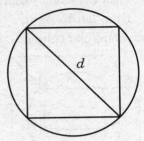

In order to find this diagonal, which is the hypotenuse in a 45-45-90 triangle, we need the length of an edge of the cube, or s. We can find s from the diagonal of the cube (not to be confused with the diagonal of a face of the cube), since the formula for the diagonal of a cube is $s\sqrt{3}$, where s is the length of an edge of the cube. The question states that the diagonal of the cube is $4\sqrt{3}$, so it follows that $s = 4$. This means that the diagonal along a single face of the cube is $4\sqrt{2}$, (using the special properties of a 45-45-90 triangle). Therefore, the radius of the cylinder is $4\sqrt{2}/2 = 2\sqrt{2}$. Plug that into the formula for the volume of the cylinder, and you get $\pi \times (2\sqrt{2})^2 \times 5 = 40\pi$.

Helpful Tips

Math Level 1 questions involving inscribed solids are much easier to solve when you know how the lines of different solids relate to one another. For instance, the previous example showed that when a cube is inscribed in a cylinder, the diagonal of a face of the cube is equal to the diameter of the cylinder. The better you know the rules of inscribed solids, the better you'll do on these questions. So without further ado, here are the rules of inscribed solids that most commonly appear on the Math Level 1.

Cylinder Inscribed in a Sphere

The diameter of the sphere is equal to the diagonal of the cylinder's height and diameter.

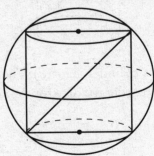

Sphere Inscribed in a Cube

The diameter of the sphere is equal to the length of the cube's edge.

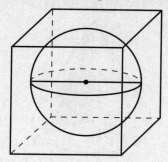

Sphere Inscribed in a Cylinder

Both the cylinder and the sphere have the same diameter and radius.

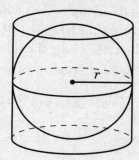

Solids Produced by Rotating Polygons

Another type of Math Level 1 question that you may come across involves a solid produced by the rotation of a polygon. The best way to explain how this type of problem works is to provide a sample question:

> **What is the surface area of the geometric solid produced by the triangle below when it is rotated 360 degrees about the axis *AB*?**

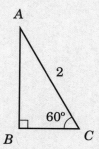

When this triangle is rotated about AB, a cone is formed. To solve the problem, the first thing you should do is sketch the cone that the triangle will form.

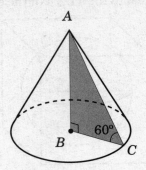

The question asks you to figure out the surface area of the cone. The formula for surface area is $\pi r^2 + \pi rl$, which means you need to know the lateral height of the cone and the radius of the circle. If you've drawn your cone correctly, you should see that the lateral height is equal to the hypotenuse of the triangle. The radius of the circle is equal to side BC of the triangle. You can easily calculate the length of BC since the triangle is a 30-60-90 triangle. If the hypotenuse is 2, then BC, being the side opposite the 30° angle, must be 1. Now plug both values of l and r into the surface area formula and then simplify:

$$\text{Total Surface Area} = \pi(1)^2 + \pi(1)(2)$$
$$= \pi + 2\pi$$
$$= 3\pi$$

Common Rotations

You don't need to learn any new techniques or formulas for problems that deal with rotating figures. You just have to be able to visualize the rotation as it's described and be aware of which parts of the polygons become which parts of the geometric solid. Below is a summary of which polygons, when rotated a specific way, produce which solids.

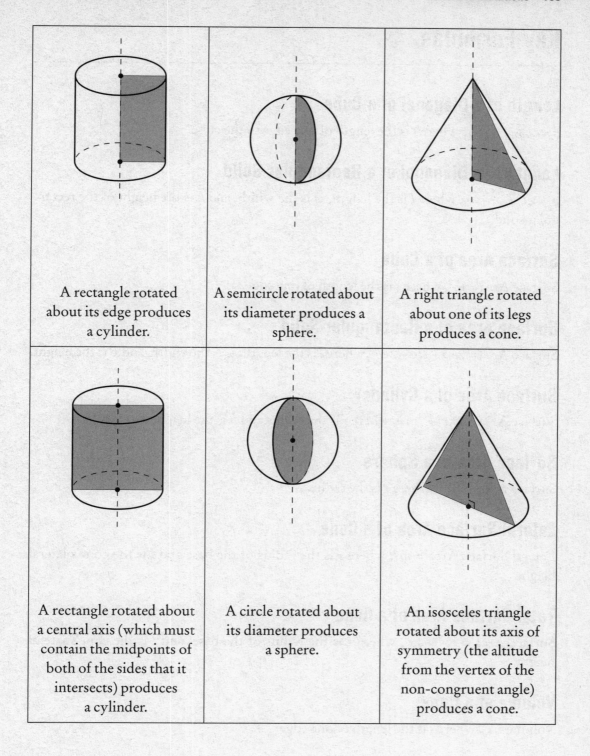

A rectangle rotated about its edge produces a cylinder.

A semicircle rotated about its diameter produces a sphere.

A right triangle rotated about one of its legs produces a cone.

A rectangle rotated about a central axis (which must contain the midpoints of both of the sides that it intersects) produces a cylinder.

A circle rotated about its diameter produces a sphere.

An isosceles triangle rotated about its axis of symmetry (the altitude from the vertex of the non-congruent angle) produces a cone.

Solid Geometry

Key Formulas

Length of a Diagonal of a Cube

$d = \sqrt{3s^2} = s\sqrt{3}$, where s is the length of one edge of the cube.

Length of a Diagonal of a Rectangular Solid

$d = \sqrt{l^2 + w^2 + h^2}$, where l is the length, w is the width, and h is the height of the rectangular solid.

Surface Area of a Cube

Surface Area $= 6s^2$, where s is the length of one edge.

Surface Area of a Rectangular Solid

Surface Area $= 2lw + 2lh + 2wh$, where l is the length, w is the width, and h is the height.

Surface Area of a Cylinder

Surface Area $= 2\pi r^2 + 2\pi rh$, where r is the radius and h is the height.

Surface Area of a Sphere

Surface Area $= 4\pi r^2$, where r is the radius.

Lateral Surface Area of a Cone

Lateral Surface Area $= \pi rl$, where r is the radius of the base and l is the cone's lateral height.

Total Surface Area of a Cone

Surface Area $= \pi r^2 + \pi rl$, where r is the radius of the base, and l is the cone's lateral height.

Volume of a Cube

Volume $= s^3$, where s is the length of one edge.

Volume of a Rectangular Solid

Volume = lwh, where l is the length, w is the width, and h is the height.

Volume of a Prism

Volume = Bh, where B is the area of the base, and h is the height.

Volume of a Cylinder

Volume = $\pi r^2 h$, where r is the radius of the circular base and h is the cylinder's height.

Volume of a Cone

Volume = $\frac{1}{3}\pi r^2 h$, where r is the radius and h is the height.

Volume of a Pyramid

Volume = $\frac{1}{3}Bh$, where B is the area of the base and h is the height.

Volume of a Sphere

Volume = $\frac{4}{3}\pi r^3$, where r is the radius.

Review Questions

1. If the length, width, and height of a rectangular solid are all doubled, by what factor is the length of its diagonal multiplied?

    (A) $\sqrt{2}$
    (B) $\sqrt{3}$
    (C) 2
    (D) 4
    (E) 8

2. A cylinder's radius is equal to its height. If its surface area is 100π, what is its volume?

    (A) 25π
    (B) 50π
    (C) 100π
    (D) 125π
    (E) 625π

Solid Geometry

3.   Cone A has volume 24. When its radius and height are multiplied by the same factor, the cone's surface area doubles. What is Cone A's new volume?

    (A) $24\sqrt{2}$
    (B)   48
    (C) $48\sqrt{2}$
    (D)   96
    (E)   Not enough information to tell

4.   A 4×6 rectangle stands so that its 6 inch side lies flat against the ground. If the rectangle is rotated around the axis of one of its two 4 inch sides, what is the volume of the resulting cylinder?

    (A) 24π
    (B) 36π
    (C) 64π
    (D) 96π
    (E) 144π

Explanations

1.   **C**

The formula for the length of the diagonal of a rectangular solid is $d = \sqrt{l^2 + w^2 + h^2}$, where l, w, and h are the dimensions of the solid. Substitute $2l$, $2w$, and $2h$ for these values:

$$d = \sqrt{(2l)^2 + (2w)^2 + (2h)^2}$$
$$= \sqrt{4l^2 + 4w^2 + 4h^2}$$
$$= \sqrt{4(l^2 + w^2 + h^2)}$$
$$= 2\sqrt{l^2 + w^2 + h^2}$$

The length of the diagonal doubles, just like the rectangular solid's other dimensions.

2.   **D**

The volume of a cylinder is given by the formula $\pi r^2 h$. In the case of this cylinder, the radius is equal to height $(r = h)$, so

$$\text{volume} = \pi r^3$$

Since we have a value only for the surface area of this cylinder, to find r, we must use the surface area formula, which is $2\pi r^2 + 2\pi r h$. Because $r = h$ in this cylinder, the surface area of this cylinder is

$$2\pi r^2 + 2\pi r^2 = 4\pi r^2$$

With the information given by the question, we can find the radius by setting either $4\pi r^2 = 100\pi$ or $r^2 = 100\pi/4\pi = 25$. Either way, the radius of the cylinder works out to 5, which means that the volume of the cylinder is $\pi 5^3 = 125\pi$.

3. **C**
The formula for a cone's surface area is $\pi r^2 + \pi r l$. A cone's volume is $\frac{1}{3}\pi r^2 h$. So if the dimensions of a cone are multiplied by the same factor, a,

$$\pi(ar)^2 + \pi(ar)(al) = \pi a^2 r^2 + \pi a^2 r l = a^2(\pi r^2 + \pi r l)$$

then its surface area multiplies by the square of that factor. If the dimensions of a cone are multiplied by the same factor, the volume becomes multiplied by the cube of that factor:

$$\frac{1}{3}\pi(ar)^2(ah) = \frac{1}{3}\pi a^2 r^2 ah = a^3\left(\frac{1}{3}\pi r^2 h\right)$$

In general, for solids, if each dimension of a cone is multiplied by the same factor, the solid's surface area is multiplied by the square of that factor, and its volume increases by the cube of that factor. If the surface area of Cone A doubles, its dimensions are multiplied by a factor of $\sqrt{2}$. Thus, the cone's volume is multiplied by a factor of $(\sqrt{2})^3 = 2\sqrt{2}$. Cone A's new volume is $24 \times 2\sqrt{2} = 48\sqrt{2}$.

4. **E**
If the rectangle is rotated about a side of length 4, then the height of the cylinder will be 4 and the radius will be 6.

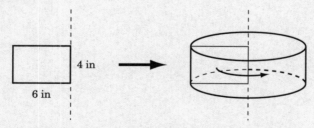

Once you visualize the cylinder, you can plug in the values for the volume of a cylinder: $\pi \times 6^2 \times 4 = 144\pi$.

Coordinate Geometry

COORDINATE GEOMETRY QUESTIONS make up about 10 percent of the Math Level 1 test. Many of the basic concepts in this chapter may be familiar to you from plane geometry, but they have a twist: the coordinate plane gives us new ways to analyze shapes and figures. Coordinate geometry also covers a number of topics that plane geometry doesn't, such as slope, parabolas, and coordinate space.

The Coordinate Plane

The coordinate plane is a plane determined by two perpendicular lines, the x-axis and the y-axis. The x-axis is the horizontal axis, and the y-axis is the vertical axis. Every point in the plane can be stated by a pair of coordinates that express the location of the point in terms of the two axes. The intersection of the x- and y-axes is designated as the origin, and its point is (0, 0).

Coordinate Geometry

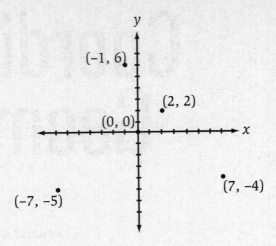

As you can see from the figure, each of the points on the coordinate plane is expressed by a pair of coordinates: (x, y). The first coordinate in a coordinate pair is called the x-coordinate. The x-coordinate is the point's location along the x-axis and can be determined by the point's distance from the y-axis (where $x = 0$). If the point is to the right of the y-axis, its x-coordinate is positive, and if the point is to the left of the y-axis, its x-coordinate is negative. The second coordinate in a coordinate pair is the y-coordinate. The y-coordinate of a point is its location along the y-axis and can be calculated as the distance from that point to the x-axis. If the point is above the x-axis, its y-coordinate is positive, and if the point is below the x-axis, its y-coordinate is negative.

The Quadrants

The coordinate plane is divided into four quadrants. Each quadrant is a specific region in the coordinate plane. The region in which $x > 0$ and $y > 0$ is Quadrant I. The region in which $x < 0$ and $y > 0$ is Quadrant II. The region in which $x < 0$ and $y < 0$ is Quadrant III. The region in which $x > 0$ and $y < 0$ is Quadrant IV.

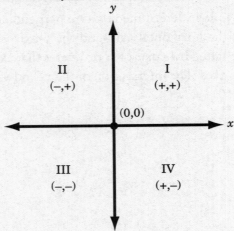

For example, the point (4, –2) lies in quadrant IV, with an x-coordinate that is 4 units to the right of the y-axis and a y-coordinate that is 2 units below the x-axis. This is how the coordinates of a point specify its exact location. The coordinates of the origin are, by definition, (0, 0).

Lines and Distance

Lines and distance are fundamental to coordinate geometry, not to mention to the Math Level 1 test. Even the most complicated coordinate geometry question uses the concepts covered in the next few sections.

Distance

Measuring distance in the coordinate plane is made possible thanks to the Pythagorean theorem. If you are given two points, (x_1, y_1), and (x_2, y_2), their distance from each other is given by the following formula:

$$\text{Distance} = \sqrt{(x_2 - x_1)^2 + (y_2 - y_1)^2}$$

The diagram below shows how the Pythagorean theorem plays a role in the formula. The distance between two points can be represented by the hypotenuse of a right triangle whose legs are lengths $(x_2 - x_1)$ and $(y_2 - y_1)$.

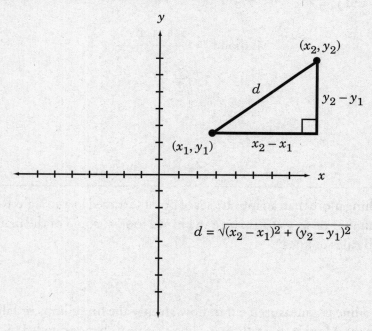

$$d = \sqrt{(x_2 - x_1)^2 + (y_2 - y_1)^2}$$

To calculate the distance from (4, –3) to (–3, 8), plug the coordinates into the formula:

$$\text{Distance} = \sqrt{(-3-4)^2 + (8-(-3))^2}$$
$$= \sqrt{49 + 121}$$
$$= \sqrt{170}$$

The distance between the points is $\sqrt{170}$, which equals approximately 13.04. You can double-check this answer by plugging it back into the Pythgorean theorem.

Finding Midpoints

The midpoint between two points in the coordinate plane can be calculated using a formula. If the endpoints of a line segment are (x_1, y_1) and (x_2, y_2), then the midpoint of the line segment is:

$$\text{Midpoint} = \left(\frac{x_1 + x_2}{2}, \frac{y_1 + y_2}{2}\right)$$

In other words, the x- and y-coordinates of the midpoint are the averages of the x- and y-coordinates of the endpoints.

Here's a practice question:

What is the midpoint of the line segment whose endpoints are (6, 0) and (3, 7)?

To solve, all you need to do is plug the points given into the midpoint formula. $x_1 = 6$, $y_1 = 0$, $x_2 = 3$, and $y_2 = 7$:

$$\text{Midpoint} = \left(\frac{6+3}{2}, \frac{0+7}{2}\right)$$
$$= \left(\frac{9}{2}, \frac{7}{2}\right)$$
$$= (4.5, 3.5)$$

Lines

Lines are nothing more than an infinite set of points arrayed in a straight formation, but there are a number of ways to analyze them. We look at some of the main properties, formulas, and rules of lines.

Slope

The **slope** of a line is a measurement of how steeply the line climbs or falls as it moves from left to right. More technically, it is a line's vertical change divided by its horizontal change, informally known as "the rise over run." Given two points on a line, call them (x_1, y_1) and (x_2, y_2), the slope of that line can be calculated using the following formula:

$$\text{Slope} = \frac{y_2 - y_1}{x_2 - x_1}$$

The variable most often used to represent slope is m.

So, for example, the slope of a line that contains the points $(-2, -4)$ and $(6, 1)$ is $m = (1 - (-4))/(6 - (-2)) = {}^5\!/_8$.

Positive and Negative Slopes

You can easily determine whether the slope of a line is positive or negative just by looking at the line. If a line slopes uphill as you trace it from left to right, the slope is positive. If a line slopes downhill as you trace it from left to right, the slope is negative. You can get a sense of the magnitude of the slope of a line by looking at the line's steepness. The steeper the line, the greater the slope will be; the flatter the line, the smaller the slope will be. Note that an extremely positive slope is *larger* then a moderately positive slope while an extremely negative slope is *smaller* then a moderately negative slope.

Look at the lines in the figure below and try to determine whether the slope of each line is negative or positive and which has the greatest slope:

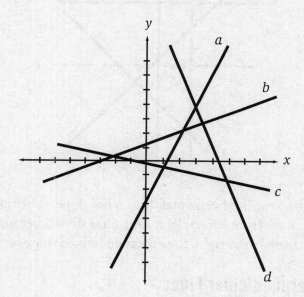

Lines a and b have positive slopes, and lines c and d have negative slopes. In terms of slope magnitude, line $a > b > c > d$.

Special Slopes

For the Math Level 1, there are a few slopes you should recognize by sight. If you can recognize one of these lines and identify its slope without having to do any calculations, you will save yourself a lot of time.

- A line that is horizontal has a slope of zero. Since there is no "rise," $y_2 - y_1 = 0$, and thus $m = y_2 - y_1 / x_2 - x_1 = 0/x_2 - x_1 = 0$.

- A line that is vertical has an undefined slope. In this case, there is no "run," and $x_2 - x_1 = 0$. Thus, $m = y_2 - y_1 / x_2 - x_1 = y_2 - y_1 / 0$, and any fraction with 0 in its denominator is, by definition, undefined.

- A line that makes a 45° angle with a horizontal line has a slope of 1 or –1. This makes sense because the rise equals the run, and $y_2 - y_1 = x_2 - x_1$, or $y_2 - y_1 = -(x_2 - x_1)$.

Of the four lines pictured below, one has a slope of 0, one has a slope of 1, another has a slope of –1, and another has undefined slope. Decide which is which.

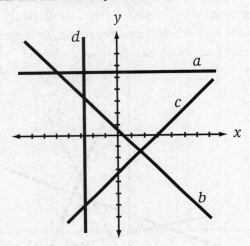

Line a has slope 0 because it is horizontal. Line b has slope –1 because it slopes downward at 45° as you move from left to right. Line c has slope 1 because it slopes upward at 45° as you move from left to right. Line d has undefined slope because it is vertical.

Parallel and Perpendicular Lines

Parallel lines are lines that don't intersect. In coordinate geometry, they can also be described as lines with the same slope.

Perpendicular lines are lines that intersect at a right angle. In coordinate geometry, perpendicular lines have opposite, reciprocal slopes. That is, a line with slope m is perpendicular to a line with a slope of $-1/m$.

In the figure below, lines q and r both have a slope of 2, so they are parallel. Line s is perpendicular to both lines q and r, and thus has a slope of $-\frac{1}{2}$.

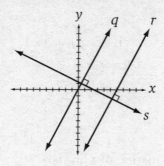

Equation of a Line

A line in coordinate geometry can be described by an equation containing the variables x and y. For the Math Level 1, you need to understand thoroughly two forms of the equation of a line: the slope-intercept form and the point-slope form.

Slope-Intercept Form

The slope-intercept form of the equation of a line is:

$$y = mx + b$$

where m is the slope of the line, and b is the y-intercept of the line. Both are constants.

The y-intercept of a line is the y-coordinate of the point where the line intersects the y-axis. Likewise, the x-intercept of a line is the x-coordinate of the point where the line intersects the x-axis. Therefore, if given the slope-intercept form of the equation of a line, you can find both intercepts.

For example, in order to find the y-intercept, simply set $x = 0$ and solve for the value of y. For the x-intercept, set $y = 0$ and solve for x.

To sketch a line given in slope-intercept form, first plot the y-intercept, and then use the slope of the line to plot another point. Connect the two points to form your line. In the figure below, the line $y = -2x + 3$ is graphed.

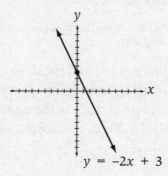

$$y = -2x + 3$$

Since the slope is equal to –2, the line descends 2 units for every 1 unit it moves in the positive x direction. The y-intercept is at 3, so the line crosses the y-axis at (0, 3). For practice, solve for the x-intercept.

$$0 = -2x + 3$$
$$2x = 3$$
$$x = \frac{3}{2}$$

Point-Slope Form

The point-slope form of the equation of a line is:

$$y - y_1 = m(x - x_1)$$

where m is the slope of the line, and (x_1, y_1) is a point on the line.

The point-slope form and slope-intercept form are alternative ways of expressing the same equation. In fact, the slope-intercept form is the point-slope form taken at the y-intercept, or the point $(0, y_1)$:

$$y - y_1 = m(x - 0)$$
$$y - y_1 = mx$$
$$y = mx + y_1$$

Since $y_1 = b$ (the y-intercept is simply the y-coordinate of the point at which $x = 0$), the two forms are equal.

The slope-intercept form of the line equation is the more common of the two, but the point-slope form is useful when your only information is the slope and a point (hence the name *point-slope* form).

Example Problems with Slope

The Math Level 1 test often asks questions that require you to understand the slope-intercept form and the point-slope form, and to be able to convert between the two.

Here are some practice questions:

What is the slope-intercept equation of the line that contains the point (3, 4) and is perpendicular to the line $y = \frac{1}{3}x - 6$?

To answer this question, you first need to find the slope of the line whose equation you are trying to determine. Fortunately, the question gives you the slope of a perpendicular line, and we know that the slope of a line is the opposite reciprocal of the slope of the line to which it is perpendicular. Thus, the slope is $-1/(\frac{1}{3}) = -3$. If the line contains the point (3, 4), its point-slope equation is $y - 4 = -3(x - 3)$. To convert this to slope-intercept form, use algebra:

$$y - 4 = -3(x - 3)$$
$$y - 4 = -3x + 9$$
$$y = -3x + 13$$

Here's another question:

What is the slope-intercept form of the equation of the line that contains the points (5, 3) and (–1, 8)?

Start by finding the slope of the line. You can calculate the slope with the two points you're given: $m = \frac{8-3}{-1-5} = -\frac{5}{6}$. To put the equation of this line in slope-intercept form, the only additional information we need is the y-intercept. To find it, use the x- and y-coordinates of a point that you know is on the line and plug them into the equation $y = -\frac{5}{6}x + b$, and solve for b. Using the point (5, 3):

$$3 = -\frac{5}{6}(5) + b$$
$$3 = -\frac{25}{6} + b$$
$$b = 3 + \frac{25}{6}$$
$$b = \frac{43}{6}$$

The slope-intercept form of the equation of this line is $y = -\frac{5}{6}x + \frac{43}{6}$.

Graphing Linear Inequalities

The graph of an inequality is a graph of a region rather than a simple graph of a line. An inequality is actually the graph of all the points on the coordinate plane that are either greater or less than a particular line. For this reason, the graph of an inequality looks similar to the graph of a line but has two major differences. First, the region on one side of the line (which side depends on the inequality) is shaded. Second, the line itself is either dotted or solid depending on whether the inequality is inclusive.

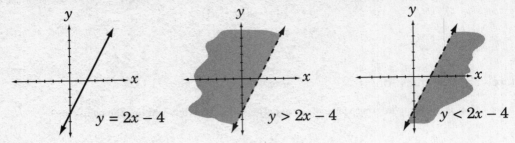

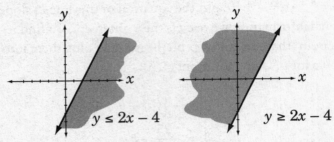

To summarize the above graphs: when the inequality is "greater than or equal to" or "less than or equal to," the line in the graph is solid; when the inequality is "greater than" or "less than," the line in the graph is dotted. Any point that satisfies the inequality lies in the shaded region, and any point that does not lies in the un-shaded region.

That's all you need to know about graphing inequalities for the Math Level 1.

Other Important Graphs and Equations

In addition to the graphs and equations of lines, the Math Level 1 will test your understanding of the graphs and equations of parabolas and circles.

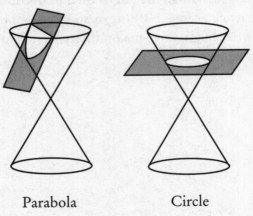

Parabola   Circle

Questions on these topics will either ask you to match the correct graph with the correct equation or give you an equation and ask you to figure out certain characteristics of the graph.

Most of the questions about parabolas and circles are straightforward. If you know the information in the sections below, you'll be able to breeze through them.

Parabolas

A **parabola** is a U-shaped curve that can open either upward or downward.

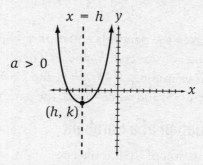

A parabola is the graph of a quadratic function, which, you may recall, is $ax^2 + bx + c$. The equation of a parabola can be expressed in two forms—the standard form and the general form. Each can help you determine different information about the nature of the parabola.

Standard Form of the Equation of a Parabola

The standard form of the equation of a parabola is perhaps the most useful and will be the one most used on the Math Level 1 test:

$$y = a(x - h)^2 + k$$

where a, h, and k are constants. From this formula, you can learn a few pieces of information:

1. The vertex of the parabola is (h, k).

2. The axis of symmetry of the parabola is the line $x = h$.

3. The parabola opens upward if $a > 0$, and downward if $a < 0$.

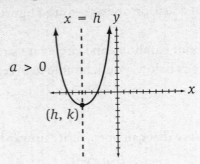

For example, if you were given the parabola equation $y = -3(x - 5)^2 + 8$, you first need to pick out the values of the constants a, h, and k. Then you can derive information about the parabola. For this example, $a = -3$, $h = 5$, and $k = 8$. So the vertex is $(5, 8)$, the axis of symmetry is the line $x = 5$, and since $-3 < 0$, the parabola opens downward.

General Form of the Equation of a Parabola

The general form of the equation of a parabola is:

$$y = ax^2 + bx + c$$

where a, b, and c are constants. If a question presents you with a parabola equation in this form, you can find the following information about the parabola:

1. The vertex of the parabola is $(-b/2a, c - b^2/4a)$.

2. The axis of symmetry of the parabola is the line $x = -b/2a$.

3. The parabola opens upward if $a > 0$, and downward if $a < 0$.

4. The y-intercept is the point $(0, c)$.

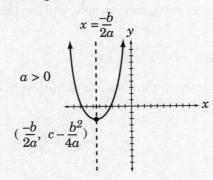

Circles

A **circle** is the collection of points equidistant from a given point, called the center of the circle. For the Math Level 1 test, there is only one equation you have to know for a circle. This equation is called the standard form:

$$(x - h)^2 + (y - k)^2 = r^2$$

where (h, k) is the center of the circle, and r is the radius. When the circle is centered at the origin, so that $h = k = 0$, then the equation simplifies to:

$$x^2 + y^2 = r^2$$

That's it. That's all you need to know about a circle in coordinate geometry. Once you know and understand this equation, you should be able to sketch a circle in its proper place on the coordinate system if you are given its equation. You will also be asked to figure out the equation of a circle if you are given a picture of its graph.

To test your knowledge, try to answer the following practice problem:

What is the equation of the circle pictured below?

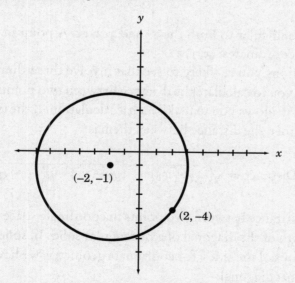

The center is given in the image: $(-2, -1)$. All you need to finish the formula is the radius. We determine this by finding the distance from the center and the point, $(2, -4)$, pictured on the circle:

$$r = \sqrt{(2 - (-2))^2 + (-4 - (-1))^2} = \sqrt{4^2 + 3^2} = 5$$

The radius of the circle is 5, so the equation of the circle can be written as $(x + 2)^2 + (y + 1)^2 = 25$.

Coordinate Space

When we add another dimension to the coordinate plane, creating a coordinate space, a new axis must be introduced. Meet the z-axis:

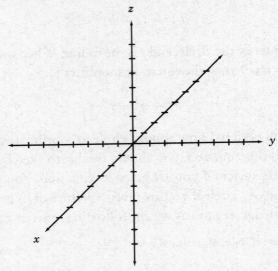

The z-axis is perpendicular to both the x- and y-axes. A point in three dimensions is specified by three coordinates: (x, y, z).

The only questions you're likely to see that involve three-dimensional coordinate geometry will ask you to calculate the distance between two points in space. There is a general formula that allows you to make such a calculation. If the two points are (x_1, y_1, z_1) and (x_2, y_2, z_2), then the distance between them is:

$$\text{Distance} = \sqrt{(x_2 - x_1)^2 + (y_2 - y_1)^2 + (z_2 - z_1)^2}$$

Determining the distance between two points in coordinate space is basically the same as finding the length of the diagonal of a rectangular solid. In solid geometry, we were given the dimensions of the sides; for coordinate geometry, we have the coordinates of the endpoints of that diagonal.

Try the example problem below:

What is the distance between the points $(4, 1, -5)$ and $(-3, 3, 6)$?

Using the formula, the answer is $\sqrt{7^2 + 2^2 + 11^2} = \sqrt{174}$, which approximately equals 13.19. To see this in diagram form, take a look at the figure below:

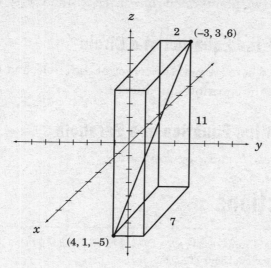

Key Formulas

Distance in the Coordinate Plane

Distance = $\sqrt{(x_2 - x_1)^2 + (y_2 - y_1)^2}$ if you're measuring the distance between the points (x_1, y_1) and (x_2, y_2).

Distance in the Coordinate Space Distance

Distance = $\sqrt{(x_2 - x_1)^2 + (y_2 - y_1)^2 + (z_2 - z_1)^2}$ if you're measuring the distance between the points (x_1, y_1, z_1) and (x_2, y_2, z_2).

Midpoint between Two Points

Midpoint = $(\frac{x_1 + x_2}{2}, \frac{y_1 + y_2}{2})$, where the endpoints of a line segment are (x_1, y_1) and (x_2, y_2).

Point-Slope Form of the Equation of a Line

$y - y_1 = m(x - x_1)$, where m is the slope of the line, and (x_1, y_1) is a point on the line.

Slope-Intercept Form of the Equation of a Line

$y = mx + b$, where m is the slope of the line, and b is the y-intercept of the line. Both m and b are constants.

Coordinate Geometry

Slope of a Line

Slope $= \frac{y_2 - y_1}{x_2 - x_1}$, where two points on the line are (x_1, y_1) and (x_2, y_2).

Standard Form of the Equation of a Circle

$(x - h)^2 + (y - k)^2 = r^2$, where (h, k) is the center of the circle, and r is the radius. When centered at the origin, the equation simplifies to $x^2 + y^2 = r^2$.

Standard Form of the Equation of a Parabola

$y = a(x - h)^2 + k$, where a, h, and k are constants.

Review Questions

1. In the line segment pictured below, $AB + CD = \frac{2}{5} AD$, and $AB = \frac{1}{2} BC$. If $AD = 15$, what is the distance between the midpoints of AD and BC?

    Note: Figure may not be drawn to scale.

    (A)   0.5
    (B)   1.5
    (C)   3
    (D)   4.5
    (E)   7.5

2. Which of the following lines is perpendicular to $y = 3x + 4$ and has 6 for its x-intercept?

    (A) $y = 3x - 6$

    (B) $y = -3x + 6$

    (C) $y = -\frac{1}{3}x + 6$

    (D) $y = -\frac{1}{3}x - 2$

    (E) $y = -\frac{1}{3}x + 2$

3.   Which of the following inequalities is graphed below?

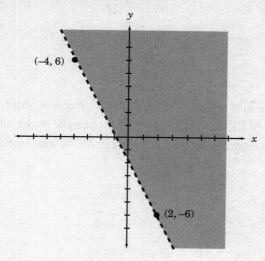

(A) $y > -2x - 2$

(B) $y \geq -2x - 2$

(C) $y < -2x - 2$

(D) $y > \dfrac{1}{2}x - 2$

(E) $y > -\dfrac{1}{2}x - 2$

4.   The following equation represents which type of graph? $2y = -6x^2 + 24x - 12$

(A)   A parabola that opens downward with vertex $(-2, 6)$
(B)   A parabola that opens upward with vertex $(6, 2)$
(C)   A parabola that opens upward with vertex $(-2, -6)$
(D)   A parabola that opens downward with vertex $(2, 6)$
(E)   A parabola that opens downward with vertex $(-6, 2)$

Explanations

1.   **B**

If you understand how to answer this question, you should be able to answer any question dealing with line segments on the Math Level 1. The question asks you to find the distance between two midpoints, so you first need to find where those midpoints are. By definition, a midpoint is a point equidistant from both ends of a line segment. So the midpoint of AD is $15 \div 2 = 7.5$ units from either end. To find the midpoint of BC, you first need to find the length of BC. From the figure, you can see that $BC = AD - AB - CD$. Since it is given that $AB + CD = \frac{2}{5} AD$,

$$BC = \frac{3}{5}AD$$
$$= \frac{3}{5}(15)$$
$$= 9$$

The midpoint of BC is $^9/_2 = 4.5$ units from B and C. But in order to measure the distance between the midpoints of BC and AD, you must situate the midpoint of BC with regard to AD. You can do this by finding out the midpoint of BC's distance from point A.

$$AB = \frac{1}{2}BC$$
$$= \frac{1}{2} \times 9$$
$$= 4.5$$

Therefore, the midpoint of BC is $4.5 + 4.5 = 9$ units from a, whereas the midpoint of AD is 7.5 units from a. The distance between these two midpoints is $9 - 7.5 = 1.5$.

2.   E
The slope of $y = 3x + 4$ is 3. A line perpendicular to this line has a slope that is the opposite of the reciprocal of 3, or $-\frac{1}{3}$. If the x-intercept of the desired line is 6, then the line contains the point (6, 0), and we have enough information to put it in point-slope form: $(y - 0) = -\frac{1}{3}(x - 6)$. This simplifies to $y = -\frac{1}{3}x + 2$.

3.   A
The slope of the line pictured is $^{-12}/_6 = -2$. The y-intercept of the line pictured is -2. So the equation of the line pictured is $y = -2x - 2$. This leaves three choices. The line in the picture is dotted; this means that the inequality is either < or >, not ≤ or ≥. Now we have two choices left. Because the region to the right and above is shaded, > is the correct inequality, but just to make sure, plug in a point or two. In this case, try the origin, (0, 0). It is in the shaded region, and must therefore satisfy the inequality. Which inequality does is satisfy? It satisfies $y > -2x - 2$, so this is the correct choice.

4.   **D**

In this equation, y is raised to the first power, and x is squared. This should lead you to believe that the graph of this equation is a parabola (in the equation of a circle, both variables are squared). Simplify the equation to arrive at the standard form:

$$2y = -6x^2 + 24x - 12$$
$$y = -3x^2 + 12x - 6$$
$$y = -3(x^2 - 4x) - 6$$
$$y = -3(x^2 - 4x + 4) - 6 + 12$$
$$y = -3(x - 2)^2 + 6$$

The equation in the question is the standard form of a parabola. From it we can see that $-3 < 0$, so the parabola opens downward, and the vertex is (2, 6).

Trigonometry

ONE OF THE MAIN DIFFERENCES BETWEEN the Math Level 1 and Math Level 2 tests is the relative emphasis the two tests place on trigonometry. Trigonometry questions make up about 20 percent of the entire Math Level 2 test. In contrast, the Math Level 1 test covers fewer trigonometry topics, and trigonometry questions comprise only about 8 percent of the test. If you don't have a strong background in trigonometry, then the Math Level 1 test is the test for you.

Basic Functions

Most of the trigonometry on the Math Level 1 test addresses the different parts of a right triangle and the relationships among these different parts. The three basic trigonometric functions—sine, cosine, and tangent—are the tools that define these relationships. Given the measure of one of the non-right angles in a right triangle, you can use these tools of trigonometry to find the characteristics of the triangle. If you are given the measure of one of the non-right angles and one of the sides, you can find all the values of the right triangle.

Basic Functions and the Right Triangle

If you know the measure of one of the non-right angles in a right triangle, the trigonometric functions tell you the ratio of the lengths of any two sides of the triangle.

In the right triangle below, one acute angle is labeled θ and the sides of the triangle are labeled hypotenuse, opposite, and adjacent, according to their position relative to the angle of measure θ.

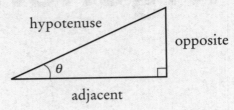

Sine

The **sine** of an angle is the ratio of the side opposite the angle to the hypotenuse.

$$\sin \theta = \frac{\text{opposite}}{\text{hypotenuse}}$$

Cosine

The **cosine** of an angle is the ratio of the side adjacent the angle to the hypotenuse.

$$\cos \theta = \frac{\text{adjacent}}{\text{hypotenuse}}$$

Tangent

The **tangent** of an angle is the ratio of the side opposite the angle to the side adjacent to the angle.

$$\tan \theta = \frac{\text{opposite}}{\text{adjacent}}$$

A handy way to remember these formulas is the acronym SOHCAHTOA. The S, C, and T stand for the three different basic trigonometric functions, and the two letters after the S, C, and T refer to the sides of the triangle that are being related by that function.

SOH: **S**ine is the side **O**pposite the angle divided by the **H**ypotenuse.

CAH: **C**osine is the side **A**djacent to the angle divided by the **H**ypotenuse.

TOA: **T**angent is the side **O**pposite divided by the **A**djacent side.

Using Your Calculator with the Basic Functions

On some questions dealing with sine, cosine, and tangent, your calculator can be extremely helpful. Using your calculator, you can quickly compute the value of one of the three trigonometric functions at any given angle. On a graphing calculator, find the button indicating the trigonometric function you want to perform, type in the value of the angle, and then hit Enter. To calculate the cosine of 45°, press the COS button, then type in 45, and press Enter.

$$\cos 45 = .707\ldots$$

On non-graphing calculators you may need to type in the value of the angle first and then press the trigonometric-function button.

Angles Larger Than 90° and the Basic Functions

Angles in a right triangle can never be larger than 90°, since the sum of all three angles must equal 180°. But on the Math Level 1, you may occasionally run into angles that are larger than 90°. It is often more intuitive to think of these in terms of the coordinate plane rather than in terms of a triangle.

Below are pictured four angles in the coordinate plane. The first is the acute angle we've already covered in this chapter; the next three are all larger than 90°.

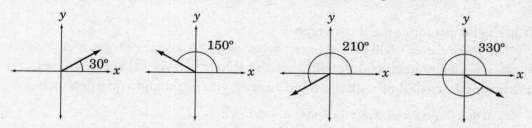

The four quadrants of the coordinate plane become very important when dealing with angles that are larger than 90°. Each angle larger than 90° can be "simplified" by looking at it in the context of its own quadrant. In the figure below, the four angles from the previous angle are defined in terms of their own quadrants:

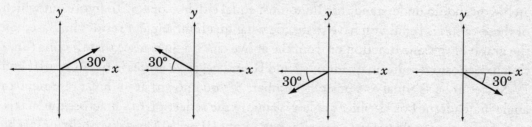

By reconsidering each angle based on its relationship to the x-axis, it becomes clear that each of the original angles can be treated as a reoriented 30° angle. In other words, a 210° angle is just the same as a 30° angle except that the 210° angle is in the third quadrant. In terms of the basic trigonometric functions, this means that the value of a 210°

angle is the same as the value of a 30° angle, except that the sign of the trigonometric function differs based on the quadrant that the angle is in. Depending on the quadrant of the coordinate plane in which an angle resides, the values of the trigonometric properties of that angle will be either positive or negative. Below is a figure illustrating the signs of the trigonometric functions according to the quadrant in which they lie.

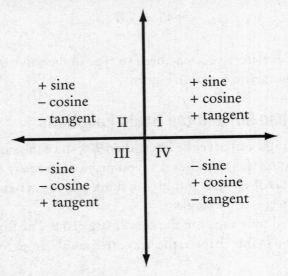

You should memorize the above graph.

The Math Level 1 will probably test whether you know the proper sign for each quadrant in an indirect way, meaning that it's unlikely that you'll have to do any heavy calculating when dealing with this topic. Instead, you might find a question such as:

If the value of sin $-\theta$ is .5, what is the value of sin θ?

This question doesn't ask you to think about sin for any specific value of θ. Instead, it tests your understanding of the quadrant signs for the sine function. The first thing you should notice is that $-\theta$ and θ have the same magnitude, even if they have different signs. This means that the magnitude of sine for $-\theta$ and θ will be the same. Immediately you should understand that sin θ must equal either .5 or $-.5$. To figure out which of these values is right, you have to decide what quadrant angle θ resides in. Based on the graph of the sine function or from the above chart, you can see that the sine function has a positive value in quadrants I and II, and negative values in quadrants III and IV. Since sin $-\theta$ is equal to a positive number, .5, you know that $-\theta$ must represent an angle in quadrant I or II. Since angle θ is simply the reflection of $-\theta$ across the x-axis, you can see that angle θ must be in either quadrant III or IV. The value of sin θ must be negative: $-.5$ is the right answer.

Solving Right Triangles

One of the most important applications of trigonometric functions is to "solve" a right triangle. By now, you should know that every right triangle has five unknowns: the lengths of its three sides and the measures of its two acute angles. Solving the triangle means finding the values of these unknowns. You can use trigonometric functions to solve a right triangle if you are given either of the following sets of information:

1. The length of one side and the measure of one acute angle

2. The lengths of two sides

Either situation might appear on the Math Level 1, so we cover both.

Given: One Angle and One Side

The right triangle below has an acute angle of 35° and a side of length 7.

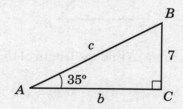

To find the measure of the other acute angle, just subtract the measures of the other two angles from 180°:

$$\angle B = 180 - 90 - 35 = 55°$$

To find the lengths of the other two sides, use trigonometric functions relating the given angle measure to the given side length. The key to problems of this type is to choose the correct trigonometric functions. In this question, you are given the measure of one angle and the length of the side opposite that angle, and two trigonometric functions relate these quantities. Since you know the length of the opposite side, the sine ($^{\text{opposite}}/_{\text{hypotenuse}}$) will allow you to solve for the length of the hypotenuse. Likewise, the tangent ($^{\text{opposite}}/_{\text{adjacent}}$) will let you solve for the length of the adjacent side.

$$\sin 35° = \frac{7}{c}$$

$$\tan 35° = \frac{7}{b}$$

You'll need your calculator to find sin 35° and tan 35°. But the basic algebra of solving right triangles is easy.

$$c = \frac{7}{\sin(35°)} = 12.2$$

$$b = \frac{7}{\tan(35°)} = 10.0$$

Given: Two Sides

The right triangle below has a leg of length 5 and a hypotenuse of length 8.

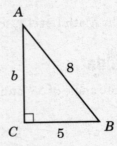

First, use the Pythagorean theorem to find the length of the third side:

$$b = \sqrt{8^2 - 5^2} = \sqrt{39} \approx 6.2$$

Next, use trigonometric functions to solve for the acute angles:

$$\sin A = \frac{5}{8}$$

$$\cos B = \frac{5}{8}$$

Now you know that $\sin A = \frac{5}{8}$, but you are trying to find out the value of $\angle A$, not sin A. To do this, you need to use some standard algebra and isolate $\angle A$. In other words, you have to find the inverse sine of both sides of the equation $\sin A = \frac{5}{8}$. Luckily, your calculator has inverse-trigonometric-function buttons labeled $\sin^{-1}$, $\cos^{-1}$, and $\tan^{-1}$. These inverse trigonometric functions are also referred to as arcsine, arccosine, and arctangent.

For this problem, use the $\sin^{-1}$ button to calculate the inverse sine of $\frac{5}{8}$. Carrying out this operation will tell you exactly which angle between 0° and 90° has a sine of $\frac{5}{8}$.

$$\sin^{-1}\sin A = \sin^{-1}\frac{5}{8}$$

$$\angle A = 38.7°$$

You can solve for $\angle B$ by using the $\cos^{-1}$ button and following the same steps. Try it out. You should come up with a value of 51.3°.

To solve this type of problem, you must know the proper math, and you also have to know how to use the inverse-trigonometric-function buttons on your calculator.

General Rules of Solving Right Triangles

We've just shown you two of the different paths you can take to solve a right triangle. The solution will depend on the specific problem, but the same three tools are always used:

1. The trigonometric functions

2. The Pythagorean theorem

3. The knowledge that the sum of the angles of a triangle is 180°

There is no "right" way to solve a right triangle. One way that is usually wrong, however, is solving for an angle or a side in the first step, approximating that measurement, and then using that approximation to finish solving the triangle. This approximation will lead to inaccurate answers, which in some cases might mean that your answer will not match the answer choices.

Trigonometric Identities

A **trigonometric identity** is an equation involving trigonometric functions that holds true for all angles. These identities are commonly called Pythagorean identities, because they come from the Pythagorean theorem.

1. $\tan \theta = {}^{\sin \theta}/_{\cos \theta}$

2. $\sin^2\theta + \cos^2\theta = 1$

The Math Level 1 will test your knowledge of the trigonometric identities by asking you to simplify a complex expression. Answering these questions has more to do with memorizing the identities and being good with algebraic substitution than it does with the theoretical concepts of trigonometry. For example:

What is $(\cos \theta \times \tan \theta) / (\sin \theta - \cos \theta^2)$?

To solve a problem like this, use the trigonometric identities to simplify the trigonometric into sines and cosines. After you have simplified the expression using the identities, it is quite likely that the expressions will simplify further due to the canceling of terms. The simplification of the expression in the example question proceeds as follows:

$$\frac{\cos\theta \times \tan\theta}{\sin\theta} - \cos^2\theta = \frac{\cos\theta\sin\theta}{\sin\theta\cos\theta} - \cos^2\theta$$
$$= 1 - \cos^2\theta$$
$$= \sin^2\theta$$

Simplifying the mess given to you by the problem, you get $\sin^2\theta$.

Here's another example:

What is $\tan^2\theta\ \cos^2\theta\ + 1 - \sin^2\theta$?

$$\tan^2\theta\cos^2\theta + 1 - \sin^2\theta = \frac{\sin^2\theta\cos^2\theta}{\cos^2\theta} + 1 - \sin^2\theta$$
$$= \sin^2\theta + 1 - \sin^2\theta$$
$$= 1$$

Graphing Trigonometric Functions

The graphs of trigonometric functions provide additional information about the functions, such as their periods, domains, and ranges. There are two ways to graph a trigonometric function, and either might appear on the test. The first method of graphing a trigonometric function involves the unit circle; the second involves the x-y coordinate plane.

The Unit Circle

The **unit circle** is a circle whose center is the origin and whose radius is 1. It is defined by equation $x^2 + y^2 = 1$.

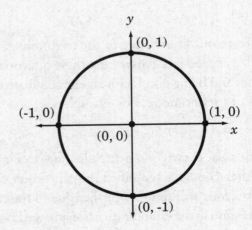

The most useful and interesting property of the unit circle is that the coordinates of a given point on the circle can be found using only the measure of the angle.

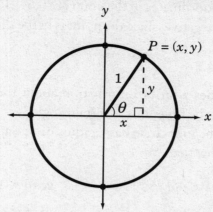

Any radius of the unit circle is the hypotenuse of a right triangle that has a (horizontal) leg of length $\cos \theta$ and a (vertical) leg of length $\sin \theta$. The angle θ is defined as the radius measured in standard position. These relationships are easy to see using the trigonometric functions:

$$\sin \theta = \frac{y}{1} = y$$
$$\cos \theta = \frac{x}{1} = x$$
$$\tan \theta = \frac{y}{x}$$

As you can see, because the radius of the unit circle is 1, the trigonometric functions sine and cosine are simplified: $\sin \theta = y$ and $\cos \theta = x$. This means that another way to write the coordinates of a point (x, y) on the unit circle is $(\cos \theta, \sin \theta)$, where θ is the measure of the angle in standard position whose terminal side contains the point.

Here's an example of a typical Math Level 1 question that tests this principle:

What are the coordinates of the point P pictured below?

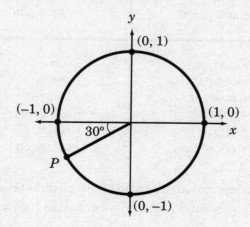

Point P is the endpoint of a radius of the unit circle that forms a 30° angle with the negative x-axis. This means that an angle of 210° in standard position would terminate in the same position. So, the coordinates of the point are (cos 210°, sin 210°) = ($-\sqrt{3}/2$, $-1/2$). Both coordinates must be negative, since the point is in the third quadrant.

Range

The unit circle also provides a lot of information about the range of trigonometric functions and the values of the functions at certain angles.

For example, because the unit circle has a radius of one and its points are all of the form (cos θ, sin θ), we know that:

$$-1 < \sin\theta < 1 \text{ and } -1 < \cos\theta < 1$$

Tangent ranges from $-\infty$ to ∞, but it is undefined at every angle whose cosine is 0. Can you guess why? Look at the formula of tan θ = $^{\sin\theta}/_{\cos\theta}$. If cos θ = 0, then division by 0 occurs, and so the quotient, tan θ, is undefined.

The Unit Circle and Important Angles

Using the unit circle makes it easy to find the values of trigonometric functions at quadrantal angles. For example, a 90° rotation from the positive x-axis puts you on the positive y-axis, which intersects the unit circle at the point (0, 1). From this, you know that (cos 90°, sin 90°) = (0, 1). Here is a graph of the values of all three trigonometric functions at each quadrantal angle:

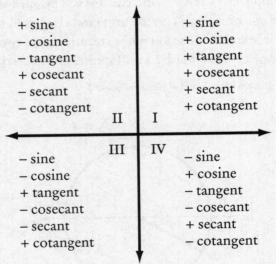

There are a few other common angles besides the quadrantal angles whose trigonometric function values you should already know. Listed below are the values of sine,

MAF $80 O'REILLY
  MASS AIR FLOW   SENSOR

    [1 MM]

    - MISC GAURILE
    - DRIVER
    - CONECTORUL INCARCARE

      COMAND 10 PLĂCI

7 7

7

0 1 2 3 4 5 6 7 8 9

7 7 7 7 7

7

cosine, and tangent taken at 30°, 45°, and 60°. You might recognize some of these values from the section on special triangles.

	$30°= \dfrac{\pi}{6}$ **rad**	$45°= \dfrac{\pi}{4}$ **rad**	$60°= \dfrac{\pi}{3}$ **rad**
$\sin \theta$	$\dfrac{1}{2}$	$\dfrac{1}{\sqrt{2}}$	$\dfrac{3}{2}$
$\cos \theta$	$\dfrac{\sqrt{3}}{2}$	$\dfrac{1}{\sqrt{2}}$	$\dfrac{1}{2}$
$\tan \theta$	$\dfrac{1}{\sqrt{3}}$	1	$\sqrt{3}$

Radians and Degrees

Radians are another way to measure angles. Sometimes radians will be used in questions, and other times you may choose to use them since they are sometimes more convenient than degrees.

A degree is equal to $^1/_{360}$ of a circle, while a radian is equal to the angle that intercepts an arc of the same length as the radius of the circle. In the figure below, arc AB has length r, and the central angle measures one radian.

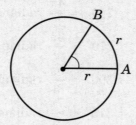

When converting between the two measurement systems, use the proportion:

$$\frac{1 \text{ degree}}{360} = \frac{1 \text{ radian}}{2\pi}$$

which can be simplified to:

$$\frac{1 \text{ degree}}{180} = \frac{1 \text{ radian}}{\pi}$$

To convert from degrees to radians: multiply the degree measure by $^\pi/_{180}$. For example, 60° is equal to $^{60\pi}/_{180} = {}^\pi/_3$ radians.

To convert from radians to degrees: multiply the measure in radians by $^{180}/\pi$. For example, $^{\pi}/_4$ radians is equal to $^{180\pi}/_{4\pi} = 45°$.

Here are the most important angle measures in degrees and radians:

$$30° = \frac{\pi}{6} \text{ radians}$$
$$45° = \frac{\pi}{4} \text{ radians}$$
$$60° = \frac{\pi}{3} \text{ radians}$$
$$90° = \frac{\pi}{2} \text{ radians}$$
$$120° = \frac{2\pi}{3} \text{ radians}$$
$$135° = \frac{3\pi}{4} \text{ radians}$$
$$150° = \frac{5\pi}{6} \text{ radians}$$
$$180° = \pi \text{ radians}$$
$$210° = \frac{7\pi}{6} \text{ radians}$$
$$225° = \frac{5\pi}{4} \text{ radians}$$
$$240° = \frac{4\pi}{3} \text{ radians}$$
$$270° = \frac{3\pi}{2} \text{ radians}$$
$$300° = \frac{5\pi}{3} \text{ radians}$$
$$315° = \frac{7\pi}{4} \text{ radians}$$
$$330° = \frac{11\pi}{6} \text{ radians}$$
$$360° = 2\pi \text{ radians}$$

On the Math Level 1, it is sometimes a better idea to work solely in radians, rather than convert back and forth between radians and degrees. Using radians is especially easy on graphing calculators that allow you to switch into radian mode.

Graphing in the Entire Coordinate Plane

The functions sine, cosine, and tangent are commonly graphed in the coordinate plane, with x representing the measure of an angle (the x units are usually given in radians) and y measuring the value of a given trigonometric function at that angle. The best way to see this is to study the graphs themselves. Image (a) is the graph of $y = \sin x$; (b) is $y = \cos x$; and (c) is $y = \tan x$.

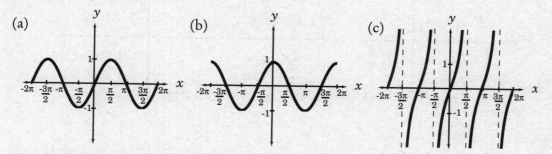

These graphs show a number of important characteristics of trigonometric functions.

Domain

The **domain** of a function is simply the x values for which the function can be calculated. In the case of the trigonometric functions, the input is an angle measure, and the output is a ratio (like $^{opposite}/_{hypotenuse}$, for example).

The domain of a trigonometric function can be seen in its graph: it is the set of all x-values for which the function is defined. For sine and cosine, the domain is the set of real numbers, because any angle measure has a sine and a cosine; there are no values of x for which sine or cosine doesn't produce a y-value.

The graph of the tangent function, however, tells a different story. It shows certain x-values for which the tangent is undefined. These undefined points occur when the cosine is zero, since $\tan x = {}^{\sin x}/_{\cos x}$, and division by zero is undefined. The x-values for the undefined tangent show up on its graph as vertical dotted lines every 180°, such that $x = n(180°) + 90°$, where n is an integer. For example, the tangent function is undefined at the x-value $2(180°) + 90° = 450°$.

Range

Like the domain, the range of the trigonometric functions can be seen in their graphs. The range of a function is the set of all possible values of the function. In other words, the range is the set of all y-values of the function.

The range of sine and cosine, as you can see in its graph or by analyzing the unit circle, is $-1 \leq y \leq 1$. The graphs of these two functions never rise above 1 or fall below -1, and every point on the unit circle has an x and y value between -1 and 1. Occasionally, you may see a question in which the answer choices are possible values of sine or cosine. If any of them are greater than 1 or less than -1, you can eliminate them.

The range of tangent is the set of real numbers. To see why there are no bounds on the value of tangent, recall that the denominator ($\cos \theta$) can get increasingly close to zero, making the quotient get infinitely large.

The chart below summarizes what has been discussed in the previous few paragraphs.

Function	Domain	Range
$y = \sin x$	$-\infty < x < \infty$	$-1 \leq y \leq 1$
$y = \cos x$	$-\infty < x < \infty$	$-1 \leq y \leq 1$
$y = \tan x$	$-\infty < x < \infty, x \neq n\pi + \pi/2; n$ is an integer	$-\infty < y < \infty$

Periodic Functions

Sine, cosine, and tangent are all periodic functions, meaning that their values repeat on a regular interval. This regular interval is called the functions period. More technically, the period of a function is the smallest domain containing a full cycle of the function. Take a look at the periods for sine, cosine, and tangent:

- For $y = \sin x$ and $y = \cos x$, the period is 2π radians. This means that every $360°$, the values of sine and cosine repeat themselves. For example, trigonometric functions of 0 and 2π radians produce the same values.

- For $y = \tan x$, the period is π radians. Thus, the tangents of $0°$ and $180°$ are equal.

If a trigonometric function contains a coefficient in front of x, its period changes. In general, the period of $y = f(bx)$ is the normal period of f divided by b. The period of $y = \sin\frac{1}{4}x = \frac{2\pi \text{ radians}}{1/4} = 8\pi \text{ radians}$.

Amplitude

Another useful property of the sine and cosine curves (but not tangent) is amplitude. The figure below shows the amplitude, *a*, for the sine and cosine functions:

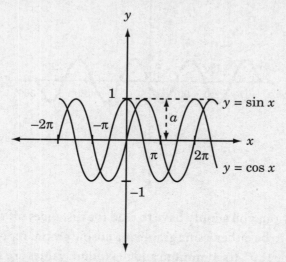

The amplitude of the sine and cosine functions is half the vertical distance between its minimum value and its maximum value. The amplitude of $y = \sin x$ and $y = \cos x$ is 1 because the minimum and maximum values of these functions are −1 and 1, respectively, and half the vertical distance between these values is 1. The tangent graph has no amplitude, because the tangent function has no minimum or maximum value. In general, the amplitude of the trigonometric function $y = af(x)$ is $|a|$. The amplitude of $\frac{1}{3} \cos x$ is $\frac{1}{3}$.

Here is an example of the type of problem on the Math Level 1 that will cover the graphs of the trigonometric functions.

> What is the period and amplitude of the function $y = 4 \sin 3x$?

As we just discussed, the period of $y = f(bx)$ is the normal period of f divided by b. For the sine function, the normal period is 360°. In this example, $b = 3$, so the period of this function is $360 \div 3 = 120°$. In general, the amplitude of the sine function $y = af(x)$ is $|a|$. In this particular case, $a = 4$. So the amplitude is 4.

Take a look at another type of question you may see on the test:

What is the period and amplitude of the function graphed below?

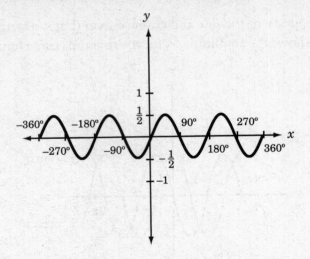

To answer this question, you simply have to read the distances off the graph. The function, which appears to be either a sine graph or a cosine graph, repeats itself every 180°. Its period is therefore 180°. Its minimum and maximum values are ±½, so its amplitude is ½.

To handle any question about the graphs of trigonometric functions, you should be able to answer questions about period and amplitude based on the equation or graph of a given function.

Key Formulas

SOHCAHTOA

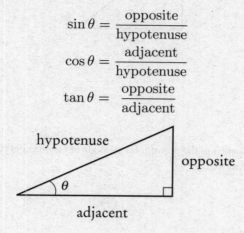

$$\sin \theta = \frac{\text{opposite}}{\text{hypotenuse}}$$

$$\cos \theta = \frac{\text{adjacent}}{\text{hypotenuse}}$$

$$\tan \theta = \frac{\text{opposite}}{\text{adjacent}}$$

Pythagorean Identities

$$\tan \theta = \frac{\sin \theta}{\cos \theta}$$

$$\sin^2 \theta + \cos^2 \theta = 1$$

Review Questions

1. In the triangle below, what is the length of *AC*?

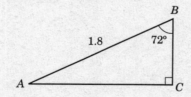

    (A)   0.56
    (B)   0.95
    (C)   1.30
    (D)   1.71
    (E)   5.54

2.   In the triangle below, what is the measure of $\angle B$?

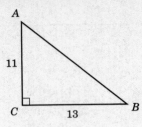

(A)   32.2°
(B)   40.2°
(C)   48.5°
(D)   49.7°
(E)   50.8°

3.   A boy flies a kite 100 feet from the ground. If the angle of elevation of the kite string is 55°, how many feet long is the kite string?

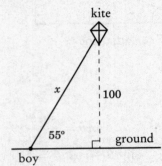

(A)   70.0
(B)   98.5
(C)   122.1
(D)   155.0
(E)   174.3

4.   If $\sqrt{\dfrac{\cos^2 x - 1}{-\cos^2 x}} = 1$, then $x = ?$

(A)   30°
(B)   45°
(C)   60°
(D)   75°
(E)   90°

5.   If $\alpha = \beta/4$, and $\sin \alpha$ and $\cos \beta$ are greater than zero, which of the following values could *not* be α?

(A)   10°
(B)   65°
(C)   90°
(D)   110°
(E)   165°

6. The graph of $y = 3 \sin(bx)$ crosses the x-axis seven times in the interval $0 \le x \le 2\pi$. What is the value of b?

   (A)   2
   (B)   7/3
   (C)   3
   (D)   4
   (E)   7

7. What is the period and amplitude of the graph of the function $y = 2 \cos(4x + 2) - 7$?

   (A)   period = $\pi/2$; amplitude = 2
   (B)   period = π; amplitude = 2
   (C)   period = $7\pi/2$; amplitude = 4
   (D)   period = 2; amplitude = 2
   (E)   period = 4; amplitude = 2π

8. Find the area of triangle ABC pictured below:

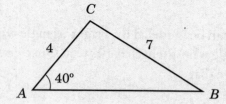

   (A)   10.44
   (B)   12.30
   (C)   14.14
   (D)   15.69
   (E)   27.47

Explanations

1.   **D**

Since the triangle is a right triangle and the figure gives the value of the angle opposite side AC, you can use the sine function to find the length of AC.

$$\sin 72° = \frac{AC}{1.8}$$
$$AC = 1.8 \sin 72°$$
$$AC \approx 1.71$$

2.   **B**

Since the figure gives only the values for the two legs of this right triangle, to find the measure of $\angle B$ you'll first need to calculate a value for tan B and then take the inverse.

$$\tan B = \frac{11}{13}$$

which means that

$$B = \arctan\frac{11}{13}$$
$$B \approx 40.2°$$

3.   **C**

The kite-flying situation can be modeled by a right triangle with an acute angle of 55°, and a leg opposite that angle whose length is 100 feet. Once you picture the situation as a right triangle, you can see that

$$\sin(55°) = \frac{100}{\text{hypotenuse}}$$

where the hypotenuse is the length of the kite string. Therefore, letting x represent the hypotenuse:

$$x = \frac{100}{\sin(55°)}$$
$$x \approx 122.1$$

4.   **B**

Simplify the left side using trigonometric identities to make this problem easier to solve. First, you need to rearrange the identity $\sin^2 x + \cos^2 x = 1$ so that you find $\cos^2 x - 1 = -\sin^2 x$. Then substitute this into the equation. Later, substitute tan x for $\sin x/\cos x$.

$$\sqrt{\frac{\cos^2(x) - 1}{-\cos^2(x)}} = \sqrt{\frac{-\sin^2(x)}{-\cos^2(x)}}$$
$$= \sqrt{\tan^2(x)}$$
$$= \tan(x)$$

Now solve the equation $\tan x = 1$. It's just a matter of taking the inverse of both sides of the equation: $\angle x = \arctan 1 = 45°$.

5.   B

If $\theta = \frac{1}{4}\theta$, we can rewrite the given conditions: $\sin \theta$ and $\cos 4\theta$ are greater than zero. These are the conditions we must meet.

   In order for $\sin a$ to be greater than zero, $0° < \theta < 180°$, because sine is only positive in the first two quadrants. This mean $0 < 4\theta < 720°$. Cosine, however, is positive only in the first and fourth quadrants. Thus, for $0° < x < 720°$, cosine is only positive in the following intervals: $(0°, 90°)$, $(270°, 450°)$, and $(630°, 720°)$. By dividing these intervals by four, the range of θ is defined: $0° < \theta < 22.5°$, $67.5° < \alpha < 112.5°$, or $157.5° < \theta < 180°$. The only answer choice that does not fall within one of these intervals is $65°$.

6.   C

The variable b adjusts the period of the standard function from 2π to $\frac{2\pi}{b}$. The standard sine function, $y = \sin x$, crosses the x-axis three times in the interval $0 \le x \le 2\pi$: at 0, π, and 2π. So, since the period of a function is the interval between each repeat of the function's curve, the only way for the graph of $y = 3 \sin bx$ to cross the x-axis more often than $y = \sin x$ is to have a shorter period. Thus, b must be greater than 1.

   To make the function cross the x-axis $\frac{7}{3}$ as many times as $y = \sin x$ does, you might be tempted to make the period $\frac{3}{7}$ as long as 2π, which would correspond to a b value of $\frac{7}{3}$. This, however, is wrong, because it counts the intersection at 2π too many times. You can check this result if you have a graphing calculator.

   By halving the period of the function, you might think that the number of crossings would double. Actually, $y = \sin 2x$ crosses the x-axis only five times because the crossing at 2π does not figure into the doubling.

   Using this logic as a guide, you see that to achieve seven crossings, you must make the period 3 times shorter so that the first 2 crossings are tripled in number and the crossing at 2π is added at the end. This means that the period of the unknown function is $\frac{2\pi}{3}$, and $b = 3$.

7.   A

In the cosine function, the amplitude is the coefficient in front of cosine and the period is 2π divided by the coefficient of x. So for the function $y = 2 \cos (4x + 2) - 7$, the amplitude is 2 and the period is $\frac{2\pi}{4} = \frac{\pi}{2}$.

8.   B

This problem takes a few steps. Your goal is to find AB and the height to vertex C. Then you can use the area formula, $A = \frac{1}{2}bh$, where b is the base and h is the height.

First, draw an altitude from C to AB.

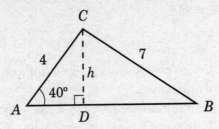

The length of this altitude is the height of the triangle. In the triangle you just formed, triangle ACD, $\sin 40° = {}^h\!/_4$. So, $h = 4 \sin 40° \approx 2.57$. The Pythagorean theorem can now be used to find lengths AD and BD:

$$AD = \sqrt{4^2 - 2.57^2} \approx 3.07$$
$$BD = \sqrt{7^2 - 2.57^2} \approx 6.51$$

The sum of AD and BD is AB, approximately 9.58. Finally, you can plug these values back into the area formula:

$$\text{Area} = \frac{1}{2}(9.58)(2.57) \approx 12.3$$

Functions

F UNCTIONS COME IN MANY SHAPES AND sizes. In fact, you've already seen quadratic functions such as $f(x) = x^2 + 7x - 5$ in the Algebra chapter and trigonometric functions such as $f(x) = \sin x$ and $f(x) = \cos x$ in the Trigonometry chapter. This chapter explains the specific notation, behavior, and properties of functions that you will need to know for the Math Level 1 test.

About six questions on the Math Level 1 cover functions. These questions can range from rather simple substitution problems to conceptual problems about the definition of a function to questions that test your ability to graph functions.

Characteristics of a Function

In order to discuss functions, you need to understand of their basic characteristics.

A **function** describes a relationship between one or more inputs and one output. The inputs to a function are variables; x is the most common letter used as a variable in the functions that appear on the Math Level 1, though you may also come across an occasional a, b, or some other letter. The output of the function for a particular value of x is usually represented as $f(x)$ or $g(x)$. When a function of a single variable is graphed on the (x,y) plane, the output of the function, $f(x)$, is graphed on the y-axis; functions are therefore commonly written as $y = x^2$ rather then $f(x) = x^2$.

Two characteristics of functions that you should become comfortable with are domain and range. The domain is the set of inputs (x values) for which the function is defined. Consider the following two functions: $f(x) = x^2$ and $g(x) = \frac{1}{x}$. In $f(x)$, any value of x can produce a valid result since any number can be squared. In $g(x)$, though, not every value of x can generate an output: when $x = 0$, $g(x)$ is undefined.

The range of a function is closely related to the domain. Whereas the domain is the set of inputs that a function can take, the range is the set of outputs that a function can produce. To help you understand this concept, let's use the examples in the last paragraph: $f(x) = x^2$ and $g(x) = 1/x$. Try to think of all the values that can be generated when a number is squared. Well, all squares are positive (or equal to 0), so $f(x)$ can never be negative. In the case of $g(x)$, almost every number is part of the range. In fact, the only number that cannot be generated by the function $g(x)$ is 0. Try it for yourself; there's no value of x for which $1/x$ equals 0. The range of the function $g(x)$ is all numbers except zero.

Once you understand the concepts of a function's domain and range, you can see how their relationship helps to define a function. A function requires that each value of x has only one value of $f(x)$; that is, each element of the domain must be paired with exactly one element of the range. Each element of the domain and its corresponding element of the range can be written (and graphed) as a coordinate pair, $(x, f(x))$.

Now consider the set of coordinates $\{(1, 5), (3, 5), (1, 3)\}$. Does this set define a function? No, because the definition of a function requires that each element of the domain be paired with only one element of the range. Specifically, 1 has been assigned to two different values in the range, 5 and 3. This rule is easy to apply when you have the coordinates listed for you. If you are presented with a graph instead, you can use the **vertical line test**, which states that any vertical line drawn anywhere along a function must not intersect it more than once.

Evaluating Functions

Evaluating a function simply means finding $f(x)$ at some specific value x. The Math Level 1 will likely ask you to evaluate a function at some particular constant. Take a look at the following example:

If $f(x) = x^2 - 3$, what is $f(5)$?

Evaluating a function at a constant involves nothing more than substituting the constant into the definition of the function. In this case, substitute 5 for x:

$$f(5) = 5^2 - 3 = 22$$

It's as simple as that.

The Math Level 1 may also ask questions in which you are asked to evaluate a function at a variable rather than a constant. For example:

If $f(x) = 3x/4 - x$, what is $f(x + 1)$?

To solve problems of this sort, follow the same method you used for evaluating a function at a constant: substitute the variable into the equation. To solve the sample question, substitute $(x + 1)$ for x in the definition of the function:

$$f(x + 1) = \frac{3(x + 1)}{4 - (x + 1)}$$

$$= \frac{3x + 3}{4 - x - 1}$$

$$= \frac{3x + 3}{3 - x}$$

Operations on Functions

Functions can be added, subtracted, multiplied, and divided like any other quantity. There are a few rules that make these operations easier. For any two functions $f(x)$ and $g(x)$:

	Rule	Example
Addition	$(f + g)(x) = f(x) + g(x)$	If $f(x) = \sin x$, and $g(x) = \cos x$: $(f + g)(x) = \sin x + \cos x$
Subtraction	$(f - g)(x) = f(x) - g(x)$	If $f(x) = x^2 + 5$, and $g(x) = x^2 + 2x + 1$: $(f - g)(x) = x^2 + 5 - x^2 - 2x - 1 = -2x + 4$
Multiplication	$(f \times g)(x) = f(x) \times g(x)$	If $f(x) = x$, and $g(x) = x^3 + 8$: $(f \times g)(x) = x \times (x^3 + 8) = x^4 + 8x$
Division	$\frac{f}{g}(x) = \frac{f(x)}{g(x)}, g(x) \neq 0$	If $f(x) = 2 \cos x$, and $g(x) = 2 \sin^2 x$: $(f \div g)(x) = \frac{2\cos x}{2\sin^2 x} = \frac{\cos x}{\sin^2 x}$

As usual, when dividing, you have to be aware of possible situations in which you inadvertently divide by zero. Since division by zero is not allowed, you should just remember that any time you are dividing functions, like $f(x)/g(x)$, the resulting function is undefined whenever the function in the denominator equals zero.

Compound Functions

A compound function is a function that operates on another function. A compound function is written as nested functions, in the form $f(g(x))$. To evaluate a compound function, first evaluate the internal function, $g(x)$. Next, evaluate the outer function at the result of $g(x)$. Work with the inner parentheses first and then the outer ones, just as in any other algebraic expression. Try the following example:

Suppose $h(x) = x^2 + 2x$ and $j(x) = |\frac{x}{4} + 2|$. What is $j(h(4))$?

To evaluate this compound function, first evaluate $h(4)$:

$$h(4) = 4^2 + 2(4)$$
$$= 16 + 8$$
$$= 24$$

Now plug 24 into the definition of j:

$$j(24) = |\frac{24}{4} + 2|$$
$$= |6 + 2|$$
$$= 8$$

It is important that you pay attention to the order in which you evaluate the compound function. Always evaluate the inner function first. For example, if we had evaluated $j(x)$ before $h(x)$ in the above question, you would get a completely different answer:

$$h(j(4)) = h(|\frac{4}{4} + 2|)$$
$$= h(|1 + 2|)$$
$$= h(3)$$
$$= 3^2 + 2(3)$$
$$= 9 + 6$$
$$= 15$$

Here's a slightly more complicated example, in which you are not given a specific point of the compound function to evaluate :

Suppose $f(x) = 3x + 1$ and $g(x) = \sqrt{5x}$. What is $g(f(x))$?

When you are not given a constant at which to evaluate a compound function, you should simply substitute the definition of $f(x)$ as the input to $g(x)$. This situation is exactly the same as a regular equation being evaluated at a variable rather than a constant.

$$g(f(x)) = g(3x + 1)$$
$$= \sqrt{5(3x + 1)}$$
$$= \sqrt{15x + 5}$$

Inverse Functions

The inverse of a function "undoes" that function. An example may be the best way to explain what this means: the inverse of x^2 is $\sqrt{x}$. Let's see how $\sqrt{x}$ "undoes" x^2:

$$x = 10$$
$$10^2 = 100$$
$$\sqrt{100} = 10$$

For the Math Level 1, it is important to know how to find the inverse of a simple function mathematically. For example:

What is the inverse of $f(x) = 3x + 2$?

The easiest way to find the inverse of a function is to break the function apart step by step. The function $f(x) = 3x + 2$ requires that for any value of x, it must be first multiplied by three and then added to 2. The inverse of this function must begin by subtracting 2 and then dividing by three, undoing the original function: $f^{-1}(x) = \frac{x-2}{3}$.

You should know how an inverse works in order to deal with any conceptual inverse questions the Math Level 1 might throw at you. But if you are ever asked to come up with the inverse of a particular function, there is an easy method that will always work.

1. Replace the variable $f(x)$ with y.

2. Switch the places of x and y.

3. Solve for y.

4. Replace y with $f^{-1}(x)$.

Here's an example of the method in action:

What is the inverse of the function $f(x) = \sqrt{\dfrac{2x^2 - 3}{5}}$?

First, replace $f(x)$ with y. Then switch the places of x and y, and solve for y.

$$x = \sqrt{\frac{2y^2 - 3}{5}}$$

$$x^2 = \frac{2y^2 - 3}{5}$$

$$5x^2 = 2y^2 - 3$$

$$5x^2 + 3 = 2y^2$$

$$\frac{5}{2}x^2 + \frac{3}{2} = y^2$$

$$y = \sqrt{\frac{5}{2}x^2 + \frac{3}{2}}$$

$$f^{-1}(x) = \sqrt{\frac{5}{2}x^2 + \frac{3}{2}}$$

Finding Whether the Inverse of a Function Is a Function

Contrary to their name, inverse functions are not necessarily functions at all. Take a look at this question:

Is the inverse of $f(x) = x^3$ a function?

Begin by writing $y = x^3$. Next, switch the places of x and y: $x = y^3$. Solve for y: $y = 3\sqrt{x}$. Now you need to analyze the inverse of the function and decide whether for every x, there is only one y. If only one y is associated with each x, you've got a function. Otherwise, you don't. In this case, every x value that falls within the domain $x \geq 0$ turns out one value for y, so $f^{-1}(x)$ is a function.

Here's another question:

What is the inverse of $f(x) = 2|x - 1|$, and is it a function?

Again, replace x with y and solve for y:

$$x = 2|y - 1|$$

$$\frac{1}{2}x = |y - 1|$$

Now, since you're dealing with an absolute value, split the equations:

$$y - 1 = \frac{1}{2}x \text{ or } 1 - y = \frac{1}{2}x$$

Therefore,

$$y = \frac{1}{2}x + 1 \text{ or } y = -\frac{1}{2}x + 1$$

The inverse of $f(x)$ is this set of two equations. As you can see, for every value of x except 0, the inverse of the function assigns two values of y. Consequently, $f^{-1}(x)$ is not a function.

Domain and Range

Several of the Math Level 1 questions about functions will focus on domain and range. These questions are straightforward if you understand the basic concepts and know what to look for.

Domain

We discussed the concept of a function's domain earlier in this chapter. The domain of a function is the set of inputs to the function that produce valid outputs. It is common for a domain to include only positive numbers, only negative numbers, or even all numbers except one or two points. As an example of a function that is undefined on a certain interval, consider $f(x) = \sqrt{x}$. A negative number has no square root defined in the real number system, so $f(x)$ is undefined for all $x < 0$.

Finding the Domain of a Function

The Math Level 1 may ask you to find the domain of a given function. When you are solving a problem of this sort, you should begin by assuming that the domain is the set of real numbers. The next step is to look for any restrictions on the domain. For example, in the case of $f(x) = \sqrt{x}$, we must restrict the domain to non-negative numbers since we know that you can't take the square root of a negative number.

In general, when finding a domain on the Math Level 1, there are two main restrictions to be on the lookout for:

1. Division by zero. Division by zero is mathematically impossible. A function is therefore undefined for all the values of x for which division by zero occurs. For example, $f(x) = \frac{1}{x-2}$ is undefined at $x = 2$, since when $x = 2$, the function is equal to $f(x) = \frac{1}{0}$.

2. Even roots. An even root (a square root, fourth root, etc.) of a negative number does not exist. A function is undefined for all values of x that cause a negative number to be the radicand of an even root.

Recognizing that these two situations cause the function to be undefined is the key to finding any restriction on the function's domain. Once you've discovered where the likely problem spots are, you can usually find the values to be eliminated from the domain easily.

By now, you must be itching for a sample problem:

What is the domain of $f(x) = \dfrac{x}{x^2 + 5x + 6}$?

In this question, $f(x)$ has variables in its denominator, which should be a red flag that alerts you to the possibility of division by zero. We may need to restrict the function's domain to ensure that division by zero does not occur. To find the values of x that cause the denominator to equal zero, set up an equation and factor the quadratic: $x^2 + 5x + 6 = (x + 2)(x + 3) = 0$. For $x = \{-2, -3\}$, the denominator is zero and $f(x)$ is undefined. Since it is defined for all other real numbers, the domain of $f(x)$ is the set of all real numbers x such that $x \neq -2, -3$. This can also be written as $\{x : x \neq -2, -3\}$.

Here's another example:

What is the domain of $f(x) = \dfrac{2\sqrt{x - 4}}{x - 7}$?

This function has both warning signs: an even root and a variable in the denominator. It's best to examine each situation separately:

1. The denominator would equal zero if $x = 7$.

2. The quantity under the square root (the radicand), $x - 4$, must be greater than or equal to zero in order for the function to be defined. Therefore, $x \geq 4$.

The domain of the function is therefore the set of real numbers x such that $x \geq 4$, $x \neq 7$.

The Domain of a Function with Two Variables

So far we have looked only at functions that take a single variable as input. Some functions on the Math Level 1 test take two variables. For example:

$$f(s, t) = \frac{s^2}{4} + \frac{6t}{7}$$

A two-variable function is not very different from the basic single-variable variety you've already seen. Essentially, the domain of this function is a set of ordered pairs of real numbers (s, t), rather than a set of single real numbers.

$$f(8, 14) = \frac{8^2}{4} + \frac{6(14)}{7}$$
$$= \frac{64}{4} + \frac{84}{7}$$
$$= 16 + 12$$
$$= 28$$

Evaluating such a function follows the same process as evaluating a single-variable function. Just substitute for the variables in the equation and do the algebra. Try to find $f(8, 14)$, using the definition of $f(s, t)$ above.

Piecewise Functions

Not all functions must have the same definition across their entire domain. Some functions have different definitions for different intervals of their domains; this type of function is called a piecewise function. Here is a typical example:

$$g(x) = 2x, \quad x < 0$$
$$x, \quad 0 \le x \le 10$$
$$-x, \quad x > 10$$

To evaluate a piecewise function, you need to find the correct interval for the given definition and evaluate as usual. For example, what is $g(6)$, using the above piecewise definition of $g(x)$?

$$0 \le 6 \le 10, \text{ so } g(6) = 6$$

Range

A function's range is the set of all values of $f(x)$ that can be generated by the function. In general, the range for most functions whose domain is unrestricted is the set of all real numbers. To visualize the concept of range, consider two trigonometric functions, $\sin x$ and $\tan x$.

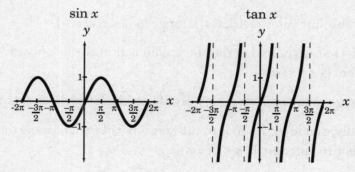

Functions

What values of the y-axis are reached on each graph? On the graph of tan x, you can see that every possible value of y, from negative infinity to positive infinity, is included in the range. The range could be written as $\{y: -\infty \le y \le \infty\}$. Contrast this with the graph of sin x, in which the range is quite limited. You'll notice that only the values between -1 and 1 are part of the range. We'll write the range using another common notation: $\{-1 \le f(x) \le 1\}$.

Of course, there are other ways that a function's range might be limited. For example, if a function has a limited domain (only certain x values are allowed), its range might be limited as well. In addition, there are two main reasons that a function's range would be restricted:

Absolute value. Remember that by definition, the absolute value of a quantity is always positive. So, in a simple case, $f(x) = |x|$, you know that $f(x)$ must always be positive, and so the range excludes all negative numbers. Be careful, though, not to assume that any function with an absolute value symbol has the same range. For example, the range of $g(x) = -|x|$ is $\{y: -\infty \le y \le 0\}$ and the range of $h(x) = 10 + |x|$ is $\{10 \le h(x) \le \infty\}$.

Even exponents. Any time you square a number (or raise it to any multiple of 2) the resulting quantity will be positive. As in the case of the absolute value, though, don't assume that the range will always be $\{y: 0 \le y \le \infty\}$.

Determining the range of a complex function is similar to finding the domain. First look for absolute values, even exponents, or other reasons that the range would be restricted. Then simply adjust that range step by step as you complete the questions. The best way to get the hang of it is to practice.

What is the range of $\dfrac{|x-3|}{2}$?

The absolute value around $|x - 3|$ tells us that the range for that term excludes negative numbers ($y: 0 \le y \le \infty$). $|x - 3|$ is then divided by 2, so we must also divide the range by 2: ($y: \%2 \le y \le \%2$). Obviously, this doesn't change the range, since both zero and infinity remain unchanged when halved. Now for a more complicated example:

What is the range of $\dfrac{\sqrt{|x-6|+4}}{2}$?

Let's tackle this example step by step.

1. The absolute value restricts the range to $\{0 \le f(x) \le \infty\}$.

2. Add 4 to each bound of the range. This action affects only the lower bound: $\{4 \le f(x) \le \infty\}$.

3. Taking the square root again only affects the lower bound: $\{2 \le f(x) \le \infty\}$.

4. Finally, divide the bounds of the range in half to determine the range of the entire function: $\{1 \le f(x) \le \infty\}$.

Note that addition, subtraction, multiplication, division, and other mathematical operations cannot affect infinity. That's why it is particularly important that you look for absolute values and even roots. Once you can find a bound on a range, then you know that the operations on the function will affect that range.

Before we move on, here is one last example that uses a slightly different range notation that you might come across on the Math Level 1:

What is the range of $f(x) = \dfrac{-3x^2}{2} + 2$?

Once again, take a step by step approach to finding the range:

1. The range of $f(x) - x^2$ is $\{0, \infty\}$.

2. The range of $f(x) - {}^3/_2\, x^2$ is $\{-\infty, 0\}$.

3. The range of $f(x) - {}^3/_2\, x^2 + 2$ is therefore $\{-\infty, 2\}$, or simply $\{f(x) \le 2\}$.

The Range of a Function with a Prescribed Domain

Occasionally the Math Level 1 will present you with a question in which the domain of a function is restricted to a given interval, and you are asked to find the range of the newly restricted function. For example:

$f(x) = 2x^2 + 4$ for $-3 < x < 5$. What is the range of f?

The best way to solve this type of problem is to manipulate the domain of x in exactly the same way that x is manipulated in the function. First x is squared, then multiplied by 2, then added to 4; we simply need to do the same operations to the bounds of the domain:

1. $-3 < x < 5$

2. $0 < x^2 < 25$

3. $0 < 2x^2 < 50$

4. $4 < 2x^2 + 4 < 54$

The range of $f(x)$ is $\{4 < f(x) < 54\}$.

Graphing Functions

While most of the function questions on the Math Level 1 will involve analysis and manipulation of the functions themselves, you will sometimes be asked a question about the graph of a function. A common question of this type asks you to match a function's graph to its definition. Understanding the next few topics will help prepare you for questions relating to functions and their graphs.

Identifying Whether a Graph Is a Function

For the Math Level 1, it's important to be able to determine if a given graph is indeed a function. A foolproof way to do this is to use the vertical line test: if a vertical line intersects a graph more than once, then the graph is not a function.

The vertical line test makes sense because the definition of a function requires that any x-value have only one y-value. A vertical line has the same x-value along the entire line; if it intersects the graph more than once, then the graph has more than one y-value associated with that x-value.

Using the vertical line test, check to see that the three graphs below are functions.

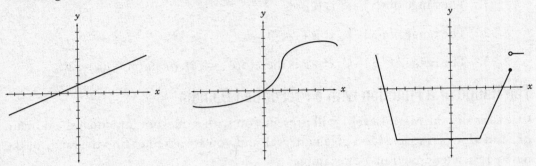

The next three graphs are not functions. In each graph, a strategically placed vertical line (depicted by the dashed line) will intersect the graph more than once.

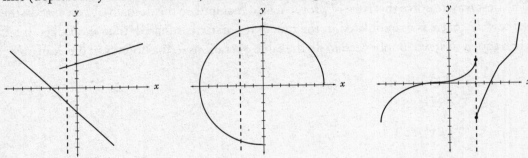

Range and Domain in Graphing

The range and domain of a function are easy enough to see in their graphs. The domain is the set of all x-values for which the function is defined. The range is the set of all y-values for which the function is defined. To find the domain and range of a graph, just look at which x- and y-values the graph includes.

Certain kinds of graphs have specific ranges and domains that are visible in their graphs. A line whose slope is not 0 (a horizontal line) or undefined (a vertical line) has the set of real numbers as its domain and range. Since a line, by definition, extends infinitely in both directions, it passes through all possible values of x and y:

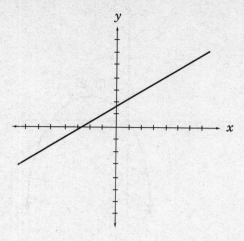

An odd-degree polynomial, which is a polynomial whose highest degree of power is an odd number, also has the set of real numbers as its domain and range:

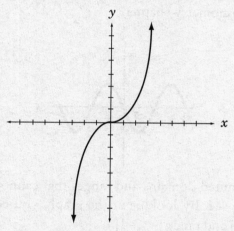

An even-degree polynomial, which is a polynomial whose highest degree of power is an even number, has the set of real numbers as its domain, but it has a restricted range. The range is usually bounded at one end and unbounded at the other. The following parabola has range $\{-\infty, 2\}$:

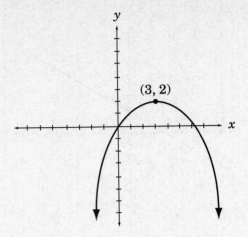

Trigonometric functions have various domains and ranges depending on the function. Sine, for example, has the real numbers for its domain and {–1, 1} for its range. A more detailed breakdown of the domains and ranges for the various trigonometric functions can be found in the Trigonometry chapter.

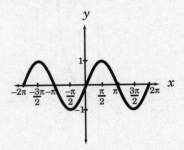

Some functions have limited domains and ranges that cannot be categorized simply, but are still obvious to see. By looking at the graph, you can see that the function below has domain {3, ∞} and range {–∞, –1}.

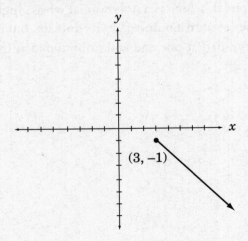

Asymptotes and Holes

There are two types of abnormalities that can further limit the domain and range of a function: asymptotes and holes. Being able to identify these abnormalities will help you to match the domain and range of a graph to its function.

An **asymptote** is a line that a graph approaches but never intersects. In graphs, asymptotes are represented as dotted lines. You'll probably only see vertical and horizontal asymptotes on the Math Level 1, though they can have other slopes as well. A function is undefined at the x value of a vertical asymptote, thus restricting the domain of the function graphed. A function's range does not include the y value of a horizontal asymptote, since the whole point of an asymptote is that the function never actually takes on that value.

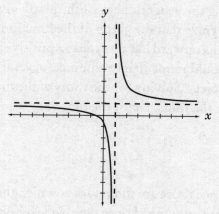

In this graph, there is a vertical asymptote at $x = 1$, and a horizontal asymptote at $y = 1$. Because of these asymptotes, the domain of the graphed function is the set of real numbers except 1 ($x \neq 1$), and the range of the function graphed is also the set of real numbers except 1 ($f(x) \neq 1$).

A **hole** is a point at which a function is undefined. You'll recognize it in a graph as an open circle at the point where the hole occurs. Find it in the following figure:

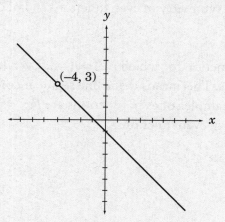

The hole in the graph above is the point (–4, 3). This means that the domain of the function is the set of real numbers except 4 ($x \neq -4$), and the range is the set of real numbers except 3 ($f(x) \neq 3$).

The Roots of a Function

The **roots** (or **zeroes**) of a function are the x values for which the function equals zero. Graphically, the roots are the values where the graph intersects the x-axis ($y = 0$). To solve for the roots of a function, set the function equal to 0 and solve for x.

A question on the Math Level 1 that tests your knowledge of roots and graphs will give you a function such as $f(x) = x^2 + x - 12$ along with five graphs and ask you to determine which graph shows that function. To approach a question like this, you should start by identifying the general shape of the graph of the function. For $f(x) = x^2 + x - 12$, you should recognize that the graph of the function in the paragraph above is a parabola and that it opens upward because it has a positive leading coefficient.

This basic analysis should immediately eliminate several possibilities, but it might still leave two or three choices. Solving for the roots of the function will usually get the right answer. To solve for the roots, factor the function:

$$f(x) = x^2 + x - 12$$
$$= (x + 4)(x - 3)$$

The roots are –4 and 3, since those are the values at which the function equals 0. Given this additional information, you can choose the answer choice with the upward-opening parabola that intersects the x-axis at –4 and 3.

Function Symmetry

Another type of question you might find on the Math Level 1 involves identifying a function's symmetry. There are only two significant types of symmetry that come up on the Math Level 1: the symmetry of even functions and of odd functions.

Even Functions

An even function is a function for which $f(x) = f(-x)$. Even functions are symmetrical with respect to the y-axis. This means that a line segment connecting $f(x)$ and $f(-x)$ is a horizontal line. Some examples of even functions are $f(x) = \cos x$, $f(x) = x^2$, and $f(x) = |x|$. Here is a figure with an even function:

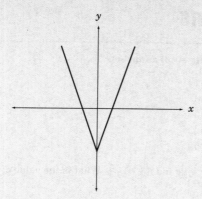

Odd Functions

An odd function is a function for which $f(x) = -f(-x)$. Odd functions are symmetrical with respect to the origin. This means that a line segment connecting $f(x)$ and $f(-x)$ contains the origin. Some examples of odd functions are $f(x) = \sin x$, and $f(x) = x$.

Here is a figure with an odd function:

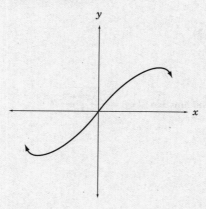

Symmetry Across the *x*-axis

No function can have symmetry across the *x*-axis, but the Math Level 1 will occasionally include a graph that is symmetrical across the *x*-axis to fool you. A quick check with the vertical line test would prove that the equations that produce such lines are not functions:

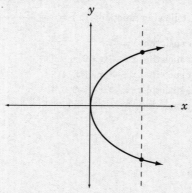

Review Questions

1. Which of the following sets is *not* a function?

   (A) $\{(0, 1,), (0, 2,), (0, 3)\}$
   (B) $\{(1, 0), (2, 0), (3, 0)\}$
   (C) $\{(1, 1), (2, 2), (3, 3)\}$
   (D) $\{(2, 3), (3, 1), (4, 0)\}$
   (E) $\{(-1, 5), (0, 4), (1, 5)\}$

2. Suppose $f(s, t) = 4s^2 - 4st + t^2$, and $f(3, t_0) = 0$. What is the value of t_0?

   (A) -6
   (B) 0
   (C) 3
   (D) 6
   (E) 12

3. Suppose $f(x) = 5x$. For which of the following functions $g(x)$ is $f/g(x)$ undefined at $x = \{1, 3\}$?

   (A) $g(x) = x^2 - 3x - 1$
   (B) $g(x) = (x + 3)(x + 1)$
   (C) $g(x) = x^2 - 4x + 3$
   (D) $g(x) = 3x + 1x$
   (E) $g(x) = 3x^3 + x^2$

4. What is the inverse of the function $f(x) = \dfrac{\sqrt{3x^2 + 4}}{2}$?

   (A) $\sqrt{\dfrac{x^2 - 4}{2}}$

   (B) $\dfrac{2}{(\sqrt{3x^2 + 4})}$

   (C) $(\dfrac{3x^2}{2} + 4)^2$

   (D) $\dfrac{4x^2}{3} - 4$

   (E) $\sqrt{\dfrac{4x^2 - 4}{3}}$

5. What is the domain of the following function: $f(x) = \dfrac{\sqrt{x + 3}}{x^3 - 2x^2 - 8x}$

   (A)   All real numbers x such that $x \geq -3$
   (B)   All real numbers x such that $x \geq -3, x \neq 0$
   (C)   All real numbers x such that $x \geq -3, x \neq \{-2, 4\}$
   (D)   All real numbers x such that $x \geq -3, x \neq \{-2, 0, 4\}$
   (E)   All real numbers x such that $-3 \leq x \leq 4, x \neq \{-2, 0\}$

6.   Suppose $3 < \dfrac{x^2 + 5}{2} < 7$. What is one possible value of $|x|$?

    (A)   −2

    (B)   0

    (C)   1

    (D)   2

    (E)   3

7.   Which of the following graphs is a function?

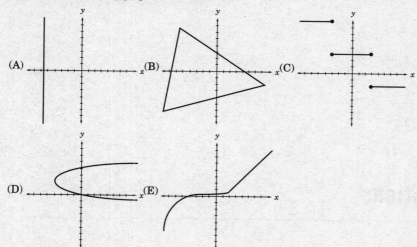

8.   What is the domain and range of the function pictured below?

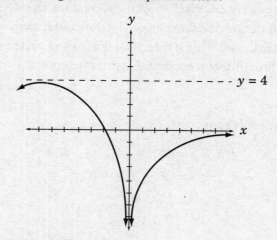

    (A)   Range: real numbers; domain: $x \le 4$

    (B)   Range: $y \le 4$; domain: $x \le 4$

    (C)   Range: $y \ne 0$; domain: real numbers

    (D)   Range: $y \le 4$; domain: $x > 0$

    (E)   Range: $y \le 4$; domain: real numbers such that $x \ne 0$

Functions

9. The graph of the function $f(x) = x^2(x - 4)(x + 3)^2(x + 7)$ has how many x-intercepts?

    (A) 1
    (B) 3
    (C) 4
    (D) 5
    (E) 6

10. If $u = (2, y)$ and $v = (x, -4)$, for what (x, y) does $2u + 3v = (10, -12)$?

    (A) $(-2, 4)$

    (B) $(6, 0)$

    (C) $(6, 12)$

    (D) $(2, 0)$

    (E) $(4, \frac{4}{3})$

Explanations

1. **A**

A function is an association between two sets such that each member of the first set, the domain, is paired with exactly one member of the second set, the range. In order for one of the sets above to be a function, the same input (x-coordinate) cannot be assigned to more than one output (y-coordinate). This is true of all the choices except the first, in which the input 0 is assigned to three different outputs. **A** is not a function.

2. **D**

Plug in 3 for s, and then solve for t_0:

$$f(3, t_0) = 4(3)^2 - 4(3)t_0 + (t_0)^2$$
$$= 36 - 12t_0 + (t_0)^2$$
$$= (t_0 - 6)^2$$
$$= 0$$

Since it is given that $f(3, t_0) = 0$, we can set $(t_0 - 6)^2 = 0$. Thus, $t_0 = 6$.

3. **C**

The function $f/g(x)$ can be simplified to $f(x)/g(x)$. Since $g(x)$ is the denominator, the function $f/g(x)$ is undefined for values at which $g(x) = 0$. From the given information, we know these values are 3 and 1. To find which function could be $g(x)$, simply test each answer choice to see if plugging 3 and 1 into the function produces zero.

4. E

To find the inverse of a function, set the function equal to y, interchange the places of y and x, and solve for y. The result is the inverse of your function:

$$x = \frac{\sqrt{3y^2 + 4}}{2}$$
$$2x = \sqrt{3y^2 + 4}$$
$$4x^2 = 3y^2 + 4$$
$$4x^2 - 4 = 3y^2$$
$$\frac{4x^2 - 4}{3} = y^2$$
$$y = \sqrt{\frac{4x^2 - 4}{3}}$$

5. D

Assume the domain of the function is all real numbers. To find the points at which the function is undefined, restrict it such that the quantity under the square root (in the numerator) is greater than or equal to zero and that the denominator is not equal to zero. The quantity under the square root, $x + 3$, is greater than or equal to zero if $x \geq -3$. The denominator can be simplified to $x^3 - 2x^2 - 8x = x(x^2 - 2x - 8) = x(x + 2)(x - 4)$. Thus, the values of x that make the denominator equal to zero are $x = \{-2, 0, 4\}$. This means that the domain of the function is the real numbers x such that $x \geq -3$, $x \neq \{-2, 0, 4\}$.

6. D

Since we're given the range for $\frac{x^2+5}{2}$, we can use algebra to find the range of $|x|$:

$$3 < \tfrac{x^2+5}{2} < 7$$
$$6 < x^2 + 5 < 14$$
$$1 < x^2 < 9$$

At this point, you can write two equations: $-3 < x < -1$ and $1 < x < 3$. From these equations, you know $1 < |x| < 3$. Thus, 2 is the only possible correct answer choice.

7. E

Use the vertical line test: the only graph that a vertical line will not cross twice is the last answer choice, **E**.

8. E

The range is the set of all y-values the graph touches, and the domain is the set of all x-values for which the graph is defined. According to these definitions, you can simply look at the graph and see that the range is all real numbers less than or equal to 4, $y \le 4$, and that the domain is the set of real numbers not equal to zero, because at $x = 0$, there is a vertical asymptote. Therefore, the last answer choice is correct.

9. **C**

The number of x-intercepts equals the number of roots. Calculate the roots of $f(x)$ by setting the function equal to 0. When $f(x) = 0$, x has four possible values: 0, 4, –3 and –7. These values are the roots of $f(x)$, so $f(x)$ has 4 roots, or 4 x-intercepts.

You can use a graphing calculator to check this answer. Graph $f(x)$ and see how many times $f(x)$ intersects the x-axis.

10. **D**

$2u + 3v = 2(2, y) + 3(x, -4) = (4, 2y) + (3x, -12) = (4 + 3x, 2y - 12)$. Set this ordered pair equal to $(10, -12)$, and simple algebra shows $x = 2$ and $y = 0$.

Statistics

STATISTICS QUESTIONS ON THE MATH Level 1 test your ability to manipulate and understand data. Only a few questions on the Math Level 1 will be devoted to statistics, and these questions don't cover many topics. In this chapter, we touch on the few major concepts you'll need to know.

Statistical Analysis

On the Math Level 1, you will occasionally be presented with a data set—a collection of measurements or quantities. For example, the set of test scores for the 20 students in Ms. McCarthy's math class is a data set:

71, 83, 57, 66, 95, 96, 68, 71, 84, 85, 87, 90, 88, 90, 84, 90, 90, 93, 97, 99

The Math Level 1 will test your ability to use the basic tools of statistics. From a given data set, you should be able to derive the following four values:

1. Arithmetic Mean

2. Median

3. Mode

4. Range

Arithmetic Mean

The **arithmetic mean** is the value of the sum of the elements contained in a data set divided by the number of elements in the set.

$$\text{Arithmetic Mean} = \frac{\text{the sum of the elements of a set}}{\text{the number of elements in the set}}$$

On the Math Level 1 and in many high school math classes, the arithmetic mean is often called an "average" or "mean."

Let's take another look at the test scores of the 20 students in Ms. McCarthy's math class. We've sorted the scores in order from lowest to highest:

57, 66, 68, 71, 71, 83, 84, 84, 85, 87, 88, 90, 90, 90, 90, 93, 95, 96, 97, 99

To find the arithmetic mean of this data set, we must sum the scores and then divide by 20—the number of scores in the set. The mean of the math test scores in Ms. McCarthy's class is:

$$\text{mean} = \frac{57 + 66 + 68 + \cdots + 96 + 97 + 99}{20}$$
$$\text{mean} = \frac{1600}{20}$$
$$\text{mean} = 80$$

While some Math Level 1 questions might cover arithmetic mean in the straightforward manner shown in this example, it is more likely the test will cover mean in a more complicated way.

The Math Level 1 might give you $n - 1$ numbers of an n-number set and the average of that set, and ask you to find the last number:

If the average of four numbers is 22, and three of the numbers are 7, 11, and 18, then what is the fourth number?

Remember that the mean of a set of numbers is intimately related to the number of terms in the set and the sum of those terms. In the question above, you know that the average of the 4 numbers is 22. This means that the four numbers, when added together, must equal 4 × 22, or 88. Based on the sum of the three terms you are given, you can easily determine the fourth number by subtraction:

7 + 11 + 18 + unknown number = 88

Solving for the unknown number is easy: all you need to do is subtract 7, 11, and 18 from 88 to get 52, which is the answer.

The test might also present you with what we call an "adjusted mean" question. For example:

> The mean age of the 14 members of a ballroom dance class is 34. When a new student enrolled, the mean age increased to 35. How old is the new student?

Here you know the original number of students in the class and the original mean of the students' ages, and you are asked to determine the mean after an additional term is introduced. To figure out the age of the new student, you simply need to find the sum of the ages in the adjusted class (with one extra student) and subtract from that the sum of the ages of the original class. To calculate the sum of the ages of the adjusted class:

$$\text{New Mean} = \frac{\text{The new sum of the students' ages}}{\text{The new class enrollment}}$$

$$35 = \frac{\text{The new sum of the students' ages}}{\text{The old class enrollment} + 1 \text{ new student}}$$

$$\text{The new sum of the students' ages} = 15 \times 25$$

$$\text{The new sum of the students' ages} = 525$$

By the same calculations, the sum of the students' ages in the original class is $14 \times 34 = 476$. So the new student added an age of $525 - 476 = 49$ years.

Median

The Math Level 1 might also ask you about the median of a set of numbers. The **median** is the number whose value is in the middle of the numbers in a particular set. Take the set: 6, 19, 3, 11, 7. Arranging the numbers in order of value results in the list below:

$$3, 6, 7, 11, 19$$

Once the numbers are listed in this ordered way, it becomes clear that the middle number in this group is 7, making 7 the median.

The set 3, 6, 7, 11, 19 contains an odd number of items; in a set with an even number of items, it's impossible to isolate a single number as the median, so calculating the median requires an extra step. Let's add one number to the set from the previous example:

$$3, 6, 7, 11, 15, 19$$

When the set contains an even number of elements, the median is found by taking the mean of the two middle numbers. The two middle numbers in this set are 7 and 11, so the median of the set is $^{7+11}/_2 = 9$.

Mode

The **mode** is the element of a set that appears most frequently. In the set 10, 11, 13, 11, 20, the mode is 11 since it appears twice and each of the other numbers appears only once. In a set in which more than one number appears with the same highest frequency, there is more than one mode: the set 2, 2, 3, 4, 4 has modes of 2 and 4. In a set in which each of the elements appears an equal number of times, there is no mode.

Mode questions are easy; unfortunately they don't often appear on the Math Level 1.

Range

The **range** measures the spread of a data set, or the difference between the smallest element and the largest. For the set of test scores in Ms. McCarthy's class:

$$57, 66, 68, 71, 71, 83, 84, 84, 85, 87, 88, 90, 90, 90, 90, 93, 95, 96, 97, 99$$

The range is $99 - 57 = 42$.

Probability

Probability is another statistics-related topic you might see on the Math Level 1. You should be familiar with the probability formula and with applying the probability formula to calculate the likely outcome of independent events.

The Probability Formula

The **probability** of an event is a number between 0 and 1 that represents the likelihood of that event occurring. You can calculate the probability of an event by dividing the number of desired outcomes by the total number of possible outcomes.

$$\text{Probability} = \frac{\text{number of times a certain event might occur}}{\text{total number of events that might occur}}$$

For example, in a deck of 52 cards, the probability of pulling one of the 13 hearts from the deck is much higher than the likelihood of pulling out the ace of spades. To calculate an exact value for the probability of drawing a heart from the deck, divide the number of hearts you could possibly draw by the total number of cards in the deck.

$$P = \frac{\text{number of hearts in the deck}}{\text{total number of cards in the deck}}$$
$$P = \frac{13}{52}$$
$$P = \frac{1}{4}$$

In contrast, the possibility of drawing the single ace of spades from the deck is:

$$P = \frac{\text{number of aces of spades in the deck}}{\text{total number of cards in the deck}}$$
$$P = \frac{1}{52}$$

After looking at these examples, you should be able to understand the general formula for calculating probability. Let's look at a more complicated example:

Joe has 3 green marbles, 2 red marbles, and 5 blue marbles. If all the marbles are dropped into a dark bag, what is the probability that Joe will pick out a green marble?

There are 3 ways for Joe to pick a green marble (since there are 3 different green marbles), but there are 10 total possible outcomes (one for each marble in the bag). Therefore, you can simply calculate the probability of picking a green marble:

$$\text{Probability} = \frac{\text{particular outcome}}{\text{total outcomes}}$$
$$= \frac{\text{green marbles}}{\text{total marbles}}$$
$$= \frac{3}{10}$$

When calculating probabilities, always be careful to count all of the possible favorable outcomes among the total possible outcomes.

The Range of Probability

The probability, P, of any event occurring will always be $0 \leq P \leq 1$. A probability of 0 for an event means that the event will *never* happen. A probability of 1 means the event will always occur. For example, drawing a green card from a standard deck of cards has a probability of 0; getting a number less than seven on a single roll of one die has a probability of 1.

If you are ever asked to calculate probability on the Math Level 1, you can automatically eliminate any answer choices that are less than 0 or greater than 1.

The Probability That an Event Will *Not* Occur

Some Math Level 1 questions ask you to determine the probability that an event will not occur. In that case, just figure out the probability of the event occurring, and subtract that number from 1.

Probability an event will not occur = 1 − probability of the event occurring

Probability and Multiple Events

The most difficult Math Level 1 probability questions deal with the probability of multiple events occurring. Such questions will always deal with independent events — events whose probability is not dependent on the outcome of any other event. For these questions, the probability of both events occurring is the product of the outcomes of each event: $P(A) \times P(B)$, where $P(A)$ is the probability of the first event and $P(B)$ is the probability of the second event.

For example, the probability of drawing a spade from a full deck of cards *and* rolling a one with a six-sided die is the product of the probability of each event.

$$P = \frac{13}{52} \times \frac{1}{6}$$
$$= \frac{1}{4} \times \frac{1}{6}$$
$$= \frac{1}{24}$$

The same principle can be applied to finding the probability of a series of events. Take a look at the following problem:

> A teacher keeps a jar full of different flavored jelly beans on her desk and hands them out randomly to her class. But one particularly picky student likes only the licorice-flavored ones. If the jar has 50 beans in all — 15 licorice, 10 cherry, 20 watermelon, and 5 blueberry — what is the probability that the first three jelly beans given out are licorice-flavored?

In order to find the probability of three consecutive events, you should first find the probability of each event separately. The first jellybean has a $^{15}/_{50}$ chance of being licorice-flavored. The second jellybean, however, is a different story. There are now only 49 jelly beans left in the jar, so the probability of getting another licorice-flavored one is $^{14}/_{49}$. The probability of getting a third licorice-flavored jellybean is $^{13}/_{48}$. The odds of getting three licorice jelly beans in a row is:

$$P = \frac{15}{50} \times \frac{14}{49} \times \frac{13}{48}$$
$$= \frac{3}{10} \times \frac{2}{7} \times \frac{13}{48}$$
$$= \frac{1}{10} \times \frac{1}{7} \times \frac{13}{8}$$
$$= \frac{13}{560}$$

Permutations and Combinations

Permutations and combinations are counting tools. They have vast applications in probability, especially in determining the number of successful outcomes and the number of total outcomes in a given scenario. Questions about permutations and combinations on the Math Level 1 will not be complex, nor will they require advanced math. But you will need to understand how they work and how to work with them. Important to both of these undertakings is a familiarity with factorials.

Factorials

The **factorial** of a number, $n!$, is the product of the natural numbers up to and including n:

$$n! = n \times (n-1) \times (n-2) \times \cdots \times 3 \times 2 \times 1$$

If you are ever asked to find the number of ways that the n elements of a group can be ordered, you simply need to calculate $n!$. For example, if you are asked how many different ways 6 people can sit at a table with six chairs, you could either list all of the possible seating arrangements (which would take a while) or just answer $6! = 6 \times 5 \times 4 \times 3 \times 2 \times 1 = 720$.

Permutations

A **permutation** is an ordering of elements. For example, say you're running for student council. There are six different offices to be filled—president, vice president, secretary, treasurer, spirit coordinator, and parliamentarian—and there are six candidates running. Assuming the candidates don't care which office they're elected to, how many different ways can the student council be composed?

The answer is $6!$ because there are 6 students running for office, and thus, 6 elements in the set.

Say that due to budgetary costs, there are now only the three offices of president, vice president, and treasurer to be filled. The same 6 candidates are still running. To handle this situation, we will now have to change our method of calculating the number of permutations.

In general, the permutation, nP_r, is the number of subgroups of size r that can be taken from a set with n elements:

$$nP_r = \frac{n!}{(n-r)!}$$

For our example, we need to find $_6P_3$:

$$_6P_3 = \frac{6!}{6-3!} = \frac{6!}{3!} = \frac{6 \times 5 \times 4 \times 3 \times 2 \times 1}{3 \times 2 \times 1} = \frac{720}{6} = 120$$

Consider the following problem:

> At a dog show, three awards are given: best in show, first runner-up, and second runner-up. A group of 10 dogs are competing in the competition. In how many different ways can the prizes be awarded?

This problem is a permutation since the question asks us to order the top three finishers among 10 contestants in a dog show. There is more than one way that the same three dogs could get first place, second place, and third place, and each arrangement is a different outcome. So, the answer is $_{10}P_3 = {}^{10!}/_{(10-3)!} = {}^{10!}/_{7!} = 720$.

Permutations and Calculators

Graphing calculators and most scientific calculators have a permutation function, labeled nP_r. In most cases, you must enter n, then press the button for permutation, and then enter r. This will calculate a permutation for you, but if n is a large number, the calculator often cannot calculate $n!$. If this happens to you, don't give up! In cases like this, your knowledge of the permutation function will save you. Since you know that $_{100}P_3$ is ${}^{100!}/_{(100-3)!}$ you can simplify it to ${}^{100!}/_{97!}$, or $100 \times 99 \times 98 = 970{,}200$.

Combinations

A **combination** is an unordered grouping of a set. An example of a scenario in which order doesn't matter is a hand of cards: a king, an ace, and a five is the same as an ace, a five, and a king.

Combinations are represented as $_nC_r$, or $\binom{n}{r}$, where unordered subgroups of size r are selected from a set of size n. Because the order of the elements in a given subgroup doesn't matter, this means that $\binom{n}{r}$ will be less than $_nP_r$. Any one combination can be turned into more than one permutation. $_nC_r$ is calculated as follows:

$$\binom{n}{r} = \frac{nP_r}{r!} = \frac{n!}{(n-r)!r!}$$

Here's an example:

> Suppose that a committee of 10 people must elect three leaders, whose duties are all the same. In how many ways can this be done?

In this example, the order in which the leaders are assigned to positions doesn't matter—the leaders aren't distinguished from one another in any way, unlike in the student council example. This distinction means that the question can be answered with a combination rather than a permutation. We are looking for how many different groups of three can be taken from a group of 10:

$$\text{Sum} = b_1 \frac{1 - r^n}{1 - r}$$

There are only 120 different ways to elect three leaders, as opposed to 720 ways when their roles were differentiated.

Combinations and Calculators

There should be a combination function on your graphing or scientific calculator labeled $_nC_r$. Use it the same way you use the permutation key.

Group Questions

Occasionally, the Math Level 1 will pose questions about groups with overlapping members. For example:

> In a particular school, the school band has 42 members and the school orchestra has 35 members. Seven students play in both the band and the orchestra, and 231 students play in neither the band nor the orchestra. How many students are in this particular school?

To answer this question, carefully count the students. $231 + 42 + 35 = 308$ is a tempting answer, but in this solution, we are counting the students who play in both the band and orchestra twice. We must subtract 7 from this total to get the right answer: $308 - 7 = 301$.

This question illustrates the formula for answering such questions. If two subgroups of a population share members, the equation that governs the total number of people in the population is:

Total Population = Group A Population + Group B Population +
Neither Group A nor B population – Group A and B population

The last term of this formula subtracts the elements that were double-counted earlier.
Try another example:

> A room contains 80 people. Thirty have curly hair, 24 have blond hair, and 40 have hair that is neither curly nor blond. How many people in the room have curly, blond hair?

Use the formula: $80 = 30 + 24 + 40 - x$. Thus, $x = 14$ (14 people in the room have curly and blond hair). This formula will work for all group problems, as long as there are only two groups involved.

Statistics

Sets

Already in this chapter we've covered how to analyze the data in a set and how to deal with two sets that have overlapping members. For the Math Level 1, there are two more concepts concerning sets that you need to understand: union and intersection.

Union

The **union** of two or more sets is the set that contains all of the elements of the two original sets. The union of two sets A and B is symbolized this way: $A \cup B$.

For example, the union of the sets $A = \{1, 2, 3, 4, 5\}$ and $B = \{4, 5, 6, 7, 8\}$ is

$$A \cup B = \{1, 2, 3, 4, 5, 6, 7, 8\}$$

This set contains every element that is in either set. If x is an element of $A \cup B$, then it must be an element of A, or of B, or of both.

Intersection

The **intersection** of two sets is the set of their overlapping elements. The intersection of the two sets A and B is symbolized as $A \cap B$.

The intersection of the sets $A = \{1, 2, 3, 4, 5\}$ and $B = \{4, 5, 6, 7, 8\}$, for example, is $A \cap B = \{4, 5\}$. If x is an element of $A \cap B$, then x must be an element of both A *and* B.

Key Formulas

Arithmetic Mean

$$\text{Mean} = \frac{\text{The sum of the elements of a set}}{\text{The number of elements in the set}}$$

Permutation

$_nP_r = \frac{n!}{(n-r)!}$, where r is the size of the subgroup taken from a set with n elements.

Combination

$\binom{n}{r} = \frac{n!}{(n-r)!r!}$, or $^nP_r/r!$, where r is the size of the subgroup taken from a set with n elements.

Probability

$$\text{Probability} = \frac{\text{number of times a certain event might occur}}{\text{total number of events that might occur}}$$

Total Elements of Overlapping Sets

If two subsets of a set share elements, the equation that governs the total number of elements in the set is:

Total Elements = Group A Elements + Group B Elements + Neither Group A nor Group B Elements − Group A and Group B Elements

Review Questions

1. On three tests, each graded on a scale of 0 to 100, Jim had an average score of 78. If Jim pulls his average up to 84 after taking two additional tests, what is the lowest possible score he could have received on one of the last two tests?

    (A)   78
    (B)   86
    (C)   88
    (D)   93
    (E)   It is impossible for him to have increased his average score by this amount after taking two additional tests.

2. Suppose the probability of the Red Sox winning the World Series is .1 and the probability of pigs flying is .01. (Assume these events are independent.) What is the probability of pigs flying and the Red Sox *not* winning the World Series?

    (A)   .001
    (B)   .009
    (C)   .01
    (D)   .09
    (E)   .099

3. To build a sandwich at a particular restaurant, customers may choose 1 of 3 types of bread, 1 of 4 different types of meat, and 2 of 5 different types of condiments. How many different sandwiches can be created at this restaurant? (Assume that the two accessories chosen must be different.)

    (A)   12
    (B)   30
    (C)   60
    (D)   120
    (E)   240

4. A sock drawer contains 6 socks, 3 of which are definitely blue and the other 3 of which are either blue or black (exactly how many of each is unknown). If the probability of picking two blue socks in a given random selection of two socks is $^2/_3$, how many black socks must the drawer contain?

 (A) 0
 (B) 1
 (C) 2
 (D) 3
 (E) Impossible to tell

5. A set contains eight distinct elements. Each element is an integer not equal to zero. If for every element x that is in this set, $-x$ is also in this set, what is the mean of the set?

 (A) 0

 (B) $\dfrac{x}{8}$

 (C) x

 (D) $\dfrac{1}{8}$

 (E) 1

6. At a local animal shelter, there are 23 animals being cared for. If 15 of the animals are brown, 5 are brown cats, and 7 of the animals are neither brown nor cats, how many cats must be in the animal shelter?

 (A) 1
 (B) 4
 (C) 5
 (D) 6
 (E) 8

Explanations

1. **B**

The average of a set of numbers is the sum of its elements divided by the number of elements in the set. If Jim averaged 78 for the first three tests of the semester, the sum of his first three test scores must have been 78 × 3 = 234. If his average after a total of five tests is 84, the sum of his scores on those five tests must be 84 × 5 = 420. The sum of Jim's last two test scores must be 420 – 234 = 186. This means that the least Jim could have scored on one of the last two tests is 86 (because the maximum possible score is 100).

2.   **B**

These events are independent, so the probability of them both occurring is the product of their respective probabilities. The probability of pigs flying is .01, and the probability of the Red Sox *not* winning the World Series is

$$P = 1 - \text{probability that Red Sox win the World Series}$$
$$= 1 - .1$$
$$= .9$$

So the probability of both events occurring is .01 × .9 = .009.

3.   **D**

This is a combination problem because the order in which you put the sandwich together doesn't matter. Recall that the equation that is used to calculate the combinations of a subgroup of size r from a group of n elements is:

$$_nC_r = \binom{n}{r}$$
$$= \frac{n!}{(n-r)!r!}$$

To figure out how many different sandwiches can be made, you have to run the calculations for each aspect of the sandwich—bread, meat, and condiment—and then multiply the answers together. Since you can choose one of three types of bread, the combination is:

$$_3C_1 = \frac{3!}{(3-1)!1!}$$
$$= \frac{3 \times 2 \times 1}{2 \times 1} \times 1$$
$$= 3$$

The meat can be chosen in $_4C_1 = 4$ different ways, and the accessories can be chosen in $_5C_2 = 10$ different ways. The total number of different sandwiches that can be created given the conditions is 3 × 4 × 10 = 120.

4.   **B**

From the information in the question, you know that there are either 3, 4, 5, or 6 blue socks in the drawer. It is easy to find the probability of randomly selecting two blue socks in each of these situations, and from this information you can use trial and error to find the answer.

1. If there are 3 blue socks in the drawer, then the probability of picking two blue socks is $\frac{3}{6} \times \frac{2}{5} = \frac{6}{30} = \frac{1}{5}$.

2. If there are 4 blue socks in the drawer, then the probability of picking two blue socks is $\frac{4}{6} \times \frac{3}{5} = \frac{12}{30} = \frac{2}{5}$.

3. If there are 5 blue socks in the drawer, then the probability of picking two blue socks is $\frac{5}{6} \times \frac{4}{5} = \frac{20}{30} = \frac{2}{3}$. This meets the conditions needed, so the drawer contains 1 black sock.

5. A

The set must contain four integers and their opposites. Thus, the sum of any integer and its opposite is zero. Since the mean is found by adding together all the elements of a set and dividing that answer by the number of elements, the mean for this set is: $\frac{0}{8} = 0$.

6. D

Using the formula for group questions:

cats + brown animals + animals neither brown nor cats − brown cats = total animals

cats + 15 + 7 − 5 = 23

cats = 6

Miscellaneous Math

Chapter Contents

W E'VE REVIEWED THE SEVEN MAJOR topics tested by the Math Level 1: algebra, plane geometry, solid geometry, coordinate geometry, trigonometry, functions, and statistics. But not all of the fifty questions on the test fall into these seven categories. This chapter rounds up those idiosyncratic, miscellaneous, odds-and-ends topics.

Logic

Logic questions don't look like math questions at all; they do not contain numbers, formulas, or variables. Instead, logic questions contain a verbal statement and a question that asks you to interpret the validity of the statement or understand how the given statement affects another statement. For example:

The statement "If Jill misses the bus, she will be late" is true. Which other statement must be true?

(A)   If Jill does not miss the bus, she will not be late.
(B)   If Jill is not late, she missed the bus.
(C)   If a student misses the bus, he or she will be late.
(D)   Jill is late because she missed the bus.
(E)   If Jill is not late, she did not miss the bus.

Even though they're stated in words, logic questions require mathematical thinking, and there are mathematical methods for finding the right answer.

A logic statement is written in the form "If p, then q," where p and q are events. "If p, then q" can also be written as $p \rightarrow q$, and it states that if event p occurs, then event q will also occur.

Every "If p, then q" statement has an equivalent statement; this second statement is known as the **contrapositive**, which is always true. The contrapositive of "If p, then q" is "If not q, then not p." In symbols, the contrapositive of $p \rightarrow q$ is $\sim q \rightarrow \sim p$ (the symbol $\sim$ means "not"). To formulate the contrapositive of any logic statement, you must change the original statement in two ways.

1. Switch the order of the two parts of the statement. For example, "If p then q" becomes "If q, then p."

2. Negate each part of the statement. "If q, then p" becomes "If not q, then not p."

When you are faced with a logic problem on the Math Level 1, remember that if a given statement is true, then that statement's contrapositive is also true. Likewise, if a given statement is false, then that statement's contrapositive is also false.

Returning to the example problem, we are told that the given statement is true, so we should look for the contrapositive among the answer choices. **E** is the contrapositive of the original statement, so we know that it is true. Here's some more practice:

What is the contrapositive of "Every book on the shelf is old"?

You need to first rewrite this statement so that it is in the "If p, then q" form. So the given statement becomes "If a book is on the shelf, then it is old." The contrapositive of the statement is now easy to see: "If a book is not old, then it is not on the shelf."

Sequences

You might see one or two sequence questions on the Math Level 1. The two types of sequences tested are arithmetic and geometric sequences.

Arithmetic Sequences

An arithmetic sequence is an ordered list of terms in which the difference between consecutive terms is constant. In other words, the same value or variable is added to each term in order to create the next term: if you subtract any two consecutive terms of the sequence, you will get the same difference. An example is $\{a_n\} = 1, 4, 7, 10, 13, ...$, where 3 is the constant increment between values.

The notation of an arithmetic sequence is

$$a_n = a_1 + (n-1)d$$

where a_n is the nth term of the sequence and d is the difference between consecutive terms. For the Math Level 1, you must first be able to determine that a given sequence is an arithmetic sequence. To figure this out, take two sets of consecutive terms and subtract the smaller term from the larger. If the difference between the terms in the two sets is equal, you've got an arithmetic sequence. To determine if the sequence $\{a_n\} = 1$, 4, 7, 10, 13, ... is arithmetic, take two sets of consecutive terms $\{1, 4\}$ and $\{10, 13\}$, and subtract the first from the second:

$$4 - 1 = 3$$
$$13 - 10 = 3$$

Since the difference is equal, you know this sequence is arithmetic. You should be able to do three things with an arithmetic sequence:

1. Find d

2. Find the nth term

3. Calculate the sum of the first n terms

Finding d

To find the difference, d, between the terms of an arithmetic sequence, just subtract one term from the next term. For the arithmetic sequence $a_n = 1, 4, 7, 10, 13, \ldots$, $d = 4 - 1 = 3$. Here's a slightly more complicated form of this question:

If $a_4 = 4$ and $a_7 = 10$, find d.

This question gives you the fourth and seventh terms of a sequence:

$$a_n = a_1, a_2, a_3, 4, a_5, a_6, 10, \ldots$$

Since in arithmetic sequences d is constant between every term, you know that $d + 4 = a_5$, $a_5 + d = a_6$, and $a_6 + d = 10$. In other words, the difference between the seventh term, 10, and the fourth term, 4, is $3d$. Stated as an equation:

$$10 = 4 + 3d$$

Solving this equation is a process of simple algebra.

$$3d = 6$$
$$d = 2$$

Miscellaneous Math

Finding the nth Term

To find the nth term in an arithmetic sequence, use the following formula:

$$a_n = a_1 + (n-1)d$$

In the example above, to find the 55th term we would have to find the value of a_1 first. Plug the values of $a_4 = 4$, $n = 4$ and $d = 2$ into the formula $a_n = a_1 + (n-1)d$ to find that a_1 equals -2. Now find the 55th term, $a_{55} = -2 + (55-1)2 = -2 + (54)2 = -2 + 108 = 106$.

Calculating the Sum of the First n Terms

In order to find the sum of the first n terms, simply find the value of the average term and then multiply that average by the number of terms you are summing.

$$\text{Sum of the first } n \text{ terms} = n\frac{a_1 + a_n}{2}$$

As you can see, this is simply n times the average of the first n terms. Using the same example, the sum of the first 55 terms would be:

$$\text{Sum} = 55\frac{-2 + 106}{2} = 52(55) = 2860$$

Geometric Sequences

A geometric sequence is a sequence in which the ratio of any term and the next term is constant. Whereas in an arithmetic sequence the *difference* between consecutive terms is always constant, in a geometric sequence the *quotient* of consecutive terms is always constant. The constant factor by which the terms of a geometric function differ is called the common ratio of the geometric sequence. The common ratio is usually represented by the variable r. Here is an example of a geometric sequence in which $r = 3$.

$$b_x = \frac{1}{3}, 1, 3, 9, 27, 81, \ldots$$

The general form of a geometric sequence is:

$$b_x = b_1, b_1 r, b_1 r^2, b_1 r^3, \ldots$$

You should be able to identify a geometric sequence from its terms, and you should be able to perform three tasks on geometric sequences:

1. Find r

2. Find the nth term

3. Calculate the sum of the first n terms

Finding r

To find the common ratio of a geometric sequence, all you have to do is divide one term by the preceding term.

For example, the value of r for the sequence 3, 6, 12, 24, ... is $\frac{6}{3} = 2$.

Finding the nth Term

To find the nth term of a geometric sequence, use the following formula:

$$b_n = b_1 r^{n-1}$$

For example, the 11th term of the sequence above is:

$$b_{11} = 3(2^{10}) = 3072$$

Calculating the Sum of the First n Terms

To find the sum of the first n terms of a geometric sequence, use the following formula:

$$\text{Sum} = b_1 \frac{1 - r^n}{1 - r}$$

So the sum of the first 10 terms of the same sequence is:

$$3\frac{1 - 2^{10}}{1 - 2} = 3069$$

Limits

For a function $f(x)$, the limit of the function is the value that the function approaches as x approaches a certain number. Here's an example:

What is the limit of $f(x) = (x + 2)/(x^2 - 2x - 8)$ as x approaches –2?

Normally, finding the limit should be easy. You would simply plug the value that x approaches, in this case –2, into the function and produce the limit. But the Math Level

1 typically asks only one type of question about limits—the limit of a function at a point at which the function is not defined. Try and plug –2 into the function.

$$f(x) = \frac{x+2}{x^2 - 2x - 8}$$

$$= \frac{-2+2}{(-2)^2 - 2(-2) - 8}$$

$$= \frac{0}{4+4-8}$$

$$= \frac{0}{0}$$

It seems that the function is not defined at $x = -2$, because division by zero is not allowed. This is precisely what the test *wants* you to think. But the assumption that this function is undefined at –2 is incorrect. Luckily, there is an easy way to solve for the limit.

First, you need to factor the function so that it is in its most simplified state. For our example, the denominator can be factored:

$$x^2 - 2x - 8 = (x+2)(x-4)$$

Once the denominator has been factored, it's easy to see that the function $\frac{x+2}{(x+2)(x-4)}$ simplifies to $\frac{1}{x-4}$. This simplified fraction *can* be evaluated at $x = -2$:

$$f(-2) = \frac{1}{-6}$$

$\frac{1}{-6}$ is the limit of $f(x)$ at $x = -2$.

You should choose "the limit does not exist at this point" answer only if a function is undefined at the point at which you wish to find a limit and the function cannot be factored any further.

Imaginary and Complex Numbers

Most of the Math Level 1 test deals with real numbers. But every so often, a question will appear that does not involve the set of real numbers. These questions deal with imaginary and complex numbers.

Imaginary Numbers

Imaginary numbers are used to represent the even roots of negative numbers. They use the quantity i, where $i = \sqrt{-1}$. For example:

$$\sqrt{-16} = \sqrt{16}\sqrt{-1} = 4i$$

Square roots of negative numbers are called imaginary numbers because they do not lie on the real number line.

Complex Numbers

A **complex number** is the sum of a real number and an imaginary number. A complex number is written in the form $a + bi$, where a and b are real numbers, and $i = \sqrt{-1}$.

There are two things you need to be able to do with complex numbers:

1. Know the powers of i

2. Know how to do operations, like addition, subtraction, and multiplication, on complex numbers

The Powers of i

The powers of i are easy to work with. For example:

Evaluate $i^2 \times i^9$.

The trick is to remember that the powers of i work in cycles of four:

- $i^1 = i$

- $i^2 = \sqrt{-1} \times \sqrt{-1} = (\sqrt{-1})^2 = -1$

- $i^3 = \sqrt{-1} \times \sqrt{-1} \times \sqrt{-1} = \sqrt{-1} \times (\sqrt{-1})^2 = -i$

- $i^4 = \sqrt{-1} \times \sqrt{-1} \times \sqrt{-1} \times \sqrt{-1} = (\sqrt{-1})^4 = 1$

This way, the expression $i^2 \times i^9$ becomes $(-1)(i) = -i$. If you know these cycles, you can reduce any exponent of i to a much more manageable size. The expression $i^2 \times i^9$ becomes $(-1)(i) = -i$.

Operations on Complex Numbers

Algebraic manipulation of complex numbers is exactly like dealing with real numbers. See for yourself:

Miscellaneous Math

Simplify the expression $(3x + i)(x - 2i)$.

$$(3x + i)(x - 2i) =$$
$$3x^2 - 6xi + xi - 2i^2 =$$
$$3x^2 - 5xi - 2(-1) = 3x^2 - 5xi + 2$$

Key Formulas

nth Term of an Arithmetic Sequence

$a_n = a_1 + (n - 1)d$, where a_1 is the first term in the sequence, and d is the common difference.

Sum of the First n Terms of an Arithmetic Sequence

$$\text{Sum} = n\frac{a_1 + a_n}{2}$$

nth Term of a Geometric Sequence

$b_n = b_1 r_{n-1}$, where b_1 is the first term of the sequence and r is the common ratio.

Sum of the First n Terms of a Geometric Sequence

$$\text{Sum} = b_1\frac{1 - r^n}{1 - r}$$

Review Questions

1. Suppose the statement "If it rains, it pours" is false. Which of the following statements must also be false?

    (A) If it pours, it rains.
    (B) If it doesn't rain, it doesn't pour.
    (C) If it doesn't pour, it doesn't rain.
    (D) If it doesn't rain, it pours.
    (E) If it doesn't pour, it rains.

Miscellaneous Math

2.   The first term of an arithmetic sequence is –3, and each term thereafter is 3 less than the previous term. What is the value of the 30th term of the sequence?

    (A)   –93
    (B)   –90
    (C)   –87
    (D)   3
    (E)   87

3.   The nth term of a sequence is given by the formula $a_n = 6n - 3$. What is the sum of the first 100 terms of this sequence?

    (A)   300
    (B)   29,700
    (C)   29,850
    (D)   30,000
    (E)   60,000

4.   In a geometric sequence, the nth term is given by the formula $bg_n = \frac{3}{2}(2n)$. What is the sum of the first 10 terms of this sequence?

    (A)   113.3
    (B)   170.0
    (C)   226.7
    (D)   3069
    (E)   3072

5.   What is the limit of $\frac{x+2}{x^2-4}$ as x approaches –2?

    (A) $-\frac{1}{4}$
    (B)   0
    (C) $\frac{1}{4}$
    (D)   2
    (E)   Impossible to tell

6.   What is $3(i^5 - i^{14})$?

    (A)   –3
    (B) $3i$
    (C)   3
    (D) $3i + 3$
    (E) $\sqrt{-3}$

Explanations

1.   **C**

If a statement is false, the contrapositive of the statement will also be false. To find the contrapositive, you need to take the opposite of both parts of the statement and then switch the order. The contrapositive of "If it rains, it pours," is "If it doesn't pour, it doesn't rain."

2. **B**

The formula for the nth term of an arithmetic sequence is $a_n = a_1 + (n-1)d$, where d is the difference between the terms of an arithmetic sequence.

If the first term of a sequence is -3, and $d = -3$, then $a_n = -3 - 3n + 3 = -3n$. So, the 30th term is $-3(30) = -90$.

3. **D**

This sequence is an arithmetic sequence since the difference between each term is constant. The formula for the sum of the first n terms of an arithmetic sequence is:

$$n\frac{a_1 + a_n}{2}$$

To use this formula for this question, first calculate the values of a_1 and a_{100} by plugging $n = 1$ and $n = 100$ into the given formula $a_n = 6n - 3$. So, we find that $a_1 = 6 - 3 = 3$ and $a_{100} = 600 - 3 = 597$. The sum of the first 100 terms is therefore:

$$100 \times \frac{600}{2} = 100 \times 300 = 30,000.$$

4. **D**

To answer this question quickly and efficiently, you need to know the formula for the sum of the first n terms of a geometric sequence:

$$\text{Sum of the first } n \text{ terms} = n\frac{a_1 + a_n}{2}$$

where r is the common ratio of the sequence. In this problem $b_1 = \frac{3}{2}(2^1) = 3$ and $r = 2$, so the formula yields the answer 3069.

5. **A**

This question throws a little curveball at you because function is undefined at $x = -2$, since $-2^2 - 4 = 0$. However, the denominator can be factored into $(x - 2)(x + 2)$. Then $(x + 2)$ can be canceled from the numerator and denominator, leaving $\frac{1}{x-2}$ as the function. Evaluating this function at $x = -2$, you see the limit is $-\frac{1}{4}$.

6. **D**

The powers of i repeat themselves in a cycle of four, that is $i^n = i^{n+4}$. Since $i^4 = 1$, i^5 must equal i. You can also reduce i^{14} by noticing that it equals $i^{12} \times i^2$. Since 12 is a multiple of 4, i^{12} equals 1, so

$$
\begin{aligned}
i^{14} &= 1 \times i^2 \\
&= 1 \times -1 \\
&= -1
\end{aligned}
$$

So $3(i - i^{14}) = 3(i - (-1)) = 3(i + 1) = 3i + 3$.

Practice Tests

Practice Tests Are Your Best Friends

BELIEVE IT OR NOT, the SAT Math Level 1 test has some redeeming qualities. One of them: reliability. The test doesn't change much from year to year. While individual questions will never repeat from test to test, the topics that are covered and the way in which they're covered *will* remain constant.

This constancy can be of great benefit to you as you study for the test. To show how you can use the similarity between different versions of SAT Math Level 1 to your advantage, we provide a case study.

Taking Advantage of the Test's Regularity

Imagine an eleventh grader named Sylvie Pascal sits down at her desk and takes an SAT Math Level 1 practice test. Because it makes this example much simpler, imagine she takes the entire test and gets only one question wrong.

The question Sylvie missed dealt with parabolas—she had misidentified the vertex. Sylvie realizes she doesn't have a firm understanding of how to graph parabolic equations, so she takes a few minutes to study up on coordinate geometry. She learns the basics of conic sections and what causes a parabola's vertex to shift from the origin. All this takes about ten minutes, after which Sylvie vows never again to miss a question involving parabolas.

Practice Tests

Analyzing Sylvie Pascal

Sylvie wasn't content simply to see what the correct answer was and get on with her day; she wanted to see *how* and *why* she got the question wrong and what she should have done, or needed to know, to get it right. She spent a little time studying the question, discovered her mistaken understanding of parabola graphs, and learned the subject thoroughly. If Sylvie were to take that same test again, she definitely wouldn't get that question wrong.

Skeptical readers might say, "But she'll never take that test again, and she'll never see that particular question again, so wasn't figuring out her mistake a waste of time?"

No! It's definitely *not* a waste of time. If you take the time to learn why you got a question wrong and to learn what you need to know to get it right, you'll probably remember what you learned the next time you're faced with a similar question. And chances are excellent that you will be faced with a similar question.

Sylvie and You

What if you take a practice test and get 15 questions wrong, and your errors span many of the major topics in math? Do exactly what Sylvie did. Take your test and *study it*. Identify every question you got wrong, figure out why you got it wrong, and then teach yourself what you should have done to get the question right. If you can't figure out your error, find someone who can.

A wrong answer on SAT Math Level 1 identifies a weakness in your test-taking, whether that weakness is an unfamiliarity with a particular topic or a tendency to be careless. As you study each wrong answer, you are actually learning how to answer questions that will appear in similar form on the real SAT Math Level 1. You are discovering your exact weaknesses and addressing them, and you are learning to understand not just the knowledge behind the question, but also the *way* that ETS asks questions.

True, if you got 15 questions wrong, studying your first practice test will take some time. But if you invest that time and study your practice test properly, you will be eliminating future mistakes. Each successive practice test you take should have fewer errors, meaning you'll spend less time studying those errors. More important, you'll be pinpointing what you need to study for the real SAT Math Level 1, identifying and overcoming your weaknesses, and learning to answer an increasing variety of questions on the specific topics covered by the test. Taking practice tests and studying them will allow you to teach yourself how to recognize and handle whatever SAT Math Level 1 throws at you.

Taking a Practice Test

Through the example of Sylvie Pascal, we've shown you why studying practice tests is an extremely powerful stratgey. Now we're going to backtrack and explain what you should do while you're actually taking a practice test.

Controlling Your Environment

Do everything in your power to make the practice test feel like the real SAT Math Level 1. The more your practice resembles the real thing, the more helpful it will be.

When taking a practice test, follow these rules:

Take the tests timed.

Don't give yourself any extra time. Be stricter with yourself than the meanest proctor you can think of. Also, don't give yourself time off for bathroom breaks. If you have to go to the bathroom, let the clock keep running; that's what will happen on the real SAT Math Level 1.

Take the test in a single sitting.

Training yourself to endure an hour of test-taking is part of your preparation.

Find a place to take the test that offers no distractions.

Don't take the practice test in a room with lots of people walking through it. Go to a library, your bedroom, a well-lit closet, anywhere quiet.

Now, having stated the rules of practice test-taking, we can relax a little bit: don't be so strict with yourself that studying and taking practice tests becomes unbearable. The most important thing is that you actually study. Do whatever you have to do in order to make your studying interesting and painless enough for you to actually do it.

Practice Test Strategy

You should take each practice test as if it were the real SAT Math Level 1. Don't be more daring than you would be on the actual test, guessing blindly even when you can't eliminate an answer. Don't carelessly speed through the test. Don't flip through this book while taking the practice exam just to sneak a peek. Follow the rules for guessing and for skipping questions that we outlined in the chapter on strategy. The more closely your attitude and strategies during the practice test reflect those you'll employ during the actual test, the more predictive the practice test will be of your strengths and weaknesses and the more fruitful your studying of the test will be.

Scoring Your Practice Test

After you take your practice test, you'll want to score it and see how you did. When you score your test, don't just write down how many questions you answered correctly and tally your score. Instead, keep a list of every question you got wrong and every question you skipped. This list will be your guide when you study your test.

Studying Your . . . No, Wait, Go Take a Break

Go relax for a while. You know how to do that.

Studying Your Practice Test

After grading your test, you should have a list of the questions you answered incorrectly and skipped. Studying your test involves going through this list and examining each question you answered incorrectly. When you look at each question, you shouldn't just look to see what the correct answer is, but rather why you got the question wrong and how you could have gotten the question right. Train yourself in the process of getting the question right.

Why Did You Get the Question Wrong?

There are three main reasons why you might have gotten an individual question wrong.

- **Reason 1**: You thought you knew the answer, but actually you didn't.

- **Reason 2**: You managed to eliminate some answer choices and then guessed among the remaining answers. Sadly, you guessed wrong.

- **Reason 3**: You knew the answer but made a careless mistake.

You should know which of these reasons applies to every question you got wrong.

What Could You Have Done to Get the Question Right?

The reasons you got a question wrong affect how you should think about it while studying your test.

If You Got a Question Wrong for Reason 1, Lack of Knowledge

A question answered incorrectly for Reason 1 identifies a weakness in your knowledge of the material tested on SAT Math Level 1. Discovering this wrong answer gives you an opportunity to target your weakness. When addressing that weakness, make sure that you don't just look at the facts.

For example, if you missed a question about factoring quadratic equations, don't just memorize the roots of certain equations. Learn the fundamental techniques that make different quadratics result in different roots. Remember, you won't see a question exactly like the one you got wrong. But you probably *will* see a question that covers the same topic. Learn the broader topic of which the question tests only a piece.

If You Got a Question Wrong for Reason 2, Guessing Wrong

If you guessed wrong, review your guessing strategy. Did you guess intelligently? Could you have eliminated more answers? If yes, why didn't you? By thinking in this critical way about the decisions you made while taking the practice test, you can train yourself to make quicker, more decisive, and better decisions.

If you took a guess and chose the incorrect answer, don't let that sour you on guessing. Even as you go over the question and figure out if there was any way for you to have answered the question without having to guess, remind yourself that if you eliminated at least one answer and guessed, even if you got the question wrong you followed the right strategy.

If You Got a Question Wrong for Reason 3, Carelessness

If you discover you got a question wrong because you were careless, it might be tempting to say to yourself, "Oh, I made a careless error," and assure yourself you won't do that again. That is not enough. You made that careless mistake for a reason, and you should try to figure out why. Whereas getting a question wrong because you didn't know the answer constitutes a weakness in your knowledge of the test subject, making a careless mistake represents a weakness in your *method of taking the test*.

To overcome this weakness, you need to approach it in the same critical way you would approach a lack of knowledge. Study your mistake. Reenact your thought process on the problem and see where and how your carelessness came about: were you rushing? Did you jump at the first answer that seemed right instead of reading all the answers? Know your error and look it in the eye. If you learn precisely what your mistake was, you are much less likely to make that mistake again.

If You Left the Question Blank

It is also a good idea to study the questions you left blank on the test, since those questions constitute a reservoir of lost points. A blank answer is a result of either:

1. Total inability to answer a question

2. Lack of time

In the case of the first possibility, you should see if there was some way you might have been able to eliminate an answer choice or two and put yourself in a better position to guess. In the second case, look over the question and see whether you think you could have answered it. If you could have, then you know that you are throwing away points by working too slowly. If you couldn't, study the relevant material and review your guessing strategy.

The Secret Weapon: Talking to Yourself

Yeah, it's embarrassing. Yeah, you may look silly. But talking to yourself is perhaps the best way to pound something into your brain. As you go through the steps of studying a question, talk it out. When you verbalize something to yourself, it makes it much harder to delude yourself into thinking that you're working if you're really not.

SAT Math Level 1
Practice Test I

SAT MATH LEVEL 1 PRACTICE TEST I ANSWER SHEET

1 (A)(B)(C)(D)(E)	11 (A)(B)(C)(D)(E)	21 (A)(B)(C)(D)(E)	31 (A)(B)(C)(D)(E)	41 (A)(B)(C)(D)(E)
2 (A)(B)(C)(D)(E)	12 (A)(B)(C)(D)(E)	22 (A)(B)(C)(D)(E)	32 (A)(B)(C)(D)(E)	42 (A)(B)(C)(D)(E)
3 (A)(B)(C)(D)(E)	13 (A)(B)(C)(D)(E)	23 (A)(B)(C)(D)(E)	33 (A)(B)(C)(D)(E)	43 (A)(B)(C)(D)(E)
4 (A)(B)(C)(D)(E)	14 (A)(B)(C)(D)(E)	24 (A)(B)(C)(D)(E)	34 (A)(B)(C)(D)(E)	44 (A)(B)(C)(D)(E)
5 (A)(B)(C)(D)(E)	15 (A)(B)(C)(D)(E)	25 (A)(B)(C)(D)(E)	35 (A)(B)(C)(D)(E)	45 (A)(B)(C)(D)(E)
6 (A)(B)(C)(D)(E)	16 (A)(B)(C)(D)(E)	26 (A)(B)(C)(D)(E)	36 (A)(B)(C)(D)(E)	46 (A)(B)(C)(D)(E)
7 (A)(B)(C)(D)(E)	17 (A)(B)(C)(D)(E)	27 (A)(B)(C)(D)(E)	37 (A)(B)(C)(D)(E)	47 (A)(B)(C)(D)(E)
8 (A)(B)(C)(D)(E)	18 (A)(B)(C)(D)(E)	28 (A)(B)(C)(D)(E)	38 (A)(B)(C)(D)(E)	48 (A)(B)(C)(D)(E)
9 (A)(B)(C)(D)(E)	19 (A)(B)(C)(D)(E)	29 (A)(B)(C)(D)(E)	39 (A)(B)(C)(D)(E)	49 (A)(B)(C)(D)(E)
10 (A)(B)(C)(D)(E)	20 (A)(B)(C)(D)(E)	30 (A)(B)(C)(D)(E)	40 (A)(B)(C)(D)(E)	50 (A)(B)(C)(D)(E)

MATHEMATICS LEVEL 1 TEST

For each of the following problems, decide which is the BEST of the choices given. If the exact numerical value is not one of the choices, select the choice that best approximates this value. Then fill in the corresponding oval on the answer sheet.

<u>Notes:</u> (1) A calculator will be necessary for answering some (but not all) of the questions in this test. For each question you will have to decide whether or not you should use a calcuator. The calculator you use must be at least a scientific calculator; programmable calculators and calculators that can display graphs are permitted.

(2) The only angle measure used on this test is degree measure. Make sure your calculator is in the degree mode.

(3) Figures that accompany problems in this test are intended to provide information useful in solving the problems. They are drawn as accurately as possible EXCEPT when it is stated in a specific problem that its figure is not drawn to scale. All figures lie in a plane unless otherwise indicated.

(4) Unless otherwise specified, the domain of any function f is assumed to be the set of all real numbers x for which $f(x)$ is a real number.

(5) Reference information that may be useful in answering the questions in this test can be found on the page preceding Question 1.

USE THIS SPACE FOR SCRATCHWORK.

1. If $\dfrac{x}{3x+2} = \dfrac{1}{4}$, then what is the value of x?

(A) $\dfrac{1}{4}$ (B) $\dfrac{1}{2}$ (C) 1   (D) 2   (E) 4

2. $\dfrac{x}{\frac{1}{4}} =$

(A) $\dfrac{4}{x}$ (B) $\dfrac{x}{4}$ (C) $\dfrac{1}{4x}$ (D) $\dfrac{4}{4x}$ (E) $4x$

3. If $x = 2$, then what is the value of $(x - 1)(x + 3)$?

(A) –5   (B) –1   (C) 3   (D) 5   (E) 7

4. What is the distance between the points $(2, -3)$ and $(-3, 6)$?

(A) 3.16   (B) 9.38   (C) 10.30   (D) 14   (E) 106

5. $(2x + 5)(x + 4) =$

(A) $x^2 + 9x + 9$
(B) $2x^2 + 9x + 9$
(C) $2x^2 + 13x + 20$
(D) $2x^2 + 20x + 19$
(E) $2x^2 + 9x + 20$

GO ON TO THE NEXT PAGE

6. What is the slope of the line $-3(x-1) + 4y = 0$?

   (A) .75   (B) 1   (C) 1.33   (D) 3   (E) 4

7. If $4x^2 = 3$, then what is the value of $(4x^2)^{4x^2}$?

   (A) 9
   (B) 12
   (C) 27
   (D) 36
   (E) 48

8. In Figure 1, lines j and k are parallel and are intersected by line q. What is the sum of the measures of angles 1 and 2?

   (A)   45
   (B)   90
   (C)   180
   (D)   300
   (E)   360

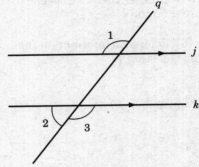

Figure 1

9. Which of the following is the **largest** possible value of x, if $11x < 23$?

   (A) 0.48
   (B) 1.19
   (C) 2.04
   (D) 2.10
   (E) 2.11

10. If a and b are nonzero real numbers, and $a^3 b^{-3} = 19$, then what is the value of $\frac{a}{b}$?

   (A) 0.22
   (B) 0.37
   (C) 1.00
   (D) 2.67
   (E) 4.36

11. A rectangular box has a volume of 144 cubic feet. If the box is 2 feet wide and 12 feet long, what is its height?

   (A) 4 ft.   (B) 6 ft.   (C) 8 ft.   (D) 12 ft.   (E) 16 ft.

GO ON TO THE NEXT PAGE

12. A pyramid fits exactly inside a box, as in Figure 2. What is the ratio of the volume of the pyramid to the volume of the box?

    (A) 1:3
    (B) 3:8
    (C) 4:5
    (D) 2:1
    (E) 3:1

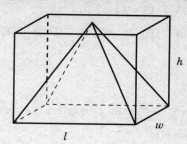

Figure 2

13. When ray OJ in Figure 3 is rotated counterclockwise 46 degrees about point O, ray OJ will be perpendicular to ray OB. What is the measure of $\angle JOB$ before this rotation?

    (A) 14°
    (B) 44°
    (C) 45°
    (D) 46°
    (E) 90°

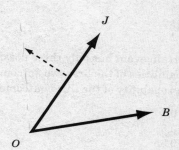

Figure 3

14. If $\sqrt{x} = \sqrt[3]{8}$, what is the value of x?

    (A) 2
    (B) $2\sqrt{2}$
    (C) 3
    (D) 4
    (E) 8

15. If $f(x) = 3x^2$, what is $f(\{0, -2, 3\})$?

    (A) $\{0, -2, 3\}$
    (B) $\{1, 6, 9\}$
    (C) $\{0, 12, 27\}$
    (D) $\{3, 7, 25\}$
    (E) $\{1, 2, 3\}$

GO ON TO THE NEXT PAGE

USE THIS SPACE FOR SCRATCHWORK.

16. $\left| -2 + \left| -1 \right| - 1 \right| = ?$

 (A) 0 (B) 1 (C) 2 (D) 3 (E) 4

17. If $7x^2y^{-3} = \dfrac{x^3}{y^3}$, and x and y are nonzero real numbers, what is the value of x?

 (A) -7
 (B) -0.14
 (C) 0.14
 (D) 7
 (E) 14

18. A certain event has only three possible outcomes. The probabilities of the first two outcomes are 0.3 and 0.4. What is the probability of the third outcome?

 (A) 0.1
 (B) 0.3
 (C) 0.35
 (D) 0.5
 (E) 0.7

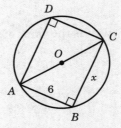

19. The perimeter of rectangle $ABCD$ in Figure 4 is 28. What is the circumference of the circle with center O?

 (A) 6π (B) 9π (C) 10π (D) 18π (E) 20π

Note: Figure not drawn to scale.
Figure 4

20. Robin walked 3 miles to a particular grocery to buy her favorite spaghetti sauce. If she doubled her pace on the way home, and the round trip took 80 minutes, what was her pace walking to the store?

 (A) 1.66 miles per hour
 (B) 3.38 miles per hour
 (C) 4.94 miles per hour
 (D) 6.75 miles per hour
 (E) 9.53 miles per hour

GO ON TO THE NEXT PAGE →

21. The coach of a basketball team is trying to pick a starting lineup. He has to fill 5 positions: a point guard, shooting guard, small forward, power forward, and center. If the team roster has 4 point guards, 2 shooting guards, 4 small forwards, 1 power forward, and 5 centers, how many different possible starting teams can he select?

    (A) 86
    (B) 94
    (C) 125
    (D) 160
    (E) 200

22. In Figure 5, *ABC* is an isosceles triangle and *ADC* is an equilateral triangle. If $x = 15°$, what is the value of *y*?

    (A) 10°
    (B) 18°
    (C) 27°
    (D) 30°
    (E) 45°

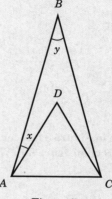

Figure 5

23. In Figure 6, what is the value of θ in terms of *x* and *y*?

    (A) $\dfrac{x}{y}$ (B) $\tan^{-1}\dfrac{y}{x}$ (C) $\tan^{-1}\dfrac{x}{y}$ (D) $\cos^{-1}\dfrac{x}{y}$ (E) $\cos^{-1}\dfrac{y}{x}$

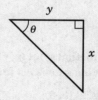

Figure 6

GO ON TO THE NEXT PAGE

24. In Figure 7, circle O has a radius of 1. What is the area of the shaded region?

(A) $\dfrac{\pi}{6}$ (B) $\dfrac{\pi}{4}$ (C) $\dfrac{2\pi}{3}$ (D) $\dfrac{3\pi}{4}$ (E) π

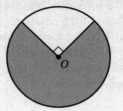

Figure 7

25. Which of the following is equal to zero if $i^2 = -1$?

(A) i
(B) $i^2 - i$
(C) i^3
(D) $i^2 + i^4$
(E) $i^2 + i^2$

26. The circle in Figure 8 has center O, a minor arc AB of length 3π, and $\angle AOB$ of measure $60°$. What is the area of circle O?

(A) 9π
(B) $27\sqrt{\pi}$
(C) 45π
(D) 81π
(E) 108π

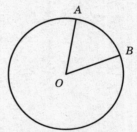

<u>Note</u>: Figure not drawn to scale.
Figure 8

27. For some function g, let (x, y) denote x and its image y. In which of the following sets is g a function?

(A) $\{(1, 1),(2, 2),(3, 3)\}$
(B) $\{(1, 2),(2, 3),(1, 3)\}$
(C) $\{(1, 5),(2, 4),(2, 3)\}$
(D) $\{(1, 1),(1, 3),(2, 2),(3, 1)\}$
(E) $\{(1, 1),(1, 2),(1, 3),(2, 3),(3, 2)\}$

GO ON TO THE NEXT PAGE

USE THIS SPACE FOR SCRATCHWORK.

28. x is an odd integer and y is an even integer. Which of the following must be equal to an odd integer?

(A) $2x + 2y$
(B) $x^2 - x + xy$
(C) $3y$
(D) $4xy - y^2$
(E) $x - 2y$

29. Let P be a point on a plane. What is the set of all points that is distance 2 from P?

(A) the region of the plane on one side of a line
(B) the interior of a square centered at P
(C) a region of the plane bounded by two horizontal lines
(D) a circle of diameter 2 centered at P
(E) a circle of radius 2 centered at P

30. Ten students received test scores whose mean is 72. What is the greatest possible number of students that could have received perfect scores (100)?

(A) 2 (B) 3 (C) 6 (D) 7 (E) 8

31. The equation for the line that passes through points (5, 7) and (7, –3) is given by which of the following?

(A) $y = -5x$
(B) $y = -5x + 18$
(C) $y = -5x + 32$
(D) $y = -3x + 18$
(E) $y = 5x - 18$

GO ON TO THE NEXT PAGE

USE THIS SPACE FOR SCRATCHWORK.

32. What is the sum of the lengths of diagonals AB and PQ in the rectangular solid in Figure 9?

    (A) 11.70
    (B) 12.73
    (C) 18.38
    (D) 25.46
    (E) 29.91

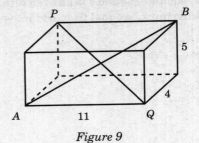

Figure 9

33. If $\frac{y}{2} = x + 1$ and $y^2 - 11x - 4 = 0$ for $x > 0$, what is the value of x?

    (A) $\frac{3}{4}$ (B) 1   (C) $\frac{7}{3}$ (D) 3   (E) 11

34. In Figure 10, circle O has an area of 49π. What is the perimeter of triangle ABC?

    (A) $7 + \sqrt{2}$
    (B) $7 + 2\sqrt{3}$
    (C) $14 + \sqrt{3}$
    (D) $7 + 7\sqrt{2}$
    (E) $14 + 14\sqrt{2}$

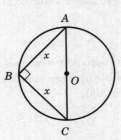

Figure 10

35. $\left(\dfrac{\sin^2\theta + \cos^2\theta}{2} \right)^2 =$

    (A) $\frac{1}{4}$ (B) $\frac{1}{2}$ (C) 1   (D) 4   (E) 16

GO ON TO THE NEXT PAGE

36. If $f(x)$ is a function, which of the following could be the graph of $y = f(x)$?

(A)

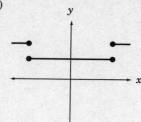

(B)

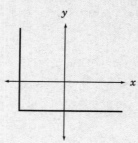

(C)

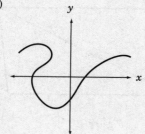

(D)

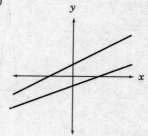

(E)

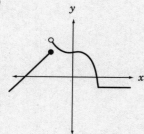

37. Jenny has invited 5 friends over for a party and wants to make conical party hats for each guest and for herself (6 hats total). How much paper (in square inches) does Jenny need if each hat has a diameter of 6 inches and is 9 inches high?

(A) 389.61
(B) 411.33
(C) 445.41
(D) 486.79
(E) 536.47

GO ON TO THE NEXT PAGE

38. A circle with center $(3, 1)$ and radius 3 is graphed on the same xy-plane as the line with the equation $y = 2x + 1$. What are the coordinates of the points of intersection of the circle and line?

    (A) $(2.4, 5.8)$ and $(3, 7)$
    (B) $(3, 4)$ and $(5.8, 0)$
    (C) $(1.3, 2)$ and $(-4.2, 3.7)$
    (D) $(0, 1)$ and $(1.2, 3.4)$
    (E) $(5.2, -1)$ and $(3.8, 8.6)$

39. In Figure 11, $BC = 21$. If the area of triangle CDE is $\frac{4}{9}$ the size of the area of parallelogram $ABCD$, what is the measurement of AE?

    (A) $1\frac{2}{3}$ (B) $2\frac{1}{3}$ (C) $3\frac{1}{4}$ (D) $4\frac{1}{2}$ (E) $5\frac{2}{3}$

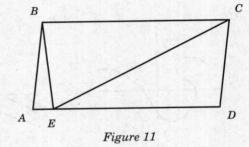

Figure 11

40. A leather jacket costs $250, but decreases in value at a rate of 4% annually. What will be the value of the jacket in 7 years?

    (A) $150
    (B) $152
    (C) $188
    (D) $212
    (E) $250

41. O and Q are the centers of the two circles shown in Figure 12. What is the area of the shaded regions?

    (A) $\dfrac{r^2(2\pi - \sqrt{3})}{2}$

    (B) $\dfrac{r^2(2\pi - \sqrt{2})}{2}$

    (C) $\dfrac{r^2(2\pi - 3\sqrt{2})}{3}$

    (D) $\dfrac{r^2(2\pi - 2\sqrt{3})}{4}$

    (E) $\dfrac{r^2(2\pi - 3\sqrt{3})}{3}$

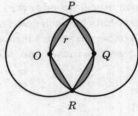

Figure 12

GO ON TO THE NEXT PAGE

USE THIS SPACE FOR SCRATCHWORK.

42. What is the range of f, if $0 \le x \le 10$, and $f(x) = |-2x - 1|$?

(A) $y \ge 0$
(B) $0 \le y \le 21$
(C) $1 \le y \le 21$
(D) $y \ge -1$
(E) $-1 \le y \le 21$

43. The base of the pyramid in Figure 13 is a square with sides of length s. The height of the pyramid is $2s$. In terms of s, what is the total surface area of the figure?

(A) $\frac{\sqrt{17}}{6}s^2$

(B) $\frac{\sqrt{17}}{2}s^2$

(C) $\frac{2\sqrt{17}}{3}s^2$

(D) $\sqrt{17}s^2$

(E) $(1 + \sqrt{17})s^2$

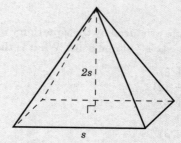

Note: Figure not drawn to scale.
Figure 13

44. In Figure 14, if $\theta = 73°$, then what is the value of $\frac{b}{c}$?

(A) 0.29
(B) 0.73
(C) 0.96
(D) 3.14
(E) 3.27

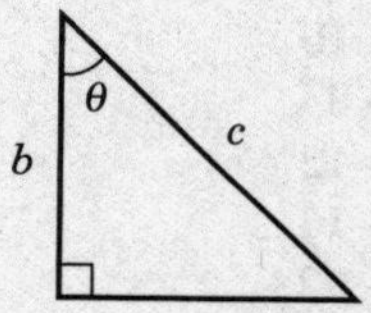

Figure 14

45. $f(x) = 3x + 2$ and $g(x) = 7x$. What is $f^{-1}(g(x) + f(3))$?

(A) $21x + 11$

(B) $21x + 33$

(C) $21x + 35$

(D) $\frac{7x}{3} + 3$

(E) $\frac{7x + 1}{3}$

46. What is the minimum value of the function $f(x) = 2x^2 + 1$?

(A) –1 (B) 0 (C) 1 (D) 3 (E) 5

GO ON TO THE NEXT PAGE

USE THIS SPACE FOR SCRATCHWORK.

47. Rhombus *ABCD* has an angle of 120 and a side of length 6. What is the area?

    (A) $6\sqrt{3}$
    (B) $18\sqrt{3}$
    (C) $24\sqrt{3}$
    (D) 36
    (E) $36\sqrt{3}$

48. The line produced by the equation $y = 3$ intersects the parabola $y = x^2 - 4x + 7$ at one point. What is the vertex of the parabola?

    (A) $(4, 3)$
    (B) $(2, 12)$
    (C) $(1, 4)$
    (D) $(0, 7)$
    (E) $(2, 3)$

49. Figure 15 depicts a courtyard with dimensions of $x \times y$ feet, and surrounded by a flower bed 2 feet wide and with a 2 foot wide walkway into the courtyard. What is the area of the flower bed, in square feet?

    (A) $2x + 2y + 16$
    (B) $2x + 4y + 8$
    (C) $4x + 4y + 12$
    (D) $4x + 4y + 16$
    (E) $4x + 4y + 32$

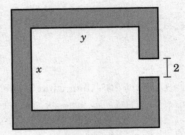

Figure 15

50. A particular brand of lemonade is made by mixing concentrate with water. How many gallons of concentrate should be mixed with 5 gallons of water so that 18 percent of the resulting lemonade is concentrate?

    (A) 1.1 (B) 1.6 (C) 1.9 (D) 2.4 (E) 3.0

S T O P

IF YOU FINISH BEFORE TIME IS CALLED, YOU MAY CHECK YOUR WORK ON THIS TEST ONLY.
DO NOT TURN TO ANY OTHER TEST IN THIS BOOK.

SAT Math Level 1 Practice Test I Explanations

Answers to SAT Math Level 1 Practice Test I

Question Number	Answer	Right	Wrong	Question Number	Answer	Right	Wrong
1	D	_____	_____	26	D	_____	_____
2	E	_____	_____	27	A	_____	_____
3	D	_____	_____	28	E	_____	_____
4	C	_____	_____	29	E	_____	_____
5	C	_____	_____	30	D	_____	_____
6	A	_____	_____	31	C	_____	_____
7	C	_____	_____	32	D	_____	_____
8	C	_____	_____	33	A	_____	_____
9	C	_____	_____	34	E	_____	_____
10	D	_____	_____	35	A	_____	_____
11	B	_____	_____	36	E	_____	_____
12	A	_____	_____	37	E	_____	_____
13	B	_____	_____	38	D	_____	_____
14	D	_____	_____	39	B	_____	_____
15	C	_____	_____	40	C	_____	_____
16	C	_____	_____	41	E	_____	_____
17	D	_____	_____	42	C	_____	_____
18	B	_____	_____	43	E	_____	_____
19	C	_____	_____	44	A	_____	_____
20	B	_____	_____	45	D	_____	_____
21	D	_____	_____	46	C	_____	_____
22	D	_____	_____	47	B	_____	_____
23	C	_____	_____	48	E	_____	_____
24	D	_____	_____	49	C	_____	_____
25	D	_____	_____	50	A	_____	_____

Calculating Your Score

Your raw score for the SAT Math Level 1 test is based on the number of questions you answer correctly and incorrectly. Once you have determined your raw score, use the conversion table on page 15 of this book to calculate your scaled score.

To Calculate Your Raw Score

1. Count the number of questions you answered correctly: _____ (A)

2. Count the number of questions you answered incorrectly, and multiply that number by ¼: _____ (B) × ¼ = _____ (C)

3. Subtract the value in (C) from value in (A): _____ (D)

4. Round the number in (D) to the nearest whole number. This is your raw score: _____ (E)

Math Level 1 Test I Explanations

1.   D   Equation Solving

The solution to this problem has two steps: first cross-multiply to break apart the fraction and then solve for x:

$$\frac{x}{3x+2} = \frac{1}{4}$$
$$1(3x+2) = 4(x)$$
$$3x+2 = 4x$$
$$x = 2$$

2.   E   Fundamentals

Recall that dividing by a fraction is equivalent to multiplying by the reciprocal of that fraction. We'll show you all the steps, but hopefully you'll be able to skip a few as you get more familiar with strategies for solving these problems.

$$\frac{x}{\frac{1}{4}} = x \times 4$$
$$x \times 4 = 4x$$

3.   D   Polynomials

Just plug 2 in for x and then carry out the operations:

$$(x-1)(x+3) = (2-1)(2+3)$$
$$= (1)(5)$$
$$= 5$$

4.   C   Lines and Distance

In order to find the distance between two points, (x_1, y_1) and (x_2, y_2), use the distance formula $d = \sqrt{(x_2-x_1)^2 + (y_2-y_1)^2}$:

$$\text{distance} = \sqrt{(-3-2)^2 + (6-(-3))^2}$$
$$= \sqrt{(-5)^2 + 9^2}$$
$$= \sqrt{106}$$
$$= 10.30$$

5.   C   Polynomials

To solve this question, simply multiply the terms; use FOIL to help you keep track of the terms.

$$(2x+5)(x+4) = 2x^2 + 8x + 5x + 20$$
$$= 2x^2 + 13x + 20$$

6. A Lines and Distance

There are several ways to find the slope of a line given its equation. One of the easiest ways to do so is to restate the equation in the slope-intercept form:

$$-3(x - 1) + 4y = 0$$
$$4y = 3(x - 1)$$
$$4y = 3x - 3$$
$$y = \frac{3x}{4} - \frac{3}{4}$$

When the equation of a line is put in slope-intercept form, the slope is equal to the coefficient of x. So, from the equation, we can see that the slope is $^3/_4 = 0.75$.

7. C Equation Solving

The most important observation to make in this problem is that you do not need to solve for x. All you have to do is substitute in $4x^2 = 3$, and you get $3^3 = 27$.

8. C Lines and Angles

Take a look at Figure 1. By definition, angles 1 and 3 are congruent, and angles 2 and 3 are supplementary (they add up to 180°). Therefore, since angles 1 and 3 have the same measure, the sum of angles 1 and 2 is also 180°.

9. C Equation Solving

Isolate the variable, x, by simply dividing both sides by 11. This will give us $x < 2.09$. The question asks for the **largest** value of x that satisfies the inequality, so x must be less than 2.09. Choices **D** and **E** are too large. The next largest possible value is 2.04, which is less than 2.09.

10. D Equation Solving

This question can be tricky if you don't remember a basic rule about negative exponents: $x^{-n} = {}^1/_{x^n}$. Armed with this knowledge, we can rewrite $a^3 b^{-3} = 19$ as $^{a^3}/_{b^3} = 19$, which is the same thing as $(a/b)^3$. Now, to solve for $^a/_b$, we just need to take the cube root of both sides to get the correct answer:

$$\frac{a}{b} = \sqrt[3]{19} = 2.67$$

11. B Prisms, Solids That Aren't Prisms

Since the volume of the box is given as 144 cubic feet, we need to work backward to find the height of the box. We know that the formula for the volume of a rectangular solid is $l \times w \times h = 144$:

$$12 \times 2 \times h = 144$$
$$24h = 144$$
$$h = 6$$

12. A Prisms, Solids That Aren't Prisms

To find the ratios of the volumes of the pyramid and box, compare their volume formulas.

$$\frac{\text{volume of pyramid}}{\text{volume of box}} = \frac{\frac{1}{3}lwh}{lwh} = \frac{1}{3}$$

13. **B** Lines and Angles

For ray OJ to be perpendicular to ray OB, the angle they form, $\angle JOB$, must be a right angle, or 90°. That means that before the 46° rotation, the measure of $\angle JOB = 90° - 46° = 44°$.

14. **D** Equation Solving

The first step is to solve for the square root of x: $\sqrt[3]{8} = 2$. Now that you know $\sqrt{x} = 2$, you can simply square both sides and find that $x = 4$.

15. **C** Evaluating Functions

In order to evaluate a function on a set, we simply evaluate the function for each member of the set:

$$
\begin{aligned}
f(\{0, -2, 3\}) &= \{f(0), f(-2), f(3)\} \\
&= \{3 \times 0^2, 3 \times (-2)^2, 3 \times 3^2\} \\
&= \{3 \times 0, 3 \times 4, 3 \times 9\} \\
&= \{0, 12, 27\}
\end{aligned}
$$

16. **C** Fundamentals

Recall that the absolute value operation does not affect positive numbers at all, and for negative numbers it simply drops the negative sign. Keeping that in mind, carry out the operations in the expression, starting with the innermost absolute value operations:

$$
\begin{aligned}
\big| -2 + |-1| - 1 \big| &= |-2 + 1 - 1| \\
&= |-2| \\
&= 2
\end{aligned}
$$

17. **D** Equation Solving

This question can be tricky if you don't remember a basic rule about negative exponents:

$$x^{-n} = \frac{1}{x^n}$$

In applying this rule to the question, we can rewrite the equation as:

$$\frac{7x^2}{y^3} = \frac{x^3}{y^3}$$

As usual, when equal fractions have equal denominators, their numerators are also equal:

$$
\begin{aligned}
7x^2y^3 &= x^3y^3 \\
7x^2 &= x^3 \\
7 &= x
\end{aligned}
$$

18. **B** Probability

The sum of the probabilities of all possible outcomes of an event is always equal to 1. So, to solve this problem simply subtract the probabilities of the first two outcomes from 1, and the result will be the probability of the third outcome: $1 - 0.3 - 0.4 = 0.3$.

19. **C**   Circles

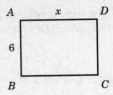

Since the value for the perimeter of rectangle *ABCD* is given, we can solve for *x*:

$$2(6) + 2x = 28$$
$$2x = 16$$
$$x = 8$$

We now know two lengths of the triangle to be 6 and 8. Hopefully you can recognize this as a multiple of the basic Pythagorean triple, 3-4-5, to figure out that this triangle has sides of length 6, 8, and 10, respectively.

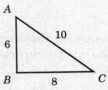

The hypotenuse also happens to be the diameter of the circle, so the circumference of the circle is $\pi d = 10\pi$.

20. **B**   Equation Solving

The best way to solve this problem is to treat Robin's trip to the store and her trip back home as two separate events whose total time was 80 minutes. Let's use *x* to represent her speed on the way to the store and 2*x* to represent her speed on the way back home. We can rearrange the standard relationship of distance = rate × time into something more useful: distance ÷ rate = time. Of course, in our problem we have two separate pieces to consider, so we have only one more modification to make: (distance to the store ÷ rate to the store) + (distance home ÷ rate home) = time. Since we know that the entire trip takes $1\frac{1}{3}$ hours, we can solve for *x*:

(distance to the store ÷ rate to the store) + (distance home ÷ rate home) = time

$$\frac{3 \text{ miles}}{x \text{ miles per hour}} + \frac{3 \text{ miles}}{2x \text{ miles per hour}} = \frac{4}{3} \text{ hours}$$

$$\frac{6 \text{ miles}}{2x \text{ miles per hour}} + \frac{3 \text{ miles}}{2x \text{ miles per hour}} = \frac{4}{3} \text{ hours}$$

$$\frac{9 \text{ miles}}{2x \text{ miles per hour}} = \frac{4}{3} \text{ hours}$$

$$9 \text{ miles} = \frac{8x}{3} \text{ miles}$$

$$27 = 8x$$

$x = 3.38$, so Robin's pace walking to the store was 3.38 miles per hour.

21. **D**   Permutations and Combinations

Each position is unrelated to the others, so the number of possibilities is simply the product of the number of choices in each category. There are $4 \times 2 \times 4 \times 1 \times 5 = 160$ possible team combinations.

22. **D**   Triangle

Triangle ADC is equilateral, meaning that all of its angles are equal to 60°.

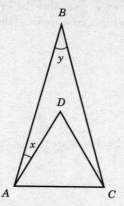

We can then figure out that $\angle BAC$ is equal to $60° + x = 60° + 15° = 75°$. Because triangle ABC is isosceles, $\angle BAC = \angle BCA = 75°$. So, you can find the value of y since the sum of the angles of ABC must be equal to 180°:

$$75° + 75° + y = 180°$$
$$150° + y = 180°$$
$$y = 30°$$

23. **C**   Basic Functions and the Right Triangle

All we know about θ from the figure are the lengths of its opposite and adjacent sides. Fortunately, the tangent of an angle is the ratio:

$$\tan \theta = \frac{\text{opposite}}{\text{adjacent}}$$

Since the question asks for θ (and not $\tan \theta$), we simply take the inverse tangent of both sides, yielding:

$$\theta = \tan^{-1} \frac{x}{y}$$

24. **D**   Circles

Because the angle that encompasses the unshaded region is 90°, the area of the unshaded region comprises $^{90}/_{360} = \frac{1}{4}$ of the area of the circle. Therefore, the shaded region takes up $^{270}/_{360} = \frac{3}{4}$ of the area of the circle:

$$\text{area of shaded region} = \frac{3}{4} \pi r^2 = \frac{3}{4} \pi (1^2) = \frac{3}{4} \pi$$

25. **D**   Imaginary and Complex Numbers

The key to this problem is remembering the basics of how to manipulate imaginary numbers:

$$i^1 = i$$
$$i^2 = -1$$
$$i^3 = -i$$
$$i^4 = 1$$

There are two basic ways to generate 0 when adding or subtracting powers of i: try to get to a variation of the expression $i - i$, or $1 - 1$. As you can see from the above equations, odd powers of i will generate imaginary results while even powers of i generate real numbers. Quickly scanning the powers of i, you can see that $i^2 + i^4 = 0$.

26. **D** Circles

We can set up a simple proportion between the length of the arc and the angle intercepting that arc. Since the 60° angle is $\frac{1}{6}$ of the circle's 360°, we can say that the length of the arc is also $\frac{1}{6}$ of the circle's circumference. Of course, once we know the circumference of the circle, we can easily find the diameter as well. To find the circumference:

$$\frac{60°}{360°} = \frac{3\pi}{c}$$

$$\frac{1}{6} = \frac{3\pi}{c}$$

$$c = 18\pi$$

In order to find the area of the circle, we need to figure out the radius:

$$c = 2\pi r$$

$$18\pi = 2\pi r$$

$$r = 9$$

So we can now solve for the area of the circle: $\pi r^2 = 81\pi$.

27. **A** Evaluating Functions

The definition of a function states that each element of its domain can be paired with only **one** element of the range. Here, the domain is the first element in the ordered pair, and the range is the second element. Of the possible choices, only **A** follows this definition of a function. The rest associate an element of the domain with more than one element of the range.

28. **E** Fundamentals

You could answer this question using the rules of even and odd integers, such as an even integer plus an odd integer results in an odd integer, but the easiest way would be to plug in odd and even values for x and y respectively (e.g., $x = 3$ and $y = 2$), and evaluate the expressions. The only answer choice that produces an odd number is **E**, since (using the example values above) $3 - 2(2) = -1$.

29. **E** Lines and Distance

As long as you remember the definition of a circle, you're all set. Recall that a circle is defined as the set of all points equidistant from a certain point (the center of the circle). Fortunately, **E** is exactly that.

30. **D** Statistical Analysis

Since the average of the ten tests is 72, the sum of all test scores is $72 \times 10 = 720$. How many of the ten tests could be perfect scores? Certainly no more than 7, since if there were 8, the total of all scores would have to be at least 800. If there are 7 perfect scores, then there are still 20 points to be distributed among the other three tests. Since we aren't told about any limitations on the minimum scores, that's no problem.

31. **C**   Lines and Distance

The first step to finding the equation of the line is to determine the slope, which we can do easily since we are given two points:

$$\frac{y_2 - y_1}{x_2 - x_1} = \frac{-3 - 7}{7 - 5}$$

$$= \frac{-10}{2}$$

$$= -5$$

Now that we've calculated the slope, we can find the y-intercept by substituting either of the given points into the equation $y = -5x + b$:

$$y = -5x + b$$
$$7 = (-5 \times 5) + b$$
$$32 = b$$

The slope of the line is -5 and the y-intercept is 32, so the equation of the line is $y = -5x + 32$.

32. **D**   Prisms, Solids That Aren't Prisms

The diagonal length, d, of a rectangular solid with length l, width w, and height h, is given by $d = \sqrt{l^2 + w^2 + h^2}$. Because $ABPQ$ is a rectangular solid, its diagonals AB and PQ are equal, and $AB = PQ = \sqrt{11^2 + 4^2 + 5^2} = \sqrt{162} \approx 12.73$. $AB + PQ = 25.46$.

33. **A**   Polynomials

Since the question gives two variables, the first step is to define one of the variables in terms of the other variable. In this case, let's try solving for y in terms of x:

$$\frac{y}{2} = x + 1$$

$$y = 2x + 2$$

Now you can eliminate y from the other equation by substituting $y = 2x + 2$ into $y^2 - 11x - 4 = 0$ and solving for x:

$$y^2 - 11x - 4 = 0$$
$$(2x + 2)^2 - 11x - 4 = 0$$
$$4x^2 + 8x + 4 - 11x - 4 = 0$$
$$4x^2 - 3x = 0$$
$$x(4x - 3) = 0$$

$$x = 0, \frac{3}{4}$$

Because the question states $x > 0$, the only possible value for x is $\frac{3}{4}$.

34. **E**   Circles

Since we're given the area of the circle, we can work backward to find the circle's radius using the formula $A = \pi r^2$:

$$\pi r^2 = 49\pi$$
$$r^2 = 49$$
$$r = 7$$

Since $\overline{AC}$ is the diameter of the circle, we can now calculate $\overline{AC} = 2(7) = 14$. Since we know that $\angle ABC$ is a right angle and $AB = BC = x$, and triangle ABC is a 45-45-90 triangle:

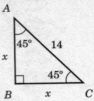

This means the lengths of its sides are in a $x: x: x\sqrt{2}$ relationship. Therefore, $x = {}^{14}/_{\sqrt{2}}$. The perimeter of the triangle is:

$$\text{perimeter} = 14 + \frac{14}{\sqrt{2}} + \frac{14}{\sqrt{2}} = 14 + \frac{28}{\sqrt{2}} = 14 + 14\sqrt{2}$$

Note that we converted ${}^{28}/_{\sqrt{2}}$ into $14\sqrt{2}$, which we can do since ${}^{2}/_{\sqrt{2}} = \sqrt{2}$.

35. **A**   Trigonometric Identities

This question requires knowledge of the Pythagorean identity, $\sin^2\theta + \cos^2\theta = 1$. Using the identity, you can substitute 1 into the numerator and work the expression out from there:

$$\left(\frac{\sin^2\theta + \cos^2\theta}{2}\right)^2 = \left(\frac{1}{2}\right)^2$$

$$= \frac{1}{4}$$

36. **E**   Graphing Functions

The vertical line test makes this problem very quick and easy. You can observe that every graph except for **E** is not the graph of a function. Each other graph fails the vertical line test: there is at least one point where a vertical line can be drawn that intersects the image more than once. Note that there is no place in the graph for **E** where a vertical line would intersect the function twice. Remember that a closed point (as in answer **A** means that the point itself is contained in the line, while an open point (choice **E**) symbolizes the limit approaching the point, but not the point itself. Thus **A** fails the vertical line test while **E** does not.

37. **E**   Prisms, Solids That Aren't Prisms

This question asks you to find the total surface area of all six cones. The formula for lateral surface area of a cone $= \frac{1}{2}Cl$, where C is the circumference and l is the slant height. See the figure below:

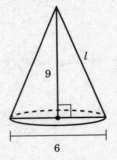

The radius is $\frac{1}{2} \times 6 = 3$ inches, and you can use the Pythagorean theorem to find l: $l = \sqrt{9^2 + 3^2} = \sqrt{90} = 3\sqrt{10}$. Therefore, the surface area of one hat is $\frac{1}{2}(6\pi)(3\sqrt{10}) = 9\sqrt{10}\,\pi$ square inches. Jenny wants 6 hats, so she needs $6 \times 9\sqrt{10}\,\pi \approx 536.47$ square inches of paper.

38. **D** Other Important Graphs and Equations

This question just asks us to find where two equations intersect, or where they have the same coordinates. We're given the equation of the line, so we first need to determine the equation of the circle. We can easily write the equation of a circle with center (h, k) and radius r:

$$(x - h)^2 + (y - k)^2 = r^2$$

So, in this case:

$$(x - 3)^2 + (y - 1)^2 = 9$$

We are given the equation of the line to be $y = 2x + 1$. To find where the circle and line intersect, plug in $2x + 1$ for y in the equation of the circle and solve for x:

$$(x - 3)^2 + ((2x + 1) - 1)^2 = 9$$
$$(x - 3)^2 + (2x)^2 = 9$$
$$x^2 - 6x + 9 + 4x^2 = 9$$
$$5x^2 - 6x = 0$$
$$x(5x - 6) = 0$$

The solution to this problem is $x = 0$ or $x = \frac{6}{5} = 1.2$, so **D** must be the correct answer.

39. **B** Polygons

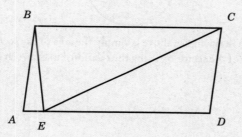

By definition, the opposite sides of a parallelogram are of equal measure, so we know that $BC = AD = 21$. $AD = AE + DE$, or more important, $AE = AD - DE$. This means that we can find AE if we know DE. We also know the formula for the area of triangle CDE is $\frac{1}{2}bh = \frac{1}{2}(DE)(h)$ and are told that the area of CDE is $\frac{4}{9}$ the area of parallelogram $ABCD$. Therefore we can set up an equation involving the areas of CDE and $ABCD$; then we can solve for DE:

$$\text{area of triangle} = \frac{4}{9} \text{ area of parallelogram}$$

$$\frac{1}{2}(DE)(h) = \frac{4}{9}bh$$

$$\frac{1}{2}(DE) = \frac{4}{9}(21)$$

$$DE = \frac{56}{3}$$

Thus, $AE = 21 - \frac{56}{3} = \frac{7}{3} = 2\frac{1}{3}$.

40. **C**   Equation Solving

We know that if the value of an object decreases at a rate of 4% per year, then the object will be worth 100 − 4 = 96% of its original value after one year. However, if another year passes, that object will again be worth 96% of the value it started the year with, but only 96% of 96% of the original value.

After the first year, the object's value is 96^1% of its initial value. After the second year, its value is 96% × 96 = 96^2% of its starting value. We can represent this mathematically, letting the initial value be P_o and its rate of depreciation be r. Since each year, the value only retains 100% − r% of its initial value, we can represent its value after the nth year as $P = P_o(1 − r)^n$.

Now that we have the general equation, we can simply plug in the values given in the problem ($P_o = 250$, $r = 4\% = 0.04$, and $n = 7$): $P = \$250(0.96)^7 \approx \$188$.

41. **E**   Circles

O is the center of the left circle and Q is on that circle, so OQ is a radius of the circle. Q is the center of the right circle and O is on that circle. So the radius of circle O is equal to the radius of Q. Also, $OP = OR = QP = QR = r$. This means that OPQ is an equilateral triangle and $\angle POQ = 60°$:

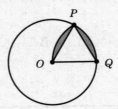

The area of the shaded region in the figure above is simply the area of the sector minus the area of triangle OPQ. First let's find the area of the sector by using the relationship between angle and sector area:

$$\frac{60°}{360°} = \frac{\text{sector area}}{\text{circle area}}$$

$$\frac{1}{6} = \frac{\text{sector area}}{\pi r^2}$$

$$\text{sector area} = \frac{\pi}{6} r^2$$

Since we know triangle OPQ is equilateral, we can find the base and height by using the properties of a 30-60-90 triangle:

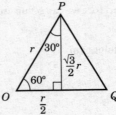

So the area of triangle OPQ is

$$\frac{1}{2}(r)(\frac{\sqrt{3}}{2} r) = \frac{\sqrt{3}}{4} r^2$$

Now, we can find the area of one of the shaded regions:

$$\text{area} = \frac{\pi}{6} r^2 − \frac{\sqrt{3}}{4} r^2 = \frac{r^2(2\pi − 3\sqrt{3})}{12}$$

Since there are four regions, the answer is

$$4 \times \frac{r^2(2\pi - 3\sqrt{3})}{12} = \frac{r^2(2\pi - 3\sqrt{3})}{3}$$

42. **C**   Domain and Range

We know that the absolute value of any number is always greater than or equal to 0, so we can immediately eliminate **D** and **E** since they are negative. We cannot, however, assume that the range of the function is simply $y \geq 0$ because the domain of this function is restricted to $0 \leq x \leq 10$. Instead, we need to find how these restrictions in the domain affect the range of the function. First, plug in the least and greatest possible values of x. For $x = 0$ we get:

$$f(0) = |(-2)(0) - 1|$$
$$= |-1|$$
$$= 1$$

For $x = 10$ we get:

$$f(10) = |(-2)(10) - 1|$$
$$= |-21|$$
$$= 21$$

This gives us a range of $1 \leq y \leq 21$, and the answer choice **C**. Note that the bounds of the domain do not always correspond to the bounds of the range, but for most polynomial functions you'll see on the Math Level 1, you can safely make that assumption.

43. **E**   Prisms, Solids That Aren't Prisms

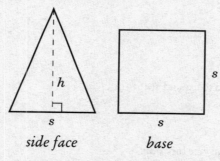

side face   base

The surface area of a pyramid is equal to the sum of the areas of all its faces. In this problem, area of base = s^2 and area of side face = $\frac{1}{2}sl$. We need to find the surface area in terms of s, so we first need to find l in terms of s. We can do this by creating a right triangle, with l as its hypotenuse; you can picture this as a slice down through the center of the pyramid, parallel to the sides of the base.

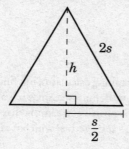

Using the Pythagorean theorem:

$$l = \sqrt{(2s)^2 + \left(\frac{s}{2}\right)^2}$$

$$l = \sqrt{4s^2 + \frac{1}{4}s^2}$$

$$= \sqrt{\frac{17}{4}s^2}$$

$$= \frac{\sqrt{17}}{2}s$$

So the area of a side face is $\frac{1}{2}(s)(\frac{1}{2}\sqrt{17}s) = \frac{\sqrt{17}}{4}s^2$. Since there are four triangular sides, their combined area is $\sqrt{17}s^2$. Add this to the area of the square base and you get $s^2 + \sqrt{17}s^2$, or $(1 + \sqrt{17})s^2$.

44. A   Basic Functions and the Right Triangle

Since we are given θ, we know several different relationships between the sides of the triangle (thanks to trig functions). All you have to know is which trig functions relate θ to sides b and c. The cosine function does just that: $\cos \theta = {}^{adjacent}/_{hypotenuse} = {}^{b}/_{c}$. In the triangle above, b is adjacent to θ and c is the hypotenuse. Therefore, we know that $\cos 73° = {}^{b}/_{c} = 0.29$.

45. D   Evaluating Functions

This problem has several parts. First, you need to find $f^{-1}(x)$, the inverse of f(x). Then you need to expand $g(x)$ and $f(3)$. We'll start with finding $f^{-1}(x)$.

$$f(x) = 3x + 2$$
$$y = 3x + 2$$
$$x = 3y + 2$$
$$x - 2 = 3y$$
$$\frac{x - 2}{3} = y$$
$$f^{-1}(x) = \frac{x - 2}{3}$$

Now that we have $f^{-1}(x)$, we need to expand $g(x) + f(3)$:

$$g(x) + f(3) = 7x + 3(3) + 2$$
$$= 7x + 11$$

Now we feed $7x + 11$ into the inverse function:

$$f^{-1}(g(x) + f(3)) = f^{-1}(7x + 11)$$
$$= \frac{(7x + 11) - 2}{3}$$
$$= \frac{7x + 9}{3}$$
$$= \frac{7x}{3} + 3$$

46. C   Domain and Range

You could graph this function on your graphing calculator, but finding an answer is even quicker if you can recognize the shape of the function from its definition. Since it is a second-degree equation, you know it is a parabola. Since the leading coefficient is positive, we know that the parabola opens upward. A parabola that opens upward has its minimum value at its vertex, which is at $x = 0$. For this function, $f(0) = 2(0)^2 + 1$ $= 0 + 1 = 1$.

47. **B** Triangle

The adjacent angles of a rhombus are supplementary and the opposite angles are congruent, so the rhombus has adjacent angles of 120 degrees and $180 - 120 = 60$ degrees. Therefore, drawing the height of the rhombus forms a 30-60-90 triangle with a height of $3\sqrt{3}$. It is given that one of the sides is length 6, so the area of the rhombus is base multiplied by the height, or $(6)(3\sqrt{3}) = 18\sqrt{3}$.

48. **E** Other Important Graphs and Equations

If a horizontal line intersects a parabola at only one point, that point must be the vertex of the parabola. Set the equation of the parabola equal to the equation of the line and solve for the x-coordinate of the vertex:

$$x^2 - 4x + 7 = 3$$
$$x^2 - 4x + 4 = 0$$
$$(x - 2)(x - 2) = 0$$

Since $x = 2$, the x-coordinate of the point is on horizontal line $y = 3$, which defines the point $(2, 3)$.

49. **C** Polygons

In order to find the area of the shaded region, we need to subtract the area of the courtyard and the walkway from the area of the entire region. The following figure should make this more clear:

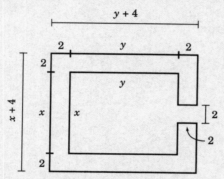

From this diagram, you should be able to identify that the area of the entire region is $(x + 4)(y + 4)$, the area of the courtyard is $x \times y$, and the walkway cuts through $2 \times 2 = 4$ square feet of the flower bed. Simply manipulating these areas, we can isolate the area of the flower bed itself:

$$\begin{aligned} \text{area of flower bed} &= (x + 4)(y + 4) - xy - (2)(2) \\ &= xy + 4x + 4y + 16 - xy - 4 \\ &= 4x + 4y + 12 \end{aligned}$$

50. **A** Equation Solving

We're looking for a particular amount of concentrate, which we'll call x. The total amount of lemonade to be made is 5 gallons of water and x gallons of concentrate. Since we're looking for an amount of concentrate such that the lemonade is 18 percent concentrate, we can set up a ratio and solve for x:

$$\frac{x}{x + 5} = .18$$
$$x = .18(x + 5)$$
$$x = .18x + .90$$
$$.82x = .90$$
$$x = 1.1$$

1.1 gallons of concentrate added to 5 gallons of water yields a mixture of lemonade that is 18% concentrate.

SAT Math Level 1
Practice Test II

SAT MATH LEVEL 1 PRACTICE TEST II ANSWER SHEET

1 Ⓐ Ⓑ Ⓒ Ⓓ Ⓔ   11 Ⓐ Ⓑ Ⓒ Ⓓ Ⓔ   21 Ⓐ Ⓑ Ⓒ Ⓓ Ⓔ   31 Ⓐ Ⓑ Ⓒ Ⓓ Ⓔ   41 Ⓐ Ⓑ Ⓒ Ⓓ Ⓔ
2 Ⓐ Ⓑ Ⓒ Ⓓ Ⓔ   12 Ⓐ Ⓑ Ⓒ Ⓓ Ⓔ   22 Ⓐ Ⓑ Ⓒ Ⓓ Ⓔ   32 Ⓐ Ⓑ Ⓒ Ⓓ Ⓔ   42 Ⓐ Ⓑ Ⓒ Ⓓ Ⓔ
3 Ⓐ Ⓑ Ⓒ Ⓓ Ⓔ   13 Ⓐ Ⓑ Ⓒ Ⓓ Ⓔ   23 Ⓐ Ⓑ Ⓒ Ⓓ Ⓔ   33 Ⓐ Ⓑ Ⓒ Ⓓ Ⓔ   43 Ⓐ Ⓑ Ⓒ Ⓓ Ⓔ
4 Ⓐ Ⓑ Ⓒ Ⓓ Ⓔ   14 Ⓐ Ⓑ Ⓒ Ⓓ Ⓔ   24 Ⓐ Ⓑ Ⓒ Ⓓ Ⓔ   34 Ⓐ Ⓑ Ⓒ Ⓓ Ⓔ   44 Ⓐ Ⓑ Ⓒ Ⓓ Ⓔ
5 Ⓐ Ⓑ Ⓒ Ⓓ Ⓔ   15 Ⓐ Ⓑ Ⓒ Ⓓ Ⓔ   25 Ⓐ Ⓑ Ⓒ Ⓓ Ⓔ   35 Ⓐ Ⓑ Ⓒ Ⓓ Ⓔ   45 Ⓐ Ⓑ Ⓒ Ⓓ Ⓔ
6 Ⓐ Ⓑ Ⓒ Ⓓ Ⓔ   16 Ⓐ Ⓑ Ⓒ Ⓓ Ⓔ   26 Ⓐ Ⓑ Ⓒ Ⓓ Ⓔ   36 Ⓐ Ⓑ Ⓒ Ⓓ Ⓔ   46 Ⓐ Ⓑ Ⓒ Ⓓ Ⓔ
7 Ⓐ Ⓑ Ⓒ Ⓓ Ⓔ   17 Ⓐ Ⓑ Ⓒ Ⓓ Ⓔ   27 Ⓐ Ⓑ Ⓒ Ⓓ Ⓔ   37 Ⓐ Ⓑ Ⓒ Ⓓ Ⓔ   47 Ⓐ Ⓑ Ⓒ Ⓓ Ⓔ
8 Ⓐ Ⓑ Ⓒ Ⓓ Ⓔ   18 Ⓐ Ⓑ Ⓒ Ⓓ Ⓔ   28 Ⓐ Ⓑ Ⓒ Ⓓ Ⓔ   38 Ⓐ Ⓑ Ⓒ Ⓓ Ⓔ   48 Ⓐ Ⓑ Ⓒ Ⓓ Ⓔ
9 Ⓐ Ⓑ Ⓒ Ⓓ Ⓔ   19 Ⓐ Ⓑ Ⓒ Ⓓ Ⓔ   29 Ⓐ Ⓑ Ⓒ Ⓓ Ⓔ   39 Ⓐ Ⓑ Ⓒ Ⓓ Ⓔ   49 Ⓐ Ⓑ Ⓒ Ⓓ Ⓔ
10 Ⓐ Ⓑ Ⓒ Ⓓ Ⓔ   20 Ⓐ Ⓑ Ⓒ Ⓓ Ⓔ   30 Ⓐ Ⓑ Ⓒ Ⓓ Ⓔ   40 Ⓐ Ⓑ Ⓒ Ⓓ Ⓔ   50 Ⓐ Ⓑ Ⓒ Ⓓ Ⓔ

MATHEMATICS LEVEL 1 TEST

For each of the following problems, decide which is the BEST of the choices given. If the exact numerical value is not one of the choices, select the choice that best approximates this value. Then fill in the corresponding oval on the answer sheet.

<u>Notes:</u> (1) A calculator will be necessary for answering some (but not all) of the questions in this test. For each question you will have to decide whether or not you should use a calcuator. The calculator you use must be at least a scientific calculator; programmable calculators and calculators that can display graphs are permitted.

(2) The only angle measure used on this test is degree measure. Make sure your calculator is in the degree mode.

(3) Figures that accompany problems in this test are intended to provide information useful in solving the problems. They are drawn as accurately as possible EXCEPT when it is stated in a specific problem that its figure is not drawn to scale. All figures lie in a plane unless otherwise indicated.

(4) Unless otherwise specified, the domain of any function f is assumed to be the set of all real numbers x for which $f(x)$ is a real number.

(5) Reference information that may be useful in answering the questions in this test can be found on the page preceding Question 1.

USE THIS SPACE FOR SCRATCHWORK.

1. If $x = 2y$ and if $x + y = 15$, then what is the value of xy?

   (A) 5
   (B) 10
   (C) 15
   (D) 18
   (E) 50

2. If $x^2 = 11$ and if $x^4 y^2 = 363$, then what is the value of y^2?

   (A) 1.73
   (B) 2.73
   (C) 3
   (D) 3.31
   (E) 5.74

3. What is the value of $(2x - 1)(5x + 7)$ if $x = -1$?

   (A) –6 (B) $-\dfrac{5}{2}$ (C) 0 (D) $\dfrac{7}{5}$ (E) 6

4. What is the sum of the distance from point $(1, 5)$ to $(3, 4)$ and from point $(3, 4)$ to $(1, 5)$?

   (A) 1.14   (B) 2.24   (C) 4.47   (D) 5   (E) 5.12

GO ON TO THE NEXT PAGE

USE THIS SPACE FOR SCRATCHWORK.

5. $(x-6)(x+6)=$

   (A) $x^2 - 6$
   (B) $x^2 - 36$
   (C) $x^2 + 6x + 6$
   (D) $x^2 + 12x + 12$
   (E) $x^2 + 12x + 36$

6. What is the slope of the straight line that passes through the points $(3, 4)$ and $(7, 6)$?

   (A) 0
   (B) 0.25
   (C) 0.33
   (D) 0.5
   (E) 1.25

7. If $y = 5x^2$ and $x = -2k$ and $k = \sqrt{3}$, what is the value of y?

   (A) 36   (B) 48   (C) 54   (D) 60   (E) 63

8. What is the measure of angle a in Figure 1?

   (A) 15   (B) 30   (C) 45   (D) 60   (E) 90

9. If $\dfrac{1}{4x-5} = \dfrac{1}{7}$, then what is the value of x?

   (A) 1   (B) 2   (C) 3   (D) 4   (E) 7

10. $\dfrac{x^{-3}}{\frac{1}{2}x^{-5}} =$

   (A) $\dfrac{1}{2x^2}$ (B) $2x^2$ (C) $\dfrac{2}{x^2}$ (D) $\dfrac{1}{x^2}$ (E) $2x$

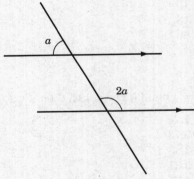

Figure 1

GO ON TO THE NEXT PAGE

11. What is the surface area of the box in Figure 2?

(A) $4x^3$
(B) $6x^2$
(C) $9x^2$
(D) $10x^3$
(E) $14x^2$

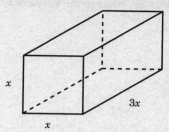

x

$3x$

x

Note: Figure not drawn to scale.
Figure 2

12. A sphere and a cone have the same radius, r, and equal volumes. What is the height of the cone in terms of r?

(A) $\frac{1}{4}r$ (B) $\frac{1}{3}r$ (C) $4r$ (D) $6r$ (E) $2\pi r$

13. Angles b and d are supplementary angles. What is $3 \times (b+d) - b - d$?

(A) 180°
(B) 360°
(C) 420°
(D) 540°
(E) 600°

14. $\left(32^{\frac{1}{3}}\right)^{\frac{3}{5}} =$

(A) $\frac{1}{5}$ (B) 1 (C) 2 (D) 4 (E) 8

15. If $f(x, y, z) = \dfrac{3x+y}{2} + (z+5)$, what is $f(3, 1, 4)$?

(A) 5 (B) 7 (C) 8 (D) 9 (E) 14

16. Of the following numbers, which has the lowest value?

(A) 100000000

(B) 100^{10}

(C) $10^{100} \times 10$

(D) $(10^{10})^{10}$

(E) $(100^{10} \times 10^{10})^{100}$

GO ON TO THE NEXT PAGE

17. If $x^2 + 1 = -2x$, what is the value of x?

    (A) −1.41
    (B) −1
    (C) 0
    (D) 1
    (E) 1.41

18. If A and B are independent events with probabilities $\frac{2}{5}$ and $\frac{3}{5}$, what is the probability that events A and B both occur?

    (A) $\frac{6}{25}$ (B) $\frac{1}{4}$ (C) $\frac{1}{2}$ (D) 1 (E) $\frac{6}{5}$

19. In Figure 3, circle O and square $ABCD$ have equal areas. If the radius of O is 6, what is the perimeter of $ABCD$?

    (A) 12π
    (B) $18\sqrt{\pi}$
    (C) 18π
    (D) $24\sqrt{\pi}$
    (E) $36\sqrt{\pi}$

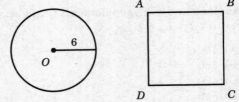

Note: Figure not drawn to scale.
Figure 3

20. For what values of x is $|4x - 7| = 17$?

    (A) −6

    (B) $-\frac{5}{2}$

    (C) $-6, \frac{5}{2}$

    (D) $-\frac{5}{2}, 6$

    (E) $\frac{5}{2}, 6$

21. Amy, Arnold, and Annika all want to take an art class, but there is only one slot left. Also, Beth and Brigette are competing for a slot in the biology class. If the principal of the school has to select who gets into the two classes, how many different possibilities does he have to choose from?

    (A) 2 (B) 3 (C) 6 (D) 9 (E) 12

GO ON TO THE NEXT PAGE

22. An isosceles triangle has two sides of lengths 3 and 7. Which of the following represents all of the possible values of the length of the third side, A?

   (A) $A = 3$
   (B) $A = 7$
   (C) $A = 3$ or $A = 7$
   (D) $3 < A < 7$
   (E) It is impossible to calculate A.

23. In Figure 4, $\dfrac{n \cos \theta}{x} =$

   (A) 0   (B) 1   (C) x (D) x^2 (E) $\dfrac{y}{x}$

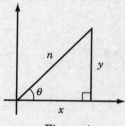

Figure 4

24. A rectangle is intersected by two semicircles in Figure 5. What is the area of the figure?

   (A) 45.73
   (B) 50.27
   (C) 79.87
   (D) 98.25
   (E) 112.38

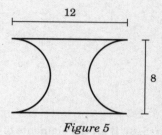

Figure 5

25. $i^5 + i^3 - i^6 =$

   (A) 1   (B) $-i$ (C) $2i$ (D) -1 (E) 2

26. What is the area of the trapezoid in Figure 6?

   (A) $72 + 16\sqrt{3}$
   (B) $88 + 16\sqrt{3}$
   (C) $96 + 24\sqrt{3}$
   (D) $108 + 12\sqrt{3}$
   (E) $144 + 24\sqrt{3}$

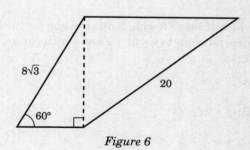

Figure 6

GO ON TO THE NEXT PAGE

27. If $f(x) = 2x + 2$, what is $f(x + 1)$?

 (A) $2x + 2$
 (B) $2x + 3$
 (C) $3x + 3$
 (D) $2x + 4$
 (E) $3x + 4$

28. Which of the following must be true if $m < l$ and $p < q$?

 (A) $m < q$
 (B) $mp < lq$
 (C) $m + p < l + q$
 (D) $m - p < l - q$
 (E) $2m + l < 2p + q$

29. If $f(x, y) = (7x, 4y + 2)$, what is the distance from $(3, 1)$ to $f(3, 1)$?

 (A) 0
 (B) 4
 (C) 16.34
 (D) 18.68
 (E) 26

30. $S = \{1, 4, 5, 5, 8\}$. If all the elements of S that are smaller than the median of S are removed, what is the mean of the new set?

 (A) 1.6
 (B) 3.75
 (C) 5.5
 (D) 6
 (E) 6.5

31. Which of the following is an equation for the line that is perpendicular to $y = 6x + 1$ and which passes through points $(4, 1)$?

 (A) $y = 6x$

 (B) $y = 6x - 23$

 (C) $y = \dfrac{x}{6} + \dfrac{1}{3}$

 (D) $y = -\dfrac{x}{6} + \dfrac{1}{3}$

 (E) $y = -\dfrac{x}{6} + \dfrac{5}{3}$

GO ON TO THE NEXT PAGE

32. The bases of the solid in Figure 7 are right triangles with legs of lengths 4 and 8. If the volume of the solid is 96, what is its height, h?

(A) 4   (B) 6   (C) 10   (D) 12   (E) 16

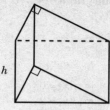

Figure 7

33. $\dfrac{x^3 - 1}{x - 1} =$

(A) $x^2 + 1$
(B) $x^2 - 1$
(C) $x^2 - x - 1$
(D) $x^2 + x + 1$
(E) $x^2 + x - 1$

34. In Figure 8, ABC is an equilateral triangle. If D and E are the midpoints of AB and BC, respectively, and $DE = 6$, what is the area of the shaded region?

(A) 9
(B) $6\sqrt{3}$
(C) $12\sqrt{3}$
(D) $27\sqrt{3}$
(E) $36\sqrt{3}$

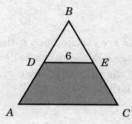

Figure 8

35. $\tan^2\theta \, \cos^2\theta + \dfrac{\sin^2\theta}{\tan^2\theta} - 2 = ?$

(A) $-2\sqrt{\pi} - 2$

(B) -1

(C) 0

(D) $\dfrac{2\sqrt{\pi}}{2}$

(E) $2\sqrt{\pi} + 2$

GO ON TO THE NEXT PAGE

36. A portion of the graph of $y = f(x)$ is shown in Figure 9. What is the range of $f(x)$?

   (A) $-\infty < f(x) < \infty$
   (B) $f(x) > 0$
   (C) $f(x) < 2$
   (D) $-\infty < f(x) < \infty, f(x) \neq 0$
   (E) $-\infty < f(x) < \infty, f(x) \neq 2$

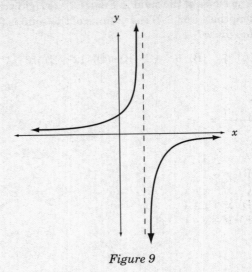

Figure 9

37. 3 tennis balls are stacked in a cylindrical canister such that there is no space between the balls and the top, bottom, or sides of the can. If the volume of the can is 20.25π, what is the volume of 1 ball?

   (A) 3.3π
   (B) 4.5π
   (C) 5.25π
   (D) 9.67π
   (E) 13.5π

38. The line with equation $y = x + 2$ is graphed on the same xy–plane as the circle with center $(-5, 2)$ and radius 5. At what points do the line and circle intersect?

   (A) $(0, 2)$ and $(-5, -3)$
   (B) $(-2, 6)$ and $(-1.4, 5.5)$
   (C) $(-7, 6.6)$ and $(-2, -2)$
   (D) $(2, 4)$ and $(0, -4)$
   (E) $(-8.3, -1.8)$ and $(-0.1, 1)$

GO ON TO THE NEXT PAGE

39. In Figure 10, the area of rhombus *ABCD* is equal to the area of an equilateral triangle. What is the length of one side of the triangle?

(A) 10
(B) $2\sqrt{6}$
(C) $4\sqrt{3}$
(D) $8\sqrt{3}$
(E) $6\sqrt{2}$

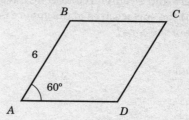

Note: Figure not drawn to scale.

Figure 10

40. A bottle of wine that increases in value at the rate of 9% per year will be worth $500 in 22 years. What is its current value?

(A) 75   (B) 94   (C) 111   (D) 198   (E) 302

41. The circle and the regular hexagon in Figure 11 have centers at *O*. The area of the circle is 64π. What is the area of the hexagon?

(A) 132.55
(B) 166.28
(C) 179.71
(D) 210.06
(E) 233.33

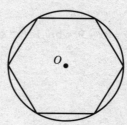

Figure 11

42. For what values of x is the expression $\dfrac{x^2-16}{2x^2+7x-4}$ undefined?

(A) 3

(B) $\dfrac{1}{2}$

(C) 0 and 3

(D) −4 and 4

(E) $\dfrac{1}{2}$ and −4

GO ON TO THE NEXT PAGE

USE THIS SPACE FOR SCRATCHWORK.

43. A sphere and a right circular cone have the same volumes and radii. If the surface area of the sphere is 36π, what is the lateral height of the cone?

(A) 3
(B) $6\sqrt{3}$
(C) $3\sqrt{17}$
(D) 9π
(E) 144

44. $\sin\theta > 0$, $\cos\theta < 0$, and $\tan\theta < 0$ for which of the following ranges of θ?

(A) $0° < \theta < 90°$
(B) $90° < \theta < 180°$
(C) $180° < \theta < 270°$
(D) $270° < \theta < 360°$
(E) none

45. If $f(g(x + 3)) = 2x + 9$, what is $f(g(2x))$?

(A) $6x$
(B) $6x - 6$
(C) $4x$
(D) $4x + 3$
(E) $4x + 6$

GO ON TO THE NEXT PAGE

46. If $f(x) = \sqrt{2x-5}$ and $g(y) = \dfrac{1}{y}$, what is the domain of $g(f(x))$?

  (A) $x > 0$

  (B) $x > \dfrac{5}{2}$

  (C) $x \neq \dfrac{5}{2}$

  (D) $0 \le x \le 5$

  (E) $x < \dfrac{5}{2}$

47. *ABCD*, in Figure 12, is a square. What is the ratio of the area of triangle *PQC* to the area of triangle *RQD*?

  (A) $\dfrac{1}{4}$ (B) $\dfrac{1}{3}$ (C) $\dfrac{\sqrt{3}}{3}$ (D) $\dfrac{\sqrt{3}}{2}$ (E) $\dfrac{2\sqrt{3}}{3}$

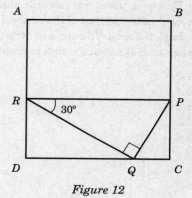

Figure 12

48. A parabola with a vertex at $(-1, 4)$ passes through the point $(1, 8)$ and is tangent to the line $y = -4(x + 1)$. At what point do the line and parabola intersect?

  (A) $(-4, 13)$
  (B) $(2, -12)$
  (C) $(0, 5)$
  (D) $(-3, 8)$
  (E) $(-1, 4)$

GO ON TO THE NEXT PAGE

49. The square and the 2 circles in Figure 13 have centers at O. The radius, r, of the larger circle is twice that of the small circle. If the area of the square is 192 and the ratio $\frac{r}{d} = \frac{1}{2}$, what is the area of the shaded region?

(A) 136.67
(B) 140.42
(C) 144.88
(D) 154.30
(E) 163.73

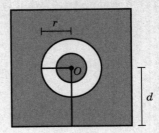

Figure 13

50. A hiker needs to cross a river. Her only option is to canoe across. However, the canoe can only support a weight that is 240 percent of the weight of the canoe. If the hiker, who weighs 120 pounds, takes up 76 percent of the canoe's weight capacity, how much does the canoe weigh in pounds?

(A) 47.2
(B) 55.4
(C) 59.2
(D) 60.3
(E) 65.8

S T O P

IF YOU FINISH BEFORE TIME IS CALLED, YOU MAY CHECK YOUR WORK ON THIS TEST ONLY.
DO NOT TURN TO ANY OTHER TEST IN THIS BOOK.

SAT Math Level 1 Practice Test II Explanations

Answers to SAT Math Level 1 Practice Test II

Question Number	Answer	Right	Wrong	Question Number	Answer	Right	Wrong
1	E			26	C		
2	C			27	D		
3	A			28	C		
4	C			29	D		
5	B			30	D		
6	D			31	E		
7	D			32	B		
8	D			33	D		
9	C			34	D		
10	B			35	B		
11	E			36	D		
12	C			37	B		
13	B			38	A		
14	C			39	E		
15	E			40	A		
16	A			41	B		
17	B			42	E		
18	A			43	C		
19	D			44	B		
20	D			45	D		
21	C			46	B		
22	B			47	B		
23	B			48	D		
24	A			49	E		
25	A			50	E		

Calculating Your Score

Your raw score for the SAT Math Level 1 test is based on the number of questions you answer correctly and incorrectly. Once you have determined your raw score, use the conversion table on page 15 of this book to calculate your scaled score.

To Calculate Your Raw Score

1. Count the number of questions you answered correctly: _____ (A)

2. Count the number of questions you answered incorrectly, and multiply that number by ¼: _____ (B) × ¼ = _____ (C)

3. Subtract the value in (C) from value in (A): _____ (D)

4. Round the number in (D) to the nearest whole number. This is your raw score: _____ (E)

Math Level 1 Test II Explanations

1. E Equation Solving

We are given two equations to solve for two unknowns. In cases like this, simply solve for one variable in one class and replace that variable in the second equation. Since we're given $x = 2y$, we don't have to do much solving; we can simply substitute $2y$ for x in $x + y = 15$. Once that substitution is made, we now have $3y = 15$. Dividing both sides by 3 gives us $y = 5$. Now that we've solved for y, it is straightforward to solve for x: $x = 2y = 2(5) = 10$. Therefore, the quantity $xy = (10)(5) = 50$.

2. C Equation Solving

Since the question asks us to find the value of y^2, our first goal is to find the other variable, x^4. Since we know that $x^2 = 11$, we can simply square that value to find the value of $x^4 = (x^2)^2 = (11)^2 = 121$. Substituting this value into the original equation we get:

$$121y^2 = 363$$

Dividing both sides by 121 gives:

$$y^2 = \frac{363}{121} = 3$$

3. A Polynomials

Just plug -1 in for x and then carry out the operations:

$$(2x - 1)(5x + 7) = (2(-1) - 1)(5(-1) + 7)$$
$$= (-2 - 1)(-5 + 7)$$
$$= -6$$

4. C Lines and Distance

It might take you a second to notice that the distance from $(1, 5)$ to $(3, 4)$ and from $(3, 4)$ to $(1, 5)$ are the same, since the endpoints of the line segment are the same. So, all we really have to do is find the distance between $(1, 5)$ and $(3, 4)$ and then double it. In order to find the distance between two points, (x_1, y_1) and (x_2, y_2), use the distance formula $d = \sqrt{(x_2 - x_1)^2 + (y_2 - y_1)^2}$:

$$\text{distance} = \sqrt{(1 - 3)^2 + (5 - 4)^2}$$
$$= \sqrt{(-2)^2 + (1)^2}$$
$$= \sqrt{5}$$
$$= 2.236; \text{ doubled, you get } 4.472, \text{ which rounds to } 4.47$$

5. B Polynomials

The straightforward way of solving this problem is to use the FOIL method to expand the binomials: $(x - 6)(x + 6) = x^2 + 6x - 6x - 36 = x^2 - 36$. However, if you can recognize these binomials as a difference of squares you can find the expansion immediately. Recall the general formula for the difference of squares: $(a + b)(a - b) = a^2 - b^2$. In this problem, $a = x$ and $b = 6$, so the answer is $x^2 - 6^2 = x^2 - 36$.

6. D Lines and Distance

The slope of a line represents the rate at which it rises or falls as x changes. Since we are given two points, we can simply use the general formula for the slope, m, of a line:

$$m = \frac{y_2 - y_1}{x_2 - x_1}$$
$$\frac{y_2 - y_1}{x_2 - x_1} = \frac{6 - 4}{7 - 3} = \frac{2}{4} = .5$$

7.　**D**　Equation Solving

Since you're given k, you can easily solve for x; once you've got x, it's pretty simple to find y. Since $k = \sqrt{3}$, $x = -2\sqrt{3}$. Plugging this value of x into $y = 5x^2$:

$$y = 5(-2\sqrt{3})^2$$
$$= 5\,(4)(3)$$
$$= 60$$

8.　**D**　Lines and Angles

As shown in the figure below, when two parallel lines are cut by a transversal, the alternate exterior angles are congruent.

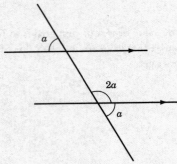

This means that angles a and $2a$ are supplementary, so $a + 2a = 3a = 180$ and $a = 60$.

9.　**C**　Equation Solving

To solve for x, you need to cross-multiply and then isolate x on one side of the equation:

$$\frac{1}{4x - 5} = \frac{1}{7}$$
$$4x - 5 = 7$$
$$4x = 12$$
$$x = 3$$

10.　**B**　Equation Solving

Since $x^{-1} = 1/x^1$ by definition, we can rearrange the expression so that we're dealing with positive exponents:

$$\frac{x^{-3}}{\frac{1}{2}x^{-5}} = \frac{2x^5}{x^3}$$

From here, we can use the division rule of exponents to simplify the expression:

$$\frac{2x^5}{x^3} = 2x^{5-3} = 2x^2$$

11.　**E**　Prisms, Solids That Aren't Prisms

The surface area of a box is just the sum of the areas of each face. This particular box has two congruent ends and four congruent sides. The area of each end is $x \times x = x^2$ and the area of each side is $3x \times x = 3x^2$. Now we just have to sum the surface areas of the six sides.

$$\text{Surface area of box} = 2(x^2) + 4(3x^2)$$
$$= 2x^2 + 12x^2$$
$$= 14x^2$$

12. **C** Prisms, Solids That Aren't Prisms

Since the two objects have equal volume, we can set their volume equations equal to each other. This will leave us with one equation and one variable, the height, which we can solve easily.

volume of sphere = volume of cone

$$\frac{4}{3}\pi r^3 = \frac{1}{3}\pi r^2 h$$
$$4r = h$$

13. **B** Lines and Angles

The first step is to remember that supplementary angles always sum to 180°. The next step is to see that $-b - d$ can be expressed as $-(b + d)$. From here, it's pretty straightforward to solve:

$$3 \times (b + d) - b - d = 3 \times (b + d) - (b + d)$$
$$= 3 \times 180 - 180$$
$$= 360$$

14. **C** Equation Solving

This question is just testing your knowledge of the power rule of exponents. Remember that when raising an exponent to another exponent, simply multiply the exponents together:

$$(32^{1/3})^{3/5} = 32^{1/3 \times 3/5}$$
$$= 32^{1/5}$$
$$= 2$$

15. **E** Evaluating Functions

In order to evaluate this function, we simply substitute the appropriate values for x, y, and z. Substituting 3 for x, 1 for y, and 4 for z gives:

$$f(x, y, z) = \frac{3x + y}{2} + (z + 5)$$
$$= \frac{3 \times 3 + 1}{2} + (4 + 5)$$
$$= 5 + 9$$
$$= 14$$

16. **A** Fundamentals

This question is made much easier because all of the choices are powers of ten. You can rewrite choice **A** as 10^8. At this point, hopefully you can see that all of the other choices are larger. If not, we'll rewrite each one as a power of 10: B = 10^{20}, C = 10^{11}, D = 10^{101}, and E = 10^{3000}. Clearly, **A** is the smallest.

17. **B** Equation Solving

To solve this quadratic equation for x, just move all the terms to one side and try to factor it. Adding $2x$ to both sides, we get $x^2 + 2x + 1 = 0$. This is a perfect square binomial, which can be factored to $(x + 1)^2$. Taking the square root of both sides, we get $x + 1 = \sqrt{0} = 0$, and $x = -1$.

18. **A** Probability

Since the two events are independent, the probability that both events occur is simply the product of their individual probabilities. In this case, the probability of events A and B occurring is probability of event A × probability of event $B = \frac{2}{5} \times \frac{3}{5} = \frac{6}{25}$.

19. D   Circles

Since you are told that the two areas are equal, you can simply set the two respective area equations equal to each other. This will leave us with one equation and only one variable, the length of a side, s, of square $ABCD$:

$$\pi r^2 = s^2$$
$$\pi(6)^2 = s^2$$
$$36\pi = s^2$$
$$s = 6\sqrt{\pi}$$

So, the perimeter of $ABCD$ is $4 \times 6\sqrt{\pi} = 24\sqrt{\pi}$.

20. D   Equation Solving

Because of the absolute value sign in the equation, you should immediately be on the lookout for two solutions, one where $4x - 7 = 17$ and another where $4x - 7 = -17$. Break this problem into two parts, and solve each one separately:

$$4x - 7 = 17$$
$$4x = 24$$
$$x = 6$$

$$4x - 7 = -17$$
$$4x = -10$$
$$x = -\frac{10}{4} = -\frac{5}{2}$$

21. C   Permutations and Combinations

Since each of his choices are independent of the other (there's no overlap), we can simply multiply the number of possible outcomes. Since he has 3 choices for the art class and two choices for the biology class, there are a total of $2 \times 3 = 6$ possibilities.

22. B   Triangle

There are two important pieces to this problem. First, since we are dealing with a triangle, you should remember the rule that no single side of a triangle can be longer than the sum of the other two sides. Second, since this particular triangle is an isosceles triangle, we know that two sides must have equal length. Here are the two ways that an isosceles triangle could satisfy the given information.

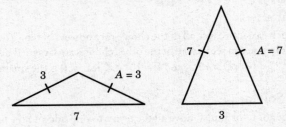

But wait! The 3-3-7 triangle violates the above rule, since $3 + 3 < 7$. So while you might be tempted to select **C**, it is the wrong answer. **B** is correct.

23. B   Basic Functions and the Right Triangle

As long as you remember that $\cos\theta = {}^{\text{adjacent}}/_{\text{hypotenuse}}$, this problem is straightforward. This means that $\cos\theta = {}^{x}/_{n}$, and the original expression becomes ${}^{n \times x}/_{n \times x}$, which simplifies to 1.

24. **A** Circles

The two semicircles together form a full circle, so the area of the figure is simply the area of the rectangle minus the area of the circle. First find the area of the rectangle:

Area of rectangle = 12 × 8 = 96

Note that **D** and **E** can be eliminated immediately, since both are greater than the area of the rectangle alone. Now we find the area, πr^2, of the circle. The circle has a diameter of 8, and therefore has a radius of 4.

Area of circle = $\pi(4)^2$ = 16 π

The area of the figure is 96 – 16π = 45.73.

25. **A** Imaginary and Complex Numbers

The most important thing about i that you need to know for the Math IC is how to raise i to powers. Here's a chart worth understanding (or memorizing):

$i^1 = i$ $\qquad\qquad$ $i^5 = i$
$i^2 = -1$ $\qquad\qquad$ $i^6 = -1$
$i^3 = -i$ $\qquad\qquad$ $i^7 = -i$
$i^4 = 1$ $\qquad\qquad$ $i^8 = 1...$

From here, it's easy to determine the values needed to solve this problem:

$$i^5 + i^3 - i^6 = i + (-i) - (-1)$$
$$= i - i + 1$$
$$= 1$$

26. **C** Polygons

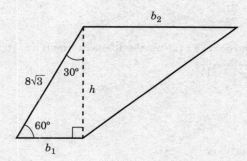

Because the height of the trapezoid makes a right angle with b_1, it creates a 30-60-90 triangle. So the sides have the x: $x\sqrt{3}$: $2x$ relationship. Since the hypotenuse of this triangle is $8\sqrt{3}$, $b_1 = {}^{b\sqrt{3}}\!/_2 = 4\sqrt{3}$ and $h = (4\sqrt{3})(\sqrt{3}) = 12$.

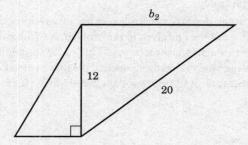

Now we have a triangle with sides that are a multiple of the 3-4-5 Pythagorean triple. Since $12 = 3 \times 4$ and $20 = 5 \times 4$, $b_2 = 4 \times 4 = 16$. Finally, you can use the area formula of a trapezoid, $\frac{1}{2}(b_1 + b_2)h$:

$$\text{Area of trapezoid} = \frac{1}{2}(16 + 4\sqrt{3})(12) = 96 + 24\sqrt{3}$$

27. D   Evaluating Functions

When asked to evaluate a function for a variable expression, all you need to do is substitute the given expression for x. In this case, replace x with $x + 1$:

$$f(x + 1) = 2(x + 1) + 2$$
$$= 2x + 4$$

28. C   Fundamentals

A sure-fire way to solve this problem is to analyze each answer choice. **A** and **E** are wrong because the question doesn't tell you anything about the relationship between m and q, or between l and p. **C** and **D** essentially say the opposite of each other, so they can't both be right, and **C** makes the most sense: the sum of the two smaller numbers will always be smaller than the sum of two larger numbers. This analysis would also seem to make choice **B** always true, but remember that the product of two large negative numbers is greater than the product of two small positive numbers. If this kind of abstract analysis is tough for you, look for an answer choice that seems false, and try to find a set of numbers that disproves it. Even if you're not able to eliminate all four wrong answers, you should be able to rule out a few quickly and put yourself in a good position to guess.

29. D   Lines and Distance

Finding the distance between two points only requires the distance formula. But first, we must find the second point, $f(3, 1)$:

$$f(3, 1) = (7 \times 3, (4 \times 1) + 2)$$
$$= (21, 6)$$

Now that we know the second point, we can use the distance formula $d = \sqrt{(x_2 - x_1)^2 + (y_2 - y_1)^2}$:

$$\text{distance} = \sqrt{(21 - 3)^2 + (6 - 1)^2}$$
$$= \sqrt{18^2 + 5^2}$$
$$= \sqrt{349}$$
$$= 18.68$$

30. D   Statistical Analysis

The median of a set is the middle element of the ordered set. S has five elements that are already in ascending order, so the median of S is the third element of the set. The median is 5, so we must remove the 1 and the 4, leaving a set with 3 numbers: $\{5, 5, 8\}$. The mean of this set is $\frac{5 + 5 + 8}{3} = \frac{18}{3} = 6$.

31. E   Lines and Distance

As long as you remember that the slopes of perpendicular lines are reciprocal and opposite, you'll be just fine on this question. The slope of the line given in the problem is 6 (the x coefficient in slope–intercept form), so the slope of the line through $(4,1)$ must be $-\frac{1}{6}$. That's a big accomplishment, because even if you do nothing else on this problem, you've already eliminated the first 3 answer choices. Now you just need to find the y–intercept by substituting $(4,1)$ into $y = -\frac{x}{6} + b$ and solving for b:

$$y = -\frac{x}{6} + b$$

$$1 = -\frac{4}{6} + b$$

$$\frac{5}{3} = b$$

32. **B** Prisms, Solids That Aren't Prisms

The formula for the volume is volume = base × height. This is all we need to solve for the height since we know the other two quantities. Just figure out the area of the base and substitute the given volume:

$$\text{volume} = \frac{1}{2}(4)(8)h$$

$$96 = 16h$$

$$h = 6$$

33. **D** Polynomials

As a sophisticated test-taker, you should be able to see some hints in this problem. Since you are not given any values to plug in, you should be expecting $(x-1)$ to be a factor of (x^3-1). After all, if it's not, there's not a whole lot you can do. If you're not comfortable factoring x^3-1, don't despair, you could, as a last resort, try multiplying $(x-1)$ by each of the answer choices until you get (x^3-1). Since that type of working backward is time-consuming, you're probably better off trying to factor the numerator. A good way to do this is to try to generate the highest term (x^3) first. Since your binomial $(x-1)$ has x as its highest term, you'll need to have an x^2 term in your new expression. So far we have $x^3 - 1 = (x-1)(x^2 + \ldots)$.

We've successfully created an x^3 term, but now we've also created a $-x^2$ term since $-1 \times x^2 = -x^2$. It looks like we'll need a positive x^2 term, which we can generate by simply adding an x to the new expression: $x^3 - 1 = (x-1)(x^2 + x + \ldots)$.

Of course, as you may have caught on, we've now created an extra $-x$, so we'll need to repeat the process and add a 1 to our new expression: $x^3 - 1 = (x-1)(x^2 + x + 1 \ldots)$. Fortunately, there's already a -1 in the term we're trying to factor, so there's no need to worry about that term. Let's double-check to make sure that the product of the two factors is indeed the original expression:

$$(x-1)(x^2 + x + 1) = x^3 - x^2 + x^2 - x + x - 1$$
$$= x^3 - 1$$

34. **D** Triangle

$\angle BDE = \angle BAC$ and $\angle BED = \angle BCA$, so triangles BDE and ABC are similar triangles. BDE is therefore an equilateral triangle, so all of its sides have length 6. Since it is given that D and E are midpoints of AB and BC, respectively, then $AB = BC = AC = (2)(6) = 12$.

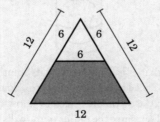

You can find the area of the shaded region by subtracting the area of the small triangle from the area of the larger triangle. But an easier method is to find the area of the shaded trapezoid. Drawing in the height of the trapezoid, we get a 30-60-90 triangle:

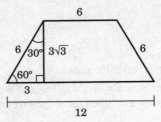

So $h = 3\sqrt{3}$, and area $= \frac{1}{2}(6 + 12)(3\sqrt{3}) = (9)(3\sqrt{3}) = 27\sqrt{3}$.

35. **B**   Trigonometric Identities

As long as you know the basic trigonometric identities, solving this problem only requires some simple substitution. First you have to remember that the tangent function can be expressed in terms of sine and cosine: $\tan \theta = \frac{\sin \theta}{\cos \theta}$. This will allow you to make some substitutions and cancel some terms. Then, all you will need is the Pythagorean Identity, $\sin^2\theta + \cos^2\theta = 1$. Substitute and solve:

$$\tan^2\theta \cos^2\theta + \frac{\sin^2\theta}{\tan^2\theta} - 2 = \frac{\sin^2\theta}{\cos^2\theta}\cos^2\theta + \frac{\sin^2\theta \cos^2\theta}{\sin^2\theta} - 2$$
$$= \sin^2\theta + \cos^2\theta - 2$$
$$= 1 - 2$$
$$= -1$$

36. **D**   Graphing Functions

The range of a function is the set of all values of $f(x)$. So, to find the range in this question, you can simply observe which values of y are included in the graph. These values include all real numbers, excluding any point where $y = 0$ (the line $y = 0$ is a horizontal asymptote).

37. **B**   Prisms, Solids That Aren't Prisms

This question sounds a little harder than it is, only because its solution may not be immediately obvious. The first step is to figure out what you need to know in order to calculate the volume of 1 ball. The formula for the volume of a sphere is $V = \frac{4}{3}\pi r^3$, so you only need to know the ball's radius. If we were given the radius of the canister, we would be all set, since the radius of the balls and the radius of the can are the same. Fortunately, since the balls are stacked so that they touch both the top and bottom of the can, we also know that the height of the can is equal to 6 times the radius of each ball. We're given the volume of the cylinder as 20.25π, so we can work backward to find r:

$$\pi r^2(h) = 20.25\pi$$
$$\pi r^2(6r) = 20.25\pi$$
$$6\pi r^3 = 20.25\pi$$
$$r^3 = 3.375$$
$$r = 1.5$$

So the volume of a ball is $\frac{4}{3}\pi(1.5)^3 = 4.5\pi$.

38. **A**   Other Important Graphs and Equations

The equation of a circle with center (h, k) and radius r is:

$$(x - h)^2 + (y - k)^2 = r^2$$

So, the equation of this circle is:

$$(x + 5)^2 + (y - 2)^2 = 25$$

We are given the equation of the line to be $y = x + 2$. To find where the circle and line intersect, plug in $x + 2$ for y in the equation of the circle and solve for x:

$$(x + 5)^2 + ((x + 2) - 2)^2 = 25$$
$$(x + 5)^2 + (x)^2 = 25$$
$$x^2 + 10x + 25 + x^2 = 25$$
$$2x^2 - 10x = 0$$
$$2x(x + 5) = 0$$

So, $x = 0$ or $x = -5$.

39. **E**   Polygons

First we need to find the area of the rhombus, which is given by the formula area = base × height. By definition, a rhombus has sides of equal length, so the base is equal to 6 as well. We just need to find the height.

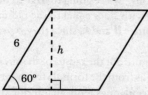

By drawing in the height of the parallelogram, we find a 30-60-90 triangle whose sides have the relationship $x : x\sqrt{3} : 2x$. The height is the side opposite the 60° angle, and is equal to $6\left(\frac{\sqrt{3}}{2}\right) = 3\sqrt{3}$. We can now solve for the area of the rhombus:

Area of rhombus $= (3\sqrt{3})(6) = 18\sqrt{3}$

The area, A, of an equilateral triangle is given by the formula $A = \frac{1}{2}sh$.

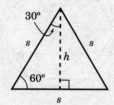

In an equilateral triangle, the height is the $x\sqrt{3}$ side of the 30-60-90 triangle, and the area of the equilateral triangle $= \frac{1}{2}(s)(\frac{\sqrt{3}}{2}s) = \frac{\sqrt{3}}{4}s^2$.

We can now set the area of the rhombus and the area of the equilateral triangle equal to each other and solve for s:

$$18\sqrt{3} = \frac{\sqrt{3}}{4}s^2$$
$$72 = s^2$$
$$s = 6\sqrt{2}$$

40. **A**   Equation Solving

You just need to remember the general formula for compounding rate problems: $P = P_o(1+r)^n$, where P is the ending price, P_o is the initial price, r is the rate, and n is the number of compounding units (in this case, years). The problem gives us almost everything we need to know:

$$P = 500$$
$$r = 9\% = 0.09$$
$$n = 22$$

Substitute these values into the equation above and solve for P_o:

$$P = P_o(1 + r)^n$$
$$500 = P_o(1+.09)^{22}$$
$$500 = P_o(1.09)^{22}$$
$$P_o = \frac{500}{1.09^{22}}$$
$$P_o \approx 75$$

41. **B**   Triangle

Since this problem is among the more difficult ones, it is a good idea to think about how you are going to solve it before you begin any calculations. We're going to have to find the area of the hexagon by breaking it up into smaller equilateral triangles with sides equal to the radius of the circle. It's also a good time to notice that you can immediately eliminate **D** and **E**, since they represent areas greater than the area of the circle alone.

The first step of the solution is to figure out the radius of the circle. Since we are told that the area of the circle is 64π, we can determine the radius from the formula for the area of a circle: $A = \pi r^2 = 64\pi$. Solving for r, we discover that $r = 8$. Since O is a regular hexagon, all interior angles are equal. The sum of the n angles in a regular polygon with n sides is $180(n-2)$, so for a hexagon, $n = 6$, and $180(6-2) = 720$. We can then figure out that each angle is $720 \div 6 = 120°$.

Now, if we draw in the diameters of the circle that bisect each angle of the hexagon, 6 equilateral triangles are created. Since the radius of the circle is 8, each side of the triangle is also 8:

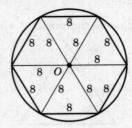

To find the area of one triangle, we draw in the height to create a 30-60-90 triangle:

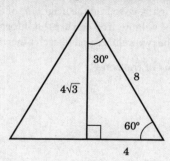

The area of the triangle is $\frac{1}{2}(8)(4\sqrt{3}) = 16\sqrt{3}$. The area of the hexagon, which is made up of 6 of these triangles, is $6 \times 16\sqrt{3} = 96\sqrt{3} \approx 166.28$.

42. E Domain and Range

A fraction is undefined when its denominator equals 0, so this function will be undefined when $2x^2 + 7x - 4 = 0$. To find the values of x that produce 0, first factor the expression:

$$2x^2 + 7x - 4 = 0$$
$$(2x - 1)(x + 4) = 0$$

So, $2x - 1 = 0$ or $x + 4 = 0$, leaving us with $x = \frac{1}{2}$ or $x = -4$. The denominator equals 0 and the fraction is undefined for $x = \frac{1}{2}$ and $x = -4$, or **E**.

   Note that the expression $(x^2 - 16)/(2x^2 + 7x - 4)$ may be factored as $\{(x - 4)(x + 4)\}/\{(2x - 1)(x + 4)\}$ and $x + 4$ can be canceled from both the numerator and denominator. However, the function is still undefined at $x = -4$, and the correct answer is still **E**. The ability to simplify this function to $(x - 4)/(2x - 1)$ means that the limit of the function as x approaches -4 can be calculated.

43. C Prisms, Solids That Aren't Prisms

In order to find the lateral height of the cone, you first need to find the radius, r, and the height, h. Then you can use the Pythagorean theorem to find l.

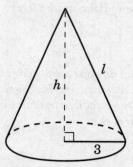

From the question, you know that the radius of the cone is equal to the radius of the sphere. Since the question tells you the surface area of the sphere is 36π, it is possible to use the formula for sphere surface area to calculate the radius of the sphere, thereby giving you the radius of the cone.

   surface area of a sphere $= 4\pi r^2$
   $36\pi = 4\pi r^2$
   $9 = r^2$
   $r = 3$

Now you just have to find the lateral height (l) of the cone to calculate the total surface area. But there's another step: in order to find l, you first have to find the height (h) of the cone. The question tells you that the sphere and the cone have the same volume. You can use this information to find the height of the cone by setting the volume equations of the two solids equal to each other:

volume of the sphere = volume of the cone

$$\frac{4}{3}\pi r^3 = \frac{1}{3}\pi r^2 h$$

$$\frac{4}{3}\pi \, 3^3 = \frac{1}{3}\pi \, 3^2 h$$

$$27\,\frac{4}{3}\pi = 9\,\frac{1}{3}\pi h$$

$$3\,\frac{4}{3}\pi = \frac{1}{3}\pi h$$

$$3\,\frac{4}{3} = \frac{1}{3}h$$

$$4 = \frac{1}{3}h$$

$$4 \times 3 = h$$

$$h = 12$$

Now you can use the Pythagorean theorem to find the lateral height of the cone:

$$l^2 = r^2 + h^2$$
$$l^2 = 3^2 + 12^2$$
$$l = \sqrt{9 + 144}$$
$$l = 3\sqrt{17}$$

44. B   Basic Functions and the Right Triangle

Recall that each of the major trigonometric functions takes on both positive and negative values depending on which quadrant the angle falls in. In the first quadrant, all three functions are positive. In the second quadrant, sine is positive and both cosine and tangent are negative. In the second quadrant, θ is between 90° and 180°.

45. D   Evaluating Functions

This question is asking "What operations do you have to perform on $(x + 3)$ to get $2x + 9$?" It then wants you to perform these operations on $2x$. Since the x term becomes $2x$, the first operation must be to multiply by 2 (so $g(x) = 2x$). Since this gives you $2x + 6$, the next operation must be to add 3, so $f(x) = x + 3$. Now you plug $2x$ into these functions to find your answer:

$$f(g(2x)) = 2(2x) + 3$$
$$= 4x + 3$$

46. B   Domain and Range

In order to find $g(f(x))$, we plug $f(x)$ into $g(y)$. That is,

$$g(f(x)) = \frac{1}{\sqrt{2x - 5}}$$

There are two rules that could potentially limit the domain of this function. First, the denominator of a fraction cannot be equal to 0, so you need to find which values of x produce a value of 0:

$$\sqrt{2x-5} \neq 0$$
$$2x-5 \neq 0$$
$$2x \neq 5$$
$$x \neq \frac{5}{2}$$

Second, you can't take the square root of a negative number, so, again, find the values of x that could cause this to happen:

$$2x-5 \geq 0$$
$$2x \geq 5$$
$$x \geq \frac{5}{2}$$

From above, we know that $x \neq \frac{5}{2}$ and $x \geq \frac{5}{2}$, so the answer must be $x > \frac{5}{2}$.

47. **B** Triangle

Let each side of the square have length s. Triangle PQR is a 30-60-90 triangle with hypotenuse $PR = s$:

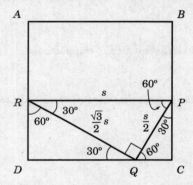

It follows that if $\angle PRQ = 30°$, then $\angle QRD = 60°$. Similarly, if $\angle RPQ = 60°$, then $\angle QPC = 30°$.

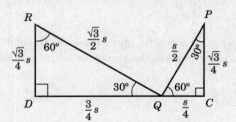

As you can see, both triangles PQC and RQD are 30-60-90 triangles. Using the values for PQ and RQ found above, we can calculate the areas of each of the triangles:

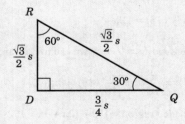

$$\text{Area of triangle } RQD = \left(\frac{1}{2}\right)\left(\frac{3}{4}s\right)\left(\frac{\sqrt{3}}{2}s\right) = \frac{3}{8}s = \frac{3\sqrt{3}}{16}s^2$$

$$\text{Area of triangle } PQC = \left(\frac{1}{2}\right)\left(\frac{s}{4}\right)\left(\frac{\sqrt{3}}{2}s\right) = \frac{\sqrt{3}}{16}s^2$$

Now we can take the ratio of the areas:

Area of triangle $RQD \div$ Area of triangle PQC

$$\frac{\sqrt{3}}{16}s \div \frac{3\sqrt{3}}{16}s = \frac{1}{3}$$

48. **D**   Other Important Graphs and Equations

The equation of a parabola with vertex (h, k) is:

$$y = a(x - h)^2 + k$$

Since we know that the vertex (h, k) is at $(-1, 4)$ and that one point on the parabola is $(1, 8)$, we can plug these values of h, k, x, and y into the equation to find a:

$$8 = a(1 + 1)^2 + 4$$
$$8 = a(4) + 4$$
$$4 = a(4)$$
$$a = 1$$

Now we can use the value of a to find the equation of this parabola:

$$y = (x + 1)^2 + 4$$

To find where the parabola and line intersect, set their equations equal to each other and solve for x:

$$(x + 1)^2 + 4 = -4(x + 1)$$
$$x^2 + 2x + 1 + 4 = -4x - 4$$
$$x^2 + 6x + 9 = 0$$
$$(x + 3)(x + 3) = 0$$

So the figures intersect at $x = -3$, eliminating all of the answer choices except **D**.

49. **E**   Circles

The area of the shaded region is just the area of the square minus the area of the larger circle and plus the area of the smaller circle. So we start by using the given area of the square to solve for d:

$$192 = (2d)^2$$
$$192 = 4d^2$$
$$48 = d^2$$
$$d = 4\sqrt{3}$$

Since we know that $r = \frac{1}{2}d$, we can find the area of the larger circle:

$$\text{area} = \pi r^2 = \pi(\frac{1}{2}d)^2 = \frac{\pi}{4}d^2 = \frac{\pi}{4}(48) = 12\pi$$

We also know that the smaller circle's radius $= \frac{1}{2}r$, so we can find its area:

$$\text{area} = \pi(\frac{r}{2})^2 = \frac{\pi}{4}r^2 = \frac{\pi}{4}(\frac{1}{2}d)^2 = \frac{\pi}{16}d^2 = \frac{\pi}{16}(48) = 3\pi$$

Putting it all together, the area of shaded region $= 192 - 12\pi + 3\pi = 192 - 9\pi \approx 163.73$.

50. **E**   Equation Solving

Let the weight of the canoe be x. It is given that her weight, 120 pounds, is 76 percent of the canoe's weight capacity, so we can write the equation 120 = .76 (weight capacity). Also, we know that the canoe's weight capacity is 240 percent the weight of the canoe, and can write this as $2.4x$. So, we can substitute the expression for the canoe's weight capacity into the first equation and solve for x:

$$120 = .76(2.4x)$$
$$x = 65.8$$

SAT Math Level 1
Practice Test III

SAT MATH LEVEL 1 PRACTICE TEST III ANSWER SHEET

1	Ⓐ Ⓑ Ⓒ Ⓓ Ⓔ	11	Ⓐ Ⓑ Ⓒ Ⓓ Ⓔ	21	Ⓐ Ⓑ Ⓒ Ⓓ Ⓔ	31	Ⓐ Ⓑ Ⓒ Ⓓ Ⓔ	41	Ⓐ Ⓑ Ⓒ Ⓓ Ⓔ
2	Ⓐ Ⓑ Ⓒ Ⓓ Ⓔ	12	Ⓐ Ⓑ Ⓒ Ⓓ Ⓔ	22	Ⓐ Ⓑ Ⓒ Ⓓ Ⓔ	32	Ⓐ Ⓑ Ⓒ Ⓓ Ⓔ	42	Ⓐ Ⓑ Ⓒ Ⓓ Ⓔ
3	Ⓐ Ⓑ Ⓒ Ⓓ Ⓔ	13	Ⓐ Ⓑ Ⓒ Ⓓ Ⓔ	23	Ⓐ Ⓑ Ⓒ Ⓓ Ⓔ	33	Ⓐ Ⓑ Ⓒ Ⓓ Ⓔ	43	Ⓐ Ⓑ Ⓒ Ⓓ Ⓔ
4	Ⓐ Ⓑ Ⓒ Ⓓ Ⓔ	14	Ⓐ Ⓑ Ⓒ Ⓓ Ⓔ	24	Ⓐ Ⓑ Ⓒ Ⓓ Ⓔ	34	Ⓐ Ⓑ Ⓒ Ⓓ Ⓔ	44	Ⓐ Ⓑ Ⓒ Ⓓ Ⓔ
5	Ⓐ Ⓑ Ⓒ Ⓓ Ⓔ	15	Ⓐ Ⓑ Ⓒ Ⓓ Ⓔ	25	Ⓐ Ⓑ Ⓒ Ⓓ Ⓔ	35	Ⓐ Ⓑ Ⓒ Ⓓ Ⓔ	45	Ⓐ Ⓑ Ⓒ Ⓓ Ⓔ
6	Ⓐ Ⓑ Ⓒ Ⓓ Ⓔ	16	Ⓐ Ⓑ Ⓒ Ⓓ Ⓔ	26	Ⓐ Ⓑ Ⓒ Ⓓ Ⓔ	36	Ⓐ Ⓑ Ⓒ Ⓓ Ⓔ	46	Ⓐ Ⓑ Ⓒ Ⓓ Ⓔ
7	Ⓐ Ⓑ Ⓒ Ⓓ Ⓔ	17	Ⓐ Ⓑ Ⓒ Ⓓ Ⓔ	27	Ⓐ Ⓑ Ⓒ Ⓓ Ⓔ	37	Ⓐ Ⓑ Ⓒ Ⓓ Ⓔ	47	Ⓐ Ⓑ Ⓒ Ⓓ Ⓔ
8	Ⓐ Ⓑ Ⓒ Ⓓ Ⓔ	18	Ⓐ Ⓑ Ⓒ Ⓓ Ⓔ	28	Ⓐ Ⓑ Ⓒ Ⓓ Ⓔ	38	Ⓐ Ⓑ Ⓒ Ⓓ Ⓔ	48	Ⓐ Ⓑ Ⓒ Ⓓ Ⓔ
9	Ⓐ Ⓑ Ⓒ Ⓓ Ⓔ	19	Ⓐ Ⓑ Ⓒ Ⓓ Ⓔ	29	Ⓐ Ⓑ Ⓒ Ⓓ Ⓔ	39	Ⓐ Ⓑ Ⓒ Ⓓ Ⓔ	49	Ⓐ Ⓑ Ⓒ Ⓓ Ⓔ
10	Ⓐ Ⓑ Ⓒ Ⓓ Ⓔ	20	Ⓐ Ⓑ Ⓒ Ⓓ Ⓔ	30	Ⓐ Ⓑ Ⓒ Ⓓ Ⓔ	40	Ⓐ Ⓑ Ⓒ Ⓓ Ⓔ	50	Ⓐ Ⓑ Ⓒ Ⓓ Ⓔ

MATHEMATICS LEVEL 1 TEST

For each of the following problems, decide which is the BEST of the choices given. If the exact numerical value is not one of the choices, select the choice that best approximates this value. Then fill in the corresponding oval on the answer sheet.

<u>Notes:</u> (1) A calculator will be necessary for answering some (but not all) of the questions in this test. For each question you will have to decide whether or not you should use a calcuator. The calculator you use must be at least a scientific calculator; programmable calculators and calculators that can display graphs are permitted.

(2) The only angle measure used on this test is degree measure. Make sure your calculator is in the degree mode.

(3) Figures that accompany problems in this test are intended to provide information useful in solving the problems. They are drawn as accurately as possible EXCEPT when it is stated in a specific problem that its figure is not drawn to scale. All figures lie in a plane unless otherwise indicated.

(4) Unless otherwise specified, the domain of any function f is assumed to be the set of all real numbers x for which $f(x)$ is a real number.

(5) Reference information that may be useful in answering the questions in this test can be found on the page preceding Question 1.

USE THIS SPACE FOR SCRATCHWORK.

1. $2x^3 = \dfrac{1}{y^2}$ and $y = \dfrac{1}{x^2}$. If x and y are nonzero real numbers, then what is the value of x?

(A) 0.25   (B) 1.41   (C) 2   (D) 4   (E) 16

2. If $a^2b = 1$, then $3a^4b^2 =$

(A) 1
(B) 1.73
(C) 2
(D) 3
(E) 6

3. If $x = 3$, then $x(x + 4)(3x + 3) =$

(A) 13
(B) 33
(C) 96
(D) 133
(E) 252

GO ON TO THE NEXT PAGE

4. What is the midpoint of the line segment described by $(1, 4)$ and $(3, 7)$?

    (A) $(3, 4)$
    (B) $(1, 7)$
    (C) $(4, 11)$
    (D) $(2, 5.5)$
    (E) $(2, 6.2)$

5. For all values in which $x \neq 1$, $\dfrac{x^2 + 13x - 14}{x - 1} =$

    (A) $x + 2$
    (B) $x - 7$
    (C) $x + 14$
    (D) $x^2 - 14$
    (E) $x^2 + 14$

6. What is the equation for the line that passes through $(1, 3)$ and is parallel to $y = 7x$?

    (A) $y = .14x + 3$
    (B) $y = .14x + 2.86$
    (C) $y = 7x + 3$
    (D) $y = 7x + 1$
    (E) $y = 7x - 4$

7. If $2^{4b} \times 2^{4b-1} = 128$, then what is the value of b?

    (A) 0   (B) 1   (C) 3   (D) 4   (E) 8

8. Angles a and c are supplementary angles. What is $2 \times (a + c)$?

    (A) $180°$
    (B) $360°$
    (C) $420°$
    (D) $540°$
    (E) $600°$

GO ON TO THE NEXT PAGE

USE THIS SPACE FOR SCRATCHWORK.

9. If $(-2x)^3 = 9$, then what is the value of $|x|$?

    (A) −1.13
    (B) −1.04
    (C) 0
    (D) 1.04
    (E) 1.13

10. If $(3^{4m})^{\frac{m}{2}} = 81$, then what is the possible value of m?

    (A) 0
    (B) $\sqrt{2}$
    (C) $2\sqrt{2}$
    (D) 3
    (E) $4\sqrt{2}$

11. What is the volume of a cone with height 10 and circumference 18π ?

    (A) 60π
    (B) 110π
    (C) 136π
    (D) 270π
    (E) 315π

12. The pyramid and cone shown in Figure 1 have equal base areas, and the volume of the cone is twice that of the pyramid. What is the height of the pyramid in terms of the height of the cone, h?

    (A) $\dfrac{h}{4}$ (B) $\dfrac{h}{2}$ (C) $\dfrac{2h}{3}$ (D) $2h$ (E) $3h$

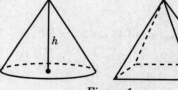

Figure 1

GO ON TO THE NEXT PAGE

13. In Figure 2, if $\overline{BC}$ is perpendicular to $\overline{CD}$, what is the value of x?

(A) 2
(B) 8
(C) 12
(D) 39
(E) 78

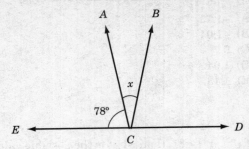

Note: Figure not drawn to scale.
Figure 2

14. At what values of x is $\left|\dfrac{x}{3} + 5\right| < 9$?

(A) $-\infty < x < 0$
(B) $0 < x < \infty$
(C) $-42 < x < 12$
(D) $-\infty < x < -12\,,\ 42 < x < \infty$
(E) $-12 < x < 42$

15. If $f(x) = 4x + \dfrac{x}{2}$, what is $f(2) + f(0)$?

(A) 1
(B) 4
(C) 8
(D) 9
(E) 10

16. What fraction of 45 is 60% of 50?

(A) $\dfrac{1}{5}$ (B) $\dfrac{2}{5}$ (C) $\dfrac{1}{2}$ (D) $\dfrac{2}{3}$ (E) $\dfrac{3}{4}$

17. If $\sqrt{x^3 + 3} = 2x\sqrt{x}$, then what is the value of x?

(A) −1.73
(B) −1
(C) 1
(D) 1.73
(E) 3

GO ON TO THE NEXT PAGE

18. Two six-sided dice are rolled, one after the other. The first roll shows an odd number. What is the probability that the second die shows an odd number?

    (A) $\frac{1}{6}$ (B) $\frac{1}{3}$ (C) $\frac{1}{2}$ (D) $\frac{2}{3}$ (E) 1

19. In Figure 3, circle O has a diameter of 10. What is the area of the shaded region?

    (A) 11.81
    (B) 16.26
    (C) 21.46
    (D) 53.54
    (E) 102.50

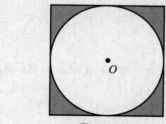

Figure 3

20. The graph in Figure 4 shows how far Matt is from his home over a period of time on Tuesday. Which of the descriptions below best explains the information in the graph?

    (A) Matt jogs from his home to the beach, and then heads to a friend's house, where he spends the rest of the morning.
    (B) Matt leaves his friend's house and jogs to the beach, where he spends the rest of the morning.
    (C) Matt leaves home and jogs to the beach, where he spends the rest of the morning.
    (D) Matt leaves home, jogs to the beach, and then jogs back home.
    (E) Matt spends the morning at his friend's house.

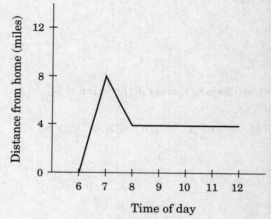

Figure 4

21. A new apartment building was just built. Each apartment in the building needs an identifying three-digit name. The set of first digits is 1, 2, 3, 4, 5, 6. The set of second digits is 0, 7. The set of third digits is A, B, C. How many possible apartment names can be made?

    (A) 14
    (B) 36
    (C) 57
    (D) 89
    (E) 113

GO ON TO THE NEXT PAGE

USE THIS SPACE FOR SCRATCHWORK.

22. What is the perimeter of parallelogram *ABCD* in Figure 5?

(A) $36 + 6\sqrt{3}$
(B) $44 + 10\sqrt{3}$
(C) $50 + 4\sqrt{2}$
(D) $52 + 6\sqrt{2}$
(E) $64 + 8\sqrt{3}$

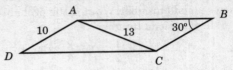

Note: Figure not drawn to scale.
Figure 5

23. In Figure 6, if $\theta = 39°$ then what is the value of x?

(A) 4.32
(B) 8.64
(C) 9.00
(D) 17.24
(E) 18.01

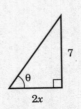

Figure 6

24. Given Figure 7, what is the value of $\frac{x + y}{30}$?

(A) 2   (B) 3   (C) 4   (D) 5   (E) 6

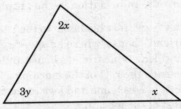

Note: Figure not drawn to scale.
Figure 7

25. If $i^2 = -1$ and if $\left(\left(i^2\right)^5\right)^j = -1$, then the least positive integer value of j is

(A) 1   (B) 2   (C) 3   (D) 5   (E) 7

26. In Figure 8, $a = c - b$ and $c = 100°$. What is the value of b?

(A) 10°
(B) 20°
(C) 40°
(D) 80°
(E) Cannot be determined.

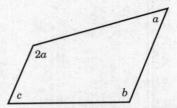

Note: Figure not drawn to scale.
Figure 8

GO ON TO THE NEXT PAGE

27. If $f(x) = x^2$, what is $2 \times \dfrac{f(2) - f(1)}{f(1)}$?

(A) 4   (B) 6   (C) 7   (D) 8   (E) 10

28. Given that j and k are nonzero integers and $j - k = jq$, which of the statements below must always be true?

I. q is an integer.
II. If m is an integer and $k = jm$, then q is an integer.
III. If j and q are negative, then k is negative.

(A) I only
(B) II only
(C) III only
(D) II and III only
(E) I, II, and III

29. What is the equation of the line that passes through points $(-3, 1)$ and $(4, 0)$?

(A) $y = \dfrac{x}{7}$

(B) $y = \dfrac{-x}{7}$

(C) $y = \dfrac{x}{7} + 1$

(D) $y = \dfrac{x}{7} + 4$

(E) $y = -\dfrac{x}{7} + \dfrac{4}{7}$

30. Suppose $S = \{2, 4, 4, 6, 7, 13\}$. Which of the following statements are true of S?

I.   The mean of S is 6.
II. The median of S is greater than the mode of S.
III. The mean, median, and mode of S are all elements of S.

(A) I only
(B) II only
(C) I and II only
(D) I and III only
(E) I, II, and III

GO ON TO THE NEXT PAGE

31. What is the midpoint of $(1, 3, -2)$ and $(11, 1, 2)$?

    (A) $(6, 2, 0)$
    (B) $(4, 2, 2)$
    (C) $(3, 1, 0)$
    (D) $(1, .33, 0)$
    (E) It cannot be determined with the information given.

32. The cylinder in Figure 9 has a volume of 90π. What is its total surface area?

    (A) 56π
    (B) 60π
    (C) 78π
    (D) 84π
    (E) 90π

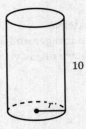

10

Figure 9

33. $3y + 1 = (6x - 2)$ and $y^2 - 3x^2 + 1 = 0$. What is the value of x?

    (A) $-3, 3$

    (B) $-\dfrac{5}{6}, \dfrac{5}{6}$

    (C) $0, \dfrac{2}{3}$

    (D) $1 + \sqrt{3}, 1 - \sqrt{3}$

    (E) $2 + \sqrt{2}, 2 - \sqrt{2}$

34. In Figure 10, what is the ratio of the perimeter of triangle ABC to the perimeter of triangle CDE?

    (A) 1:2
    (B) 1.5:1
    (C) 2:1
    (D) 3:1
    (E) 5:2

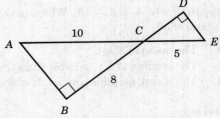

Note: Figure not drawn to scale.
Figure 10

GO ON TO THE NEXT PAGE

35. $\sin \theta = 0.75$ and $1 - \cos^2 \theta = x$. What is the value of x?

(A) 0.56
(B) 0.68
(C) 0.88
(D) 0.91
(E) 1

36. $f(x)$ is a function such that $f(x) = c^2$ for $x \geq 0$, and $f(x) = ax + b$ for $x < 0$. If a, b, and c are nonzero numbers, what could be the graph of $y = f(x)$?

(A)

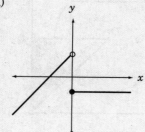

(B)

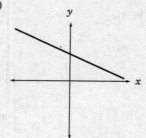

(C)

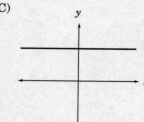

(D)

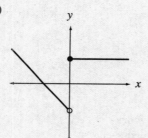

(E)

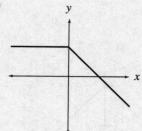

37. The volume of the wedge in Figure 11 is 180. What is the area of the shaded surface?

(A) 54 (B) 66 (C) 72 (D) 78 (E) 96

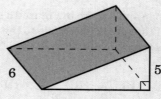

Figure 11

GO ON TO THE NEXT PAGE

USE THIS SPACE FOR SCRATCHWORK.

38. The line $y = 2x + 3$ is graphed on the same xy–plane as a parabola with vertex at $(3, 1)$ that passes through the point $(4, 2)$. At what points do the line and parabola intersect?

    (A) $(8, 26)$ and $(4.6, 3.5)$
    (B) $(1, 5)$ and $(7, 17)$
    (C) $(2.3, 1.5)$ and $(9, 37)$
    (D) $(2, 7)$ and $(0, 3)$
    (E) $(0, 10)$ and $(1, 9.3)$

39. In Figure 12, a square with side x is inscribed in the circle with center O. OP is a radius of the circle. $ABCD$ is a square with side $2x$ and center O, and OE bisects AB. What is the area of the shaded region?

    (A) $\dfrac{x^2(8 - \pi)}{16}$

    (B) $\dfrac{x^2(4 - \pi)}{8}$

    (C) $\dfrac{x^2(3 - \pi)}{6}$

    (D) $\dfrac{x^2(4 - \pi)}{16}$

    (E) $\dfrac{x^2(2 - \pi)}{8}$

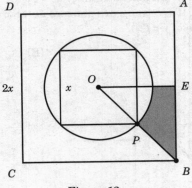

Figure 12

40. Seth works at a museum for $8 an hour and makes $256 a week. He is given a 20 percent raise. Assuming he works the same number of hours per day, how much more money does he make a week after getting the raise?

    (A) $21.00
    (B) $36.40
    (C) $51.20
    (D) $64.30
    (E) $88.90

41. The circle and square in Figure 13 both have centers at O. If the ratio of the area of the circle to the area of the square is 1:4, what is the ratio of r:t?

    (A) $\sqrt{\dfrac{\pi}{4}}$ (B) $\sqrt{\dfrac{\pi}{2}}$ (C) $\sqrt{\dfrac{1}{2\pi}}$ (D) $\sqrt{2\pi}$ (E) $\dfrac{2}{\pi}$

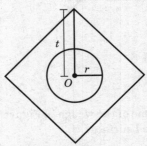

<u>Note:</u> Figure not drawn to scale.
Figure 13

GO ON TO THE NEXT PAGE

USE THIS SPACE FOR SCRATCHWORK.

42. The function $f(x) = 12x + 3$ has a domain of $-1 < x < 1$. What is the range of f?

    (A) $-15 < y < 15$
    (B) $3 < y < 15$
    (C) $y < 15$
    (D) $y < -9$ or $y > 15$
    (E) $-9 < y < 15$

43. The rectangle in Figure 14 is rotated about side AD to form a solid. It is then rotated again about the line connecting the two midpoints of AB and DC. The two axes are indicated in the figure by dotted lines. What is the ratio of the volume of the first solid to the volume of the second solid?

    (A) 1:2
    (B) 1:1
    (C) 1.5:1
    (D) 2:1
    (E) 4:1

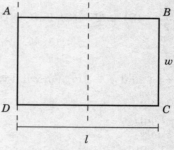

Figure 14

44. In Figure 15, $a = 3$ and $b = 6$. What is the perimeter of the triangle?

    (A) 6.71
    (B) 9.00
    (C) 15.71
    (D) 18.00
    (E) 45.00

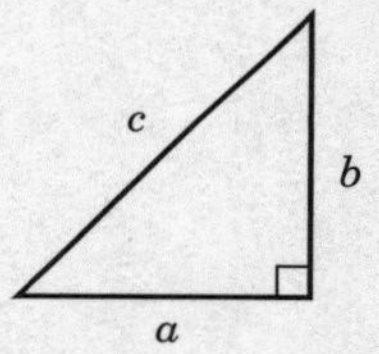

Figure 15

45. $f(x) = (a \times x) + (b \times 3)$, $f(0) = 3$, and $f(5) = 18$. What is $a - b$?

    (A) -2 (B) 0 (C) 1 (D) 2 (E) 3

46. What is the domain of the function $f(x) = \dfrac{1}{x^3 + 2x^2 - 8x}$?

    (A) $x < -4$ or $x > 2$
    (B) $-4 < x < 2$
    (C) $x \neq -4, 0, 2$
    (D) $x > 0$
    (E) All real numbers

47. $\dfrac{0! \times 4!}{2!} =$

    (A) 0 (B) 2 (C) 8 (D) 12 (E) 16

GO ON TO THE NEXT PAGE

USE THIS SPACE FOR SCRATCHWORK.

48. The vertex of the parabola $y = (x-3)^2 + 5$ lies on the circle defined by the equation $(x-1)^2 + (y-1)^2 = a$. What is the value of a?

(A) 8 (B) 16 (C) 20 (D) 32 (E) 52

49. Parallelogram $ABCD$ in Figure 16 has an area equal to the area of a rectangle with width x and length $2x$. What is the value of x?

(A) $\dfrac{\sqrt{3}}{2}$ (B) $2\sqrt{2}$ (C) $2\sqrt{3}$ (D) $3\sqrt{2}$ (E) 4

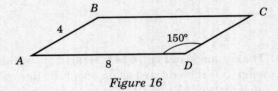

Figure 16

50. $x = t + 1$ and $y = 2\sqrt{t}$. For what value(s) of t will $y = x$?

(A) 0 only
(B) −1 only
(C) 1 only
(D) −1 and 1
(E) −1, 0, and 1

S T O P

IF YOU FINISH BEFORE TIME IS CALLED, YOU MAY CHECK YOUR WORK ON THIS TEST ONLY.
DO NOT TURN TO ANY OTHER TEST IN THIS BOOK.

SAT Math Level 1
Practice Test III
Explanations

Answers to SAT Math Level 1 Practice Test III

Question Number	Answer	Right	Wrong	Question Number	Answer	Right	Wrong
1	C	___	___	26	B	___	___
2	D	___	___	27	B	___	___
3	E	___	___	28	D	___	___
4	D	___	___	29	E	___	___
5	C	___	___	30	C	___	___
6	E	___	___	31	A	___	___
7	B	___	___	32	C	___	___
8	B	___	___	33	E	___	___
9	D	___	___	34	C	___	___
10	B	___	___	35	A	___	___
11	D	___	___	36	D	___	___
12	B	___	___	37	D	___	___
13	C	___	___	38	B	___	___
14	C	___	___	39	A	___	___
15	D	___	___	40	C	___	___
16	D	___	___	41	C	___	___
17	C	___	___	42	E	___	___
18	C	___	___	43	E	___	___
19	C	___	___	44	C	___	___
20	A	___	___	45	D	___	___
21	B	___	___	46	C	___	___
22	B	___	___	47	D	___	___
23	A	___	___	48	C	___	___
24	A	___	___	49	B	___	___
25	A	___	___	50	C	___	___

Calculating Your Score

Your raw score for the SAT Math Level 1 test is based on the number of questions you answer correctly and incorrectly. Once you have determined your raw score, use the conversion table on page 15 of this book to calculate your scaled score.

To Calculate Your Raw Score

1. Count the number of questions you answered correctly: _____ (A)

2. Count the number of questions you answered incorrectly, and multiply that number by ¼: _____ (B) × ¼ = _____ (C)

3. Subtract the value in (C) from value in (A): _____ (D)

4. Round the number in (D) to the nearest whole number. This is your raw score: _____ (E)

Math Level 1 Test III Explanations

1. C Equation Solving

Since we know $y = {}^1\!/x^2$, we can substitute $y^2 = {}^1\!/x^4$ into the equation $2x^3 = {}^1\!/y^2$. Doing so gives us

$$2x^3 = \frac{1}{\frac{1}{x^4}} = x^4$$

We can then divide both sides by x^3, and get $x = 2$.

2. D Equation Solving

The trick to solving this problem is noticing that $3a^4b^2 = 3(a^2b)^2$. Since we are given that $a^2b = 1$, we can simply make the substitution and get $3a^4b^2 = 3(a^2b)^2 = 3(1)^2 = 3$.

3. E Polynomials

Just plug 3 in for x and then carry out the operations:

$$x(x + 4)(3x + 3) = 3(3 + 4)(3(3) + 3)$$
$$= 3(7)(9 + 3)$$
$$= 3(7)(12)$$
$$= 252$$

4. D Lines and Distance

The coordinates of the midpoint are the averages of the coordinates of the two points:

$$(x_{\text{mid}}, y_{\text{mid}}) = (\frac{x_1 + x_2}{2}, \frac{y_1 + y_2}{2})$$
$$= (\frac{1 + 3}{2}, \frac{4 + 7}{2})$$
$$= (2, 5.5)$$

5. C Polynomials

This is essentially a factoring question. In questions like this, a term in the denominator is usually a factor of the numerator. In this case:

$$\frac{x^2 + 13x - 14}{x - 1} = \frac{(x + 14)(x - 1)}{x - 1}$$

The $x - 1$ cancels out, and the other factor is $x + 14$. If you found it difficult to factor the numerator, you could have tried $x - 1$ as a factor or you could have tried each of the answer choices.

6. E Lines and Distance

Because the slopes of parallel lines are equal, the slope of the line through the point $(1, 3)$ is 7. We can find the y–intercept of the line by substituting $(1, 3)$ into $y = 7x + b$:

$$y = 7x + b$$
$$3 = 7 \times 1 + b$$
$$-4 = b$$

7. **B** Equation Solving

This question relies on the multiplication rule of exponents: $x^a \times x^b = x^{a+b}$. So $2^{4b} \times 2^{4b-1} = 2^{4b+4b-1}$. Since $128 = 2^7$, we can set the exponents on the left and right sides of the equation equal to each other and solve for b:

$$4b + 4b - 1 = 7$$
$$8b - 1 = 7$$
$$8b = 8$$
$$b = 1$$

8. **B** Lines and Angles

As long as you know what supplementary angles are, you're all set. By definition, the sum of two supplementary angles is 180°. Therefore, $2 \times (a + c) = 2 \times 180° = 360°$.

9. **D** Equation Solving

To solve for x we must first take the cube root of both sides of the equation. This will give us $-2x = \sqrt[3]{9}$. Then, we divide both sides by -2 to get $x = -\sqrt[3]{9}/2 = -1.04$. The question, however, asks for the value of $|x|$ (the absolute value of x).

By definition, the absolute value of a number is always positive. Therefore, the absolute value of x is 1.04.

10. **B** Equation Solving

This question makes use of the power rule of exponents: $x^{a^b} = x^{ab}$. Since $81 = 3^4$, we can set the exponent in the question equal to 4 and then solve for m:

$$(4m)(\frac{m}{2}) = 4$$
$$\frac{4m^2}{2} = 4$$
$$2m^2 = 4$$
$$m^2 = 2$$
$$m = \sqrt{2}$$

11. **D** Prisms, Solids That Aren't Prisms

The volume of cone $= \frac{1}{3}\pi r^2 h$, so in order to find the volume, as we're asked, we just need to find the radius r. Fortunately, since we know the circumference, we can easily solve for r:

$$\text{circumference} = 18\pi$$
$$2\pi r = 18\pi$$
$$r = 9$$

The volume of the cone is $\frac{1}{3}\pi(9^2)(10) = 270\pi$.

12. **B** Prisms, Solids That Aren't Prisms

Let's call the height of the pyramid x and the base area for both figures B. Since the volume for each figure is $1/3(B \times height)$, and the volume of the cone is twice that of the pyramid, you can set up an equation and solve for x in terms of h:

$$\text{volume of cone} = 2(\text{volume of pyramid})$$

$$\frac{1}{3}(B \times h) = 2\left(\frac{1}{3}(B \times x)\right)$$

$$h = 2x$$
$$x = \frac{1}{2}h$$

13. **C**   Lines and Angles

If BC is perpendicular to CD, that means $\angle BCD = 90°$ and $\angle BCE = x + 78° = 90°$. Solving for x, we see that $x = 90° - 78° = 12°$.

14. **C**   Equation Solving

Remember that questions involving absolute values often involve two solutions, one where the argument of the absolute value is positive and one where it is negative. We can rewrite the equation in the problem in two parts: $\frac{x}{3} + 5 < 9$ and $-(\frac{x}{3} + 5) < 9$. Now we can solve each equation separately; let's try the positive one first:

$$\frac{x}{3} + 5 < 9$$
$$\frac{x}{3} < 4$$
$$x < 12$$

Finally, we need to solve the negative half of the equation. Don't forget to reverse the inequality sign when dividing by a negative number.

$$-(\frac{x}{3} + 5) < 9$$
$$\frac{x}{3} + 5 > -9$$
$$\frac{x}{3} > -14$$
$$x > -42$$

15. **D**   Evaluating Functions

When evaluating the sum of two functions, first evaluate each function separately and then add them together. Luckily, this function is very straightforward:

$$f(2) + f(0) = (4 \times 2 + \frac{4}{2}) + (4 \times 0 + \frac{0}{2})$$
$$= (8 + 1) + (0 + 0)$$
$$= 9$$

16. **D**   Fundamentals

60% of 50 is simply $.60 \times 50 = 30$. Now, you can just divide 30 by 45 to find the fraction asked for in the question. In reduced form, $\frac{30}{45} = \frac{2}{3}$.

17. **C**   Equation Solving

Imagine how much easier this question would be without those square roots. Let's get rid of the radicals by squaring both sides:

$$x^3 + 3 = (2x)^2(x)$$
$$= 4x^2(x)$$
$$= 4x^3$$

Now we need to subtract x^3 from both sides, simplifying the equation to $3x^3 = 3$. Dividing both sides by 3 leaves us with $x^3 = 1$, and thus $x = 1$.

18. **C**   Probability

The key to this question is recognizing that the first roll of the dice and the second roll of the dice are independent of each other. What happened to the first die has no effect on what will happen to the second die. You can treat the second roll as if the first roll did not exist. Obviously, 1, 3, and 5 are the possible odd rolls and 2, 4, and 6 are the possible even rolls. So, the probability of rolling an odd is $\frac{3}{6} = \frac{1}{2}$.

19. **C**   Circles

The area of the shaded region is simply the area of the square minus the area of the circle. The diameter of the circle is also the length of a side of the square, we can solve for its area: $A = 10^2 = 100$. You can immediately eliminate (E), since it is greater than the area of the square alone. The area of circle O is πr^2, and since a circle's radius is half the measurement of its diameter, the area of the circle is simply $A = \pi(5)^2 = 25\pi$. The area of the shaded region is: $100 - 25\pi \approx 21.46$.

20. **A**   Fundamentals

According to the graph, Matt starts 0 miles from his home, which means that he starts at home. Thus, we can immediately eliminate **B** and **E**. We then see that Matt goes to a location 8 miles from home, and then immediately goes to a destination 4 miles from home. So, we know that Matt goes to two different places after leaving home. Therefore, we can eliminate **C** and **D**, and are left with **A**. So, Matt jogs from home to the beach, and then heads to a friend's house where he spends the rest of the morning. This also makes sense, since according to the graph, Matt spends the rest of the morning at a location 4 miles away from home.

21. **B**   Permutations and Combinations

Each digit selection is unrelated, so the number of possibilities is simply the product of the number of choices for each space. There are $6 \times 2 \times 3 = 36$ possibilities.

22. **B**   Triangle

By definition, in a parallelogram, $\angle ADC = \angle ABC = 30°$. If we draw a vertical line from A down to DC, we get the following figure:

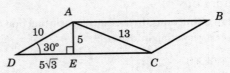

Triangle ADE is a 30-60-90 triangle, so the sides have the $x: x\sqrt{3} : 2x$ relationship. That means that $AE = 10 \div 2 = 5$ and $DE = 5\sqrt{3}$ and we see that triangle AEC is a 5-12-13 (a Pythagorean triple) triangle. $EC = 12$ and $DC = 5\sqrt{3} + 12$, so the perimeter of the parallelogram is $2(10) + 2(5\sqrt{3} + 12) = 20 + 10\sqrt{3} + 24 = 44 + 4\sqrt{3}$.

23. **A**   Basic Functions and the Right Triangle

We're given the measure of an angle, θ, and we know the lengths of the sides adjacent to and opposite of θ. You should immediately realize that you're going to need a trigonometric function to solve this problem and that the tangent function is the one you want: $\tan \theta = {}^{\text{opposite}}/_{\text{adjacent}}$.

From here, we set $\tan 39° = {}^7/_{2x}$ and solve for x:

$$\tan 39° = \frac{7}{2x}$$
$$.81 = \frac{7}{2x}$$
$$2x \times .81 = 7$$
$$1.62x = 7$$
$$x = \frac{7}{1.62}$$
$$x = 4.32$$

24. **A**   Triangle

The first step is to translate the diagram into an equation. Since we know that the three interior angles of a triangle add up 180°, we can write an equation and try to manipulate it:

$$x + 2x + 3y = 180°$$
$$3x + 3y = 180°$$
$$3(x + y) = 180°$$
$$x + y = 60°$$

Conveniently, knowing the sum of $x + y$ is enough to solve the problem: $\frac{x+y}{30} = \frac{60}{30} = 2$.

25. **A**   Imaginary and Complex Numbers

Substitute $i^2 = -1$ into the given equation: in order for $(-1)^j = -1$, j must be an odd integer and the smallest positive odd integer is 1.

26. **B**   Polygons

Since it is given that $a = c - b$ and $c = 100°$, we know that $a = 100° - b$. Also, like all four-sided polygons, the sum of the angles is 360°:

$$a + 2a + b + c = 360°$$
$$3a + b + 100° = 360°$$
$$3a + b = 260°$$

We can now substitute $a = 100° - b$ into $3a + b = 260°$:

$$3(100° - b) + b = 260°$$
$$300° - 3b + b = 260°$$
$$-2b = -40°$$
$$b = 20°$$

27. **B**   Evaluating Functions

In this problem you're asked to evaluate a series of operations on a function. Before you can manipulate the equation you must evaluate the functions and substitute the values into the equation. Only once you've replaced all of the references to f can you begin the computations.

$$2 \times \frac{f(2) - f(1)}{f(1)} = 2 \times \frac{2^2 - 1^2}{1^2}$$
$$= 2 \times \frac{4 - 1}{1}$$
$$= 2 \times \frac{3}{1}$$
$$= 2 \times 3$$
$$= 6$$

28. D   Fundamentals

There are definitely algebraic ways to solve this problem, but hopefully your intuition tells you that such an approach would be time-consuming. Strategically, you should make sure not to let this problem take too much time; you might even want to skip it and come back to it at the end. When dealing with a question that has three statements, it's a good strategy to try to prove or disprove them in order of easiest to hardest. In this case, statement I looks the easiest and statement II looks the hardest.

Starting with statement I, we should try to determine whether it is true or false. Let's try to find a non-integer value for q. If we let $q = \frac{1}{2}$ (a pretty easy fraction to work with), then we can manipulate the given equation:

$$j - k = \frac{1}{2}j$$
$$2j - 2k = j$$
$$j = 2k$$

Are there integers j and k such that $j = 2k$? Of course! Statement I must be false, so we can eliminate answers A and E.

Next let's attack statement III. If j and q are negative, then $j \times q$ must be positive. Since j is negative, k cannot be positive, since a negative number minus a positive number is always a negative number. k must be negative, so statement III is true and you can eliminate **B**.

Finally, let's look at statement II. It says $k = jm$, so let's substitute: $j - jm = jq$, and $1 - m = q$. We also know that m is an integer, so $(1 - m)$ must be an integer, and therefore q must be an integer. Statement II may look funny because we've never seen m before, but given our previous information it's true. The answer is **D**.

29. E   Lines and Distance

In order to find the equation of a line, we must first find the slope. Since the slope is the line's vertical change divided by its horizontal change, we can get the slope from the two points we are given:

$$\frac{y_2 - y_1}{x_2 - x_1} = \frac{0 - 1}{4 - (-3)}$$
$$= -\frac{1}{7}$$

Now, we must find the y-intercept by substituting one of our points into the equation $y = -\frac{x}{7} + b$. Let's use the point $(-3, 1)$:

$$y = -\frac{x}{7} + b$$
$$1 = \frac{3}{7} + b$$
$$\frac{4}{7} = b$$

30. C   Statistical Analysis

Begin by calculating the mean, median, and mode of the data set, since each of the statements relies on them. The mean is simply the sum of terms divided by the number of terms, in this case six: $(2 + 4 + 4 + 6 + 7 + 13)$ $/6 = \frac{36}{6} = 6$. The median is the middle term of the set when the elements are arranged in ascending (or descending) order. Since there is an even number of terms in the set, the median is the average of the third and fourth terms. The median is $(4 + 6)/2 = \frac{10}{2} = 5$. Finally, the mode is the most frequently occurring element, which is 4.

Now we are well prepared with the values of the mean, median, and mode of S. We can easily attack the three statements. The first statement is obviously true, since we already calculated the mean to be 6. The second statement is also true, since the median, 5, is greater than the mode, 4. Finally, the third statement is false, since 5 is not a member of S. Since statements I and II are true, the answer is **C**.

31. **A**   Lines and Distance

Calculating the midpoint of a line in three-dimensional coordinates is not much harder than finding the midpoint of a line with two-dimensional coordinates. Instead of just taking the average of the x- and y-coordinates, we also must find the average of the z-coordinate. So, the midpoint is $\left(\frac{1+11}{2}, \frac{1+3}{2}, \frac{-2+2}{2}\right) = (6, 2, 0)$.

32. **C**   Prisms, Solids That Aren't Prisms

The formula for the total surface area of a cylinder with radius r and height h is:

$$\text{surface area} = 2\pi r^2 + 2\pi r(h)$$

The height is given as 10, and since we're given the volume of the cylinder, we can work backward to find r.

$$V = \pi r^2 h$$
$$90\pi = \pi r^2 (10)$$
$$9 = r^2$$
$$r = 3$$

So the surface area is $2\pi(3)^2 + 2\pi(3)(10) = 18\pi + 60\pi = 78\pi$.

33. **E**   Polynomials

To solve systems of equations, you must use the two variables to solve for each other. First, solve for y in terms of x:

$$3y + 1 = 6x - 2$$
$$3y = 6x - 3$$
$$y = 2x - 1$$

Now you can substitute $y = 2x - 1$ into $y^2 - 3x^2 + 1 = 0$ and solve for x:

$$y^2 - 3x^2 + 1 = 0$$
$$(2x - 1)^2 - 3x^2 + 1 = 0$$
$$4x^2 - 4x + 1 - 3x^2 + 1 = 0$$
$$x^2 - 4x + 2 = 0$$

This quadratic cannot be factored into integers since there are no two numbers that sum to –4 and whose product is 2. Don't despair, we can use the quadratic equation to find the roots of the equation:

$$\text{quadratic equation} = \frac{-b \pm \sqrt{b^2 - 4ac}}{2a}$$
$$= \frac{-(-4) \pm \sqrt{(-4)^2 - 4(1)(2)}}{2(1)}$$
$$= \frac{4 \pm \sqrt{16 - (8)}}{2}$$
$$= \frac{4 \pm \sqrt{8}}{2}$$
$$= \frac{4 \pm 2\sqrt{2}}{2}$$
$$= 2 \pm \sqrt{2}$$

34. **C** Triangle

This question asks us to find the relationship between two triangles. Since $\angle ACB = \angle DCE$, and $\angle ABC = \angle CDE = 90°$, we know that $\angle BAC = \angle CED$, and the two triangles are therefore similar.

So, since $AC = 10$ and $CE = 5$, the common ratio of a side of ACE to a side of CDE is 2:1. Since each pair of sides has this ratio, their sums (the perimeter) will also have this ratio, and so the answer is also 2:1.

35. **A** Trigonometric Identities

This question requires knowledge of the Pythagorean identity $\sin^2\theta + \cos^2\theta = 1$. From this equation, you can solve for x:

$$x = 1 - \cos^2\theta$$
$$= \sin^2\theta$$
$$= (0.75)^2$$
$$= 0.56$$

36. **D** Graphing Functions

The first condition to check is that $f(x) = c^2$ for $x \geq 0$. c^2 is a positive constant, so the graph of $y = f(x)$ will contain a horizontal line for all $x \geq 0$. This condition eliminates answers **A**, **B**, and **E**. This leaves **C** and **D** as possible answers.

The graph in **C**, however, shows that f is constant for all x in its domain, not just $x \geq 0$. If this were true, then a would have to equal 0, and the graph of f would be a horizontal line at $y = 0$. The graph in **C**, though, is a horizontal line at $y = m$, for some $m > 0$. Thus, this can't be the correct answer, which leaves only **D**.

37. **D** Prisms, Solids That Aren't Prisms

The volume of this solid is equal to the area of its base multiplied by its height. There are a few ways to look at any solid: for instance, you could flip it toward you so that its base is the triangle and its height is 6. As it sits on your page, its *average* height is $(5 + 0)/2 = 2.5$ and its base is a rectangle with one side of length 6 and the other side of unknown length that we'll call x. This gives us a base area of $6x$ and we can set up an equation for the volume of the solid:

$$\text{volume} = \text{base area} \times \text{height}$$
$$180 = (6x)(2.5)$$
$$180 = 15x$$
$$x = 12$$

Since the figure has right angles, the front and back faces are right triangles with legs 5 and 12 and the hypotenuse is 13 (this is the 5-12-13 Pythagorean triple).

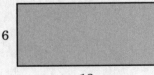

The area of the shaded surface is $6 \times 13 = 78$.

38. **B**   Other Important Graphs and Equations

The equation of a parabola with vertex (h, k) is $y = a(x - h)^2 + k$. If we plug in $(4, 2)$ for x and y we get $a = 1$, i.e., the equation of this parabola is $y = (x - 3)^2 + 1$. The given line has equation $y = 2x + 3$. To find where the parabola and line intersect, set these two equations equal to each other and solve for x:

$$(x - 3)^2 + 1 = 2x + 3$$
$$x^2 - 6x + 9 + 1 = 2x + 3$$
$$x^2 - 8x + 7 = 0$$
$$(x - 7)(x - 1) = 0$$

So $x = 7$ or $x = 1$.

39. **A**   Polygons

The area of the shaded region is simply the area of the triangle OEB minus the area of sector OPT. Since O is the center of square $ABCD$ and OE bisects AB, triangle OEB is a 45-45-90 triangle with base and height both equal to x.

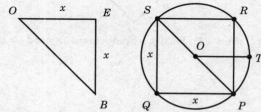

$A_{OEB} = \frac{1}{2}x^2$. Since O is also the center of the smaller square, SP is a diagonal of this square and $OP = \frac{1}{2}SP$. Triangle PQS is also a 45-45-90 triangle with base and height both equal to x. So $OP = \frac{1}{2}SP = \frac{1}{2}x\sqrt{2} = \frac{x}{\sqrt{2}}$ and the radius of the circle is $\frac{x}{\sqrt{2}}$. We know that $\angle EOB = 45°$, so we can set up the relationship:

$$\frac{\text{arc angle}}{360°} = \frac{\text{sector area}}{\text{circle area}}$$

$$\frac{45°}{360°} = \frac{\text{sector area}}{\frac{\pi}{2}x^2}$$

$$\frac{1}{8} = \frac{\text{sector area}}{\frac{\pi}{2}x^2}$$

$$\text{sector area} = \frac{\pi}{16}x^2$$

Now, we can find the area of the shaded region:

$$\text{area} = \frac{1}{2}x^2 - \frac{\pi}{16}x^2 = \frac{x^2(8 - \pi)}{16}$$

40. **C**   Equation Solving

Assuming that he works the same number of hours each week, a 20% raise in hourly wages will mean a 20% raise in weekly wages. Since the problem tells us that Seth's hours worked don't change, the answer to the question is simply 20% of his current weekly wage: $256 \times 20\% = 256 \times .20 = \$51.50$.

41. C   Circles

Let the side of the square be s. We can solve for s in terms of r and t, and then solve for the ratio $r{:}t$. Since the ratio of the areas is 4:1, we can set the area of the square equal to four times the area of the circle and solve for s:

$$4\pi r^2 = s^2$$
$$s = 2\sqrt{\pi}\,r$$

Now we need to find s in terms of t:

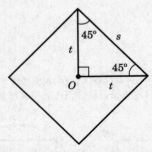

A 45-45-90 triangle is formed, so $s = \sqrt{2}\,t$. Finally, we can set $s = 2\sqrt{\pi}\,r$ and $s = \sqrt{2}\,t$ equal to each other:

$$2\sqrt{\pi}\,r = \sqrt{2}\,t$$
$$r = \frac{\sqrt{2}}{2\sqrt{\pi}}\,t$$
$$\frac{r}{t} = \sqrt{\frac{1}{2\pi}}$$

42. E   Domain and Range

Since $f(x)$ is a linear function, we simply plug in the endpoints of the domain in order to find the range. For $x = -1$ we get:

$$f(-1) = 12 \times -1 + 3$$
$$= -12 + 3$$
$$= -9$$

And for $x = 1$ we get:

$$f(1) = 12 \times 1 + 3$$
$$= 12 + 3$$
$$= 15$$

Keep in mind that the range of $f(x)$ does not actually include −9 and 15, since the domain of the function is every number between −1 and 1, excluding −1 and 1 themselves. Thus, the range of $f(x)$ includes every number between −9 to 15 (and not including −9 and 15).

Test III Explanations

43. **E** Inscribed Solids, Solids Produced by Rotating Polygons

Both rotating rectangles produce cylinders. However, in the first case, a cylinder with radius l is formed, and in the second case, a cylinder of radius $l/2$ is formed.

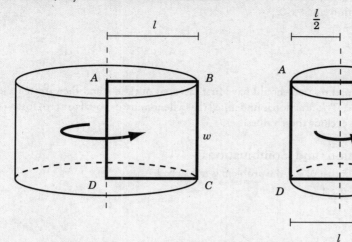

The volume of a cylinder is simply the area of its base times its height. Because the cylinders' heights are the same, the ratio of their volumes is the same as the ratio of their bases. So the ratio of the volumes of the two cylinders is:

$$\frac{\pi l^2}{\pi\left(\frac{l}{2}\right)^2} = \frac{\pi l^2}{\pi \frac{l^2}{4}}$$

$$= 4$$

44. **C** Basic Functions and the Right Triangle

If we are given two sides of a right triangle, we can always calculate the third using the Pythagorean Theorem: $a^2 + b^2 = c^2$ where a and b are legs and c is the hypotenuse. In this problem, we know the two legs, and so to calculate the length of the hypotenuse, we need to find $c = \sqrt{a^2 + b^2} = \sqrt{3^2 + 6^2} = \sqrt{45}$. However, we are not finished yet, since we are asked to find the perimeter. To do so, we simply add the lengths of the sides: $a + b + c = 3 + 6 + \sqrt{45} = 15.71$.

45. **D** Evaluating Functions

It's important to distinguish the variables and constants: a and b are constants, x is the variable. We need to try to isolate either of the constants, which is done when $x = 0$:

$f(0) = 3$
$(a \times 0) + (b \times 3) = 3$
$3b = 3$
$b = 1$

Now that we have found the value of b, we have also isolated the other constant, a:

$f(5) = 18$
$(a \times 5) + 3 = 18$
$5a = 15$
$a = 3$

So, $a - b = 3 - 1 = 2$.

46. **C**   Domain and Range

The domain of a function must exclude any numbers for which $f(x)$ is undefined, which occurs when its denominator is equal to 0. So, in order to find out what x-values make the function undefined, we set the denominator of the fraction equal to 0:

$$x^3 + 2x^2 - 8x = 0$$
$$x(x^2 + 2x - 8) = 0$$
$$x(x - 2)(x + 4) = 0$$

When factoring this equation, you should have first factored out the x and then treated the remaining expression as a quadratic. The function is undefined (has a denominator equal to zero) for $x = 0$, $x = 2$, and $x = -4$; the domain must exclude these values.

47. **D**   Permutations and Combinations

As long as you remember that $0! = 1$, the problem is not so bad:

$$\frac{0!4!}{2!} = \frac{1 \times 4 \times 3 \times 2 \times 1}{2 \times 1}$$
$$= \frac{24}{2}$$
$$= 12$$

48. **C**   Other Important Graphs and Equations

The equation of a circle with center (h, k) and radius r is $(x - h)^2 + (y - k)^2 = r^2$. In this case, $a = r^2$, and the center of the circle is $(1, 1)$. Since we know that the parabola intersects the circle, we can find that point on the equation of the circle. The distance from the center to the point of intersection will equal the radius of the circle, so we need to find the vertex of the parabola. The equation of a parabola with vertex (h, k) is $y = (x - h)^2 + k$, so the vertex of this parabola is $(3, 5)$.

The radius of the circle is the distance from $(1, 1)$ to $(3, 5)$. We can use the distance formula to find r:

$$r = \sqrt{(3 - 1)^2 + (5 - 1)^2}$$
$$r = \sqrt{2^2 + 4^2}$$
$$r = \sqrt{4 + 16}$$
$$r = \sqrt{20}$$

Since $a = r^2$, we get $a = (\sqrt{20})^2 = 20$.

49. **B**   Polygons

First, we need to find the area of parallelogram $ABCD$. In parallelograms, opposite angles are congruent and the sum of the interior angles is 360°. So $\angle B = \angle D$, $\angle A = \angle C$, and $2\angle A + 2\angle D = 360°$. Since we know that $\angle D = 150°$, we can figure out that $\angle A = 180° - 150° = 30°$. By drawing in the height of the parallelogram, a 30-60-90 triangle can be created:

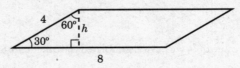

So $h = 2$ and the area of the parallelogram = $8 \times 2 = 16$.

Now we can set the area of the parallelogram equal to the area of the rectangle with width x and length $2x$.

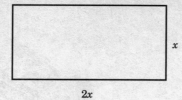

$2x$

$16 = (x)(2x)$

$8 = x^2$

$x = \sqrt{8}$

$x = 2\sqrt{2}$

50. **C** Equation Solving

This question looks harder than it is. Since we are given expressions for both x and y, we can simply set them equal to each other and solve for t:

$x = y$

$t + 1 = 2\sqrt{t}$

$t - 2\sqrt{t} + 1 = 0$

To factor this equation, it's helpful to remember that equations of the form $a^2 - 2ab + b^2 = (a-b)^2$. Here, we see that $a = \sqrt{t}$ and $b = 1$, so this equation can be factored into $(\sqrt{t})^2 - 2\sqrt{t} + 1 = (\sqrt{t} - 1)^2 = 0$. Now you can see that $\sqrt{t} - 1 = 0$, so $\sqrt{t} = 1$ and $t = 1$.